Life Behind the Lobby

Life Behind the Lobby

Indian American Motel Owners and

the American Dream

Pawan Dhingra

Stanford University Press
Stanford, California

Stanford University Press
Stanford, California

Printed in the United States of America on acid-free, archival-quality paper.

Library of Congress Cataloging-in-Publication Data

Dhingra, Pawan, author.
    Life behind the lobby : Indian American motel owners and the American dream /
Pawan Dhingra.
        pages cm.
    Includes bibliographical references and index.
    ISBN 978-0-8047-7882-4 (cloth : alk. paper) — ISBN 978-0-8047-7883-1
(pbk. : alk. paper)
    1. East Indian American businesspeople.   2. Motels—United States.   3. East
Indian Americans—Social conditions.   4. East Indian Americans—Economic
conditions.   I. Title.
    HD2358.5.U6D45 2012
    647.94089'91411073—dc23   2011039933

Typeset by Westchester Book Group in 10/14 Minion.

Contents

Acknowledgments

ALTHOUGH I HAD NO PERSONAL CONNECTION to motels or hotels and did not know any owners before I started researching this project, I have become highly sensitive to the industry's ups and downs and, of course, to the lives of those in it. This is despite the fact that I still have no formal relationship to the industry. My now emotional response to hearing reports of someone's RevPAR (revenue per room based on the number of rooms available) and of motel occupancy tax plans stems from my respect for the owners and families I have met in the course of this research. Practically all were gracious with their time, information, and (no pun intended) hospitality. My deeply sincere appreciation goes to the men and women I met, including owners, family members, employees, vendors, Asian American Hotel Owners Association staff, community leaders, and everyone else whose insights have informed this book.

This book is not meant to represent the lives of all motel owners, nor of all Indian American owners or even those from whom it draws. Instead, it takes from the information I learned and constructs an argument that speaks to the academic and lay audiences I know best. This information stemmed from the questions I asked and the observations I made over the past several years. The questions were shaped by my interest in the role(s), if any, that race, neoliberal ideology, postcolonialism, gender, class, and other factors have played in the emergence of a group that appears to embody the American dream. Where are we now as a country in our relationship with these forms of oppression? Such an accomplished minority group can offer novel insights into these topics. My academic interest expanded over the course of the project, but I never lost sight of what motivated me in the first place. This means some topics are not addressed that otherwise could have been, but this is the nature of any writing. Because this is the first full-length book on Indian American motel owners, expectations of all that could be discussed will not be met.

I also want to thank colleagues who offered guidance on this project. These include academics researching Asian Americans and immigration and racial inequality, of whom I only name very few: Vivek Bald, Jigna Desai, Joanna Dreby, Steven Gold, Monisha Das Gupta, Philip Kasinitz, Nazli Kibria, Nadia Kim, Prema Kurien, Pyong Gap Min, Dina Okamoto, Bandana Purkayastha, Junaid Rana, Sharmila Rudrappa, Jiannbin Shiao, Jane Yamashiro, and Min Zhou. Colleagues at Oberlin College provided both intellectual and social support. These include Rick Baldoz, Michael Fisher, Daphne John, Shelley Lee, Pablo Mitchell, Gina Perez, Meredith Raimondo, and other members of the sociology department and the comparative American studies program. Many students—too many to mention—also assisted in this project. Some of these excellent former undergraduates include Tuyet Ngo, Munib Raad, and James Tompsett.

I am very pleased to be publishing again with Kate Wahl, who has been a true model of professionalism: supportive and straightforward. Luckily for the readers, two anonymous reviewers gave critical insights into a first version of the text. They set a high bar that I hope to match in my future reviews.

On a personal level, I would like to thank my family for putting up with my curt answers to questions of how the book was proceeding. I am indebted to my parents and my mother-in-law, whose own immigrant stories have yet to be told. My brother, siblings-in-law, and nephews and niece have been joys to visit. My own children are my main source of inspiration to finish any project so that I can spend more time with them.

And to my wife: my source of advice, support, and calm. Without whom this project would be just half-started interviews, a reading list, and a weak opening paragraph.

Introduction

You are part of this economy, integral to the health of the U.S.,
accounting for $40 billion in commerce each year. . . . It won't be
long before you are known as people and families who are deeply,
passionately, knowledgeably, involved in making our beloved United
States of America what it should be.

WHEN FORMER VICE PRESIDENT Al Gore spoke these words at a 2002 convention of motel owners, he was not the first—nor would he be the last—
high-profile politician to do so.[1] President Bill Clinton, Senator Bob Dole,
Senator Christopher Dodd, Congressman Newt Gingrich, and two-time
presidential candidate and publisher Steve Forbes, among other nota-
bles, also have addressed this group. Such a lineup is especially noteworthy because the attendees of this convention are not the typical collection of U.S. business owners. Practically all of the audience members
were Asian Indian American. These motel owners have created what
likely is the largest ethnic enterprise in U.S. history. They claim about
half of all the nation's motels and hotels, with a concentration in
lower- and middle-budget motels.[2] Indeed, these leading Indian
American motel owners have accrued enough wealth and resources
to command attention and bring powerful, wealthy, white men in as
speakers.

Indian American motel owners appear as the American dream
incarnate—self-employed, self-sufficient, boot-strapping immigrants
who have become successful without government intervention. Regardless of their political ideology, these keynote speakers invoke the

"model minority" stereotype to describe Indian American motel owners, praising them as a group that has overcome obstacles on the road to great achievements and implying that racial or cultural inequality is no longer an issue. In his address to the 2004 Asian American Hotel Owners Association (AAHOA) convention attendees, former Speaker of the House Newt Gingrich said: "I am proud to be here with you. You are what the American dream is all about. . . . You will make America a better country for us and our kids and grandkids."[3]

Nor is it just politicians who have embraced this narrative. Popular media have made similar points. For instance, a 2004 *New York Times* story complimented the growth of motels owned by first- and second-generation (that is, immigrant parents and their U.S.-born children) Patels by profiling a typical owner, saying:

> Morning and night, Mr. Patel, an immigrant from the Indian state of Gujarat, manned the front desk and did repairs on a 60-room Econo Lodge in Bordentown, New Jersey, while his wife, Indu, and two children hauled suitcases, made up beds, and vacuumed rooms. And the work paid off. At age 57, Mr. Patel owns not only the Econo Lodge but, with relatives, four other hotels. . . . At hotel schools like those at Cornell University, New York University, and San Diego State University, as well as more general business schools, the children are studying how to manage chains of hotels, work in corporate offices of name-brand franchisors, and acquire more upscale properties like Marriott and Hilton. Call them the Cornell hotel Patels.[4]

Similarly, a *USA Today* article published in 2007 conveys this motel phenomenon through the lens of an everyday Indian American, Dinu Patel, and his upscale Four Points motel in Connecticut:

> Thirty-five years after the arrival in the United States of the first Indian motel keepers—almost all with roots in the western India state of Gujarat and most with the surname Patel—up-by-the-bootstraps tales like that of Dinu Patel have become common. . . . The influence of Mahatma Gandhi, a Gujarati who preached self-reliance and simplicity, may also have an influence in their business culture.[5]

A second-generation Indian American, owner of a lower-budget franchise in Ohio, works the morning shift.

Although these newspaper articles note challenges owners can face, the narrative of Indian Americans having pulled themselves up by their *ethnic* bootstraps has become accepted doctrine.[6]

Other depictions of the challenges faced by Indian American motel owners, however, are far less positive. The celebrated film *Mississippi Masala*, by director Mira Nair, depicts an Indian American family from Uganda that works in a motel in a small town in the South, a region with a large representation of Indian American motel owners (Bal 2006). They encounter racist comments from customers who decry seeing yet another motel owned by Indian immigrants. Worried about bringing in money, they occasionally rent out rooms by the hour for likely illicit affairs. Nor are their personal lives content. They are caught up in the class hierarchies of their local Indian community and harbor longings for the country they left behind. Indeed, films and television programs routinely depict motels, no matter the ethnicity of the owners, as isolated, run-down, and possible havens for crime.

Although both portrayals of motel owners are exaggerated, which more accurately reflects Indian Americans' experiences and small business owners more generally? And how can they both have relevance at the same time for the same owners? Using observations and in-depth interviews, I concentrate primarily on Indian Americans who own lower-budget establishments—both independent and franchise—and secondarily on those with middle-budget franchises. These two groups make up the bulk of Indian American owners and have received both the praise and the critique indicated. Lower-budget (broadly defined) motel brands that Indian Americans commonly own include Comfort Inn, Days Inn, EconoLodge, Knights Inn, Sleep Inn, Super 8, and Travelodge. Middle-budget motels include Best Western, Country Inn and Suites, Hampton Inn, and Holiday Inn (and Express). Indian Americans have slowly been entering the higher-end motel market and even the full-service hotel market (for example, boutique hotels, Courtyard by Marriott, and Hilton).[7] To appreciate better the contradiction in appraisals of motel owners, I elaborate on both.

Indian Americans' Motel Success Story

Chances are that anyone who has stayed in motels in the last decade has stayed in at least one owned by an Indian American, even if that is not apparent to the guests. Indian Americans own almost two million rooms with property values of well over $100 billion.[8] About a third of Indian American owners have independent properties, typically all lower budget.[9] Indian Americans own about 60 percent of budget-oriented motels generally and over half of some motel chains.[10] Of franchise motels built in the last few years, those owned by Indian Americans comprise more than 50 percent. The motels can be found nationwide. They are in major cities, suburbs, and exurbs, and off interstate highways. This accomplishment is all the more remarkable when one considers the small segment of India from which most owners descend. Seventy percent of Indian American owners share the same surname, Patel, although they are not all related.[11] They come from the Indian state of Gujarat, either directly or from elsewhere in the diaspora (for example, the United Kingdom or East Africa). And a majority originate not just from Gujarat but from within a 100-mile radius of the central region of the state. Patels alone own about one-third of all the nation's motels. It is no wonder that politicians and the news media often celebrate them.

Contrary to popular perception, Patels did not own motels before emigrating. In fact, they arrived with few resources, entered the motel industry at the lowest level, and typically generated sufficient income to provide for their families. Although often familiar with English, many are not fluent. And they do not live and work in ethnic enclaves that serve co-ethnics, as is often the case for immigrant entrepreneurs. Instead, with motels, they are at the nexus of the expanding highway system and the growth of leisure time—quintessential markers of American life.

Citizenship, Neoliberalism, and Entrepreneurship

Political rhetoric and media discourse suggest that Indian American motel owners have attained full citizenship, that is, economic opportunities, respect of culture, and political opportunities equal to the majority (Glenn 2002; Maira 2009). This suggestion contrasts with more common depictions of Indian and other Asian Americans as foreigners (Lal 2008; Tuan 1998) and is challenged in the next section, but it can shape impressions of them and the nation. This presumed full citizenship results not just from the economic progress of Indian American motel owners but from the means of their progress: small business ownership. Small business owners embody neoliberal ideology, which in turn helps them gain acceptance.[12] Along with increased privatization and a limited government that promotes free markets, neoliberalism values self-sufficiency (Melamed 2006; Ong 2006). Ong (2003) writes that within today's neoliberal state, "increasingly, citizenship is defined as the civic duty of the individual to reduce his or her burden on society" (p. 12).

Entrepreneurship and small business are inherently part of neoliberalism (Harvey 2005). A neoliberal state frames its citizens as entrepreneurs, that is, as people who take care of their own needs without relying on public assistance (Brown 2006). Entrepreneurs are perceived as being self-initiated, autonomous, creative, and able to handle ambiguity, all desirable traits for citizens generally (Swedberg 2000). Family-run businesses represent neoliberal aspirations more than other types of businesses. In addition, they frequently employ or otherwise support other immigrants, often kin of the owners, and so absolve the government from a responsibility to assist newcomers, even as their labor is needed to support the economy (Reddy 2005). In other words, Indian American moteliers have attained their level of industry dominance because of their hard work, and they receive praise because of their perceived ideological fit with the nation.

The bootstrap, Horatio Alger–style aspect of this narrative not only serves Indian Americans' public image but also benefits the image—not to mention the economy—of the nation. Their success and resulting "acceptance" represent what is possible in the United States. In turn, the notion of U.S. exceptionalism is strengthened (Pease 2000). The United States appears as a morally just country when its immigrants and minorities attain full citizenship. This also makes the nation's global economic and political hegemony appear benign and even beneficial, rather than imperial, which furthers the United States' global status (Melamed 2006). With this public front, inequalities that the United States inflicts on its own minorities and on other nations can more easily be ignored or explained away.

Uncovering Inequalities

The rise of Indian Americans in the motel industry has national and international implications. As immigrant business owners, they become framed publicly within the rhetoric of the American dream, regardless of their economic and social realities (Abelmann and Lie 1995). But how much do their actual professional and personal experiences fit this model? Framing moteliers' success solely within neoliberal doctrine and as conferring full citizenship obscures the reality of their tenuous position within the hierarchies of capitalism, race, gender, economic and political opportunity, and culture. Economic recessions and other challenges to leisure or business travel (for example, the September 11, 2001, attacks) create severe financial burdens for owners. For instance, at a 2010 convention held by AAHOA—a professional association representing almost exclusively Indian Americans (at whose past conventions the noted politicians spoke)—about half of the hundreds of owners at a plenary session indicated they would seriously consider leaving the industry completely given how poor the economy had been.[13]

Furthermore, a wide variety of individuals with diverse experiences comprise the Indian Americans who dominate the motel industry. Although some own middle-budget and higher-budget establishments, Indian Americans most commonly own lower-budget establishments and as such do not fit the standard depiction of Indian Americans as elite professionals (for example, physicians, venture capitalists, hedge fund managers). Owners of lower-budget motels and their families often work with limited or no staff, struggle to make ends meet, go without health care for themselves and their workers, and lack social prestige in their local community even while the ethnic group as a whole is praised. They worry about the proliferation of motels and oversaturation of the market. They refer to themselves as laborers at the mercy of customers, franchisors, and/or the government. Very low-budget motels have become associated with prostitution, drug dealing, and other crimes (a stereotype that is often misplaced and that ignores similar activities within upscale motels). Cities depend on motels to house otherwise homeless persons (Jain 1989).

Indian American owners of middle- and higher-budget properties have not encountered the same degree of marginalization. Still, they complain of a lack of autonomy from the franchisors, as seen, for example, in the franchisors' collection of fees that are not based on the owners' earnings (see Mathew 2005). Female motel owners cite disrespect in their daily negotiations with vendors. A number of Indian Americans also note that franchisors give them due attention but still seem to view them differently from other owners—as immigrants rather than "ordinary" Americans. Such problems, although not debilitating, lie in sharp

contrast to the presumably equal treatment granted to successful entrepreneurial immigrants. In addition, customers may still avoid Indian-
owned motels across all budget levels. Indian American motels can be
racialized as dirty, poorly run, and managed by "untrustworthy foreigners." "Patel motels," a common industry phrase, have been maligned as
smelling like curry (Lal 2008).

Tied to the professional challenges have been the personal hurdles
facing owners and their families, in particular the large percentage in
lower-budget establishments. Not only did they emigrate from a country halfway around the world, but they also moved repeatedly across the
United States looking for a good deal on a motel. The search for an affordable property could land them off interstate highways, in rural areas, or in commercial districts, apart from the support provided by
co-ethnic networks. In these settings, they can face cultural and racial
schisms with local residents. When they do reside near fellow co-ethnic
motel owners, relationships may be compromised by business tensions.
Also, living inside their motels contradicts the standard notion of a home.
As a result, some owners and their families have felt resigned to their
business and personal lives rather than enthusiastic about them. Sometimes their businesses perform poorly and their family life suffers, and
although most families find ways to respond to these problems, a few
regret having migrated to the United States. So, Indian American
motel owners often have a precarious relationship to the image of the
small business owner promulgated by Al Gore and Newt Gingrich and
instead resonate with the depictions in popular film. By focusing on
those in lower- and middle-budget motels, *Life Behind the Lobby* moves
away from a depiction of Asian Americans as only highly successful
professionals.

Theorizing Immigrant Adaptation Within the Diaspora

The world of Indian American moteliers holds a paradox: their entrepreneurial acumen, business ownership, and industry dominance represent the American dream, but owners and their families are caught up
in embedded economic, racial, gender, and immigrant-specific hierar-

chies. How can these dual trends coexist, and should one side be read as truer than the other?

This paradoxical dynamic also applies to other groups outside the white, masculine, heteronormative ideal. For instance, other Asian Americans, Caribbean Americans, Jewish Americans, and certain Latinos and African Americans also are considered successful and hard working but are not fully accepted as Americans. Women make up a greater percentage of college students than men but still live within a patriarchal education system, labor market, and domestic sphere. Gays and lesbians are sought-after members of cities because of the seeming advantage of "diversity" to creative growth even while homophobia remains entrenched in legislation, the labor market, and public opinion.[14] And the denial of full equality to such groups despite their meaningful gains has historical roots in white, male, capitalist privilege (Glenn 2002).

In the case of Indian American moteliers, however, this dilemma is all the more perplexing and unexpected given how synonymous their ethnicity has become with the hospitality industry. How should we make sense of their simultaneous achievements and upward mobility alongside their continued challenges? How immigrant minorities experience and respond to such dilemmas, which are relatively common, has not been adequately explained.

Current formulations of immigrant adaptation typically pick a side in this paradox and characterize nonimpoverished communities either as increasingly integrated and generally free of troubles or as defined by their troubles—a perspective that downplays the significance of their accomplishments. A large number of academics who study immigration have argued that ethnic minorities in the United States can gradually achieve socioeconomic mobility and possibly full citizenship. I call this camp "integrationists." Integrationists recognize that poverty, racism, and other constraints can handicap immigrants. Yet integrationists do not consider such barriers to be endemic. There are no hierarchies embedded in white privilege, capitalism, or patriarchy. Groups can gradually integrate as they take advantage of economic and educational opportunities and adopt useful parts of mainstream culture (for example, standard English) while also relying on resources within their ethnic group (Alba and Nee 2003; Gibson 1988; Portes and Rumbaut 2006; Zhou and Bankston 1998).[15] The integrationist perspective prioritizes groups' success even as it recognizes challenges. As evidence of a group's successful integration, scholars point to educational attainment, economic status, interracial marriage rates, and other measures (Sakamoto, Goyette, and Kim 2009).

From this cautiously optimistic perspective, Indian American motel owners' trajectory of gradual integration and economic security, especially relative to their other occupational options, becomes highlighted (Cohen and Tyree 1994; Portes and Bach 1985; Yoon 1997). Motel owners may face prejudiced customers, oversaturation of the market, and a compromised personal life, but the emphasis falls on how they are able to handle these problems effectively (Lee 2002; Min 2008). According to the integrationists, the success of these entrepreneurs is real and should come as no surprise. It stems from having a fortunate set of resources, access to business opportunities, and a lack of significant hurdles. The challenges facing Indian American motel owners in building professional and personal lives are downplayed within this perspective and, instead, are read as temporary inconveniences that can be overcome.

According to the second camp on immigrants' livelihood, which I refer to broadly as "critical race theorists," the nation is defined by inequalities that bestow privilege on heterosexual, U.S.-born, white men (Bonilla Silva 2003; Glenn 2002; Lipsitz 1998; Spickard 2007). The paradox of success along with marginalization tilts heavily toward defining immigrant minorities by their troubles, thereby downplaying their accomplishments. As Golash-Boza (2006) writes of Portes and Rumbaut (who consider race more than do other integrationists), "These scholars do not address the extent to which whiteness is a prerequisite for assimilation into dominant culture" (p. 29). The United States is an imperial, not immigrant, nation that has uplifted white men through genocide, slavery, colonization, internment, patriarchy, and war (Glick Schiller 2005; Pease 2000). Even economically successful immigrant groups, such as many

Asian Americans, experience a "differential inclusion" into the nation (Espiritu 2003; Kim 2008). They receive praise when assisting white elites but overall encounter an economic and social subordination. To demonstrate immigrants' inequalities, scholars highlight variables that are different from those within integration studies. These measures include a lack of promotions in the workplace, the "model minority" rhetoric that attributes success to a foreign culture, hate crimes, resistant transnational ties, and everyday experiences of racism (Chou and Feagin 2008; Das Gupta 2006).

Ethnic entrepreneurs' experiences, including those of Indian American motel owners, can be understood within this perspective as well (Kim 2000; Light and Bonacich 1991; Park 1997). Owners may accrue profit, but it requires exploiting themselves, for they often serve big capital while being scapegoats for other minorities' frustrations (Min 1996). In addition, business competition strains ties to one's ethnic community (Yoon 1997). Strain also arises from tense relations with various other constituencies, as well as from the long hours and having to live where one works. Owners' collective agency to resist their problems may bear some fruit, but it furthers divisions and hostilities from other groups (Bonacich 1973). The result is not the American dream for ethnic entrepreneurs like Indian Americans, but a weak economic position and the denial of full belonging (Abelmann and Lie 1995).

The academic literature's depictions of ethnic entrepreneurs correspond to those in popular media. These appraisals of immigrant minorities' adaptation have merit but are individually insufficient. Racialization and anti-imperialism theories have not adequately explained how some immigrant minorities readily identify with the American dream and have considerable achievements even while being differentially included. As a result, integration scholars can downplay this highly critical perspective as less consequential compared with their "more substantial" variables of income, educational attainment, and so on. Conversely, because integration literature glosses over the degrading treatment of immigrant minorities and their personal sacrifices, its claims of multiculturalism and gradual equality ring hollow. These competing theories talk past one another, leaving the experiences of such immigrant minorities insufficiently understood.

Bridging Mutually Exclusive Perspectives

Life Behind the Lobby explains not only Indian American motel owners' accomplishments and simultaneous economic and social marginalization, but also how individuals respond in ways that sustain this duality. First, invoking a transnational perspective on Patels' origins in Gujarat and elsewhere in the diaspora, it explains why Indian Americans immigrated to the United States (Chapter 1) and how they became so prolific as business owners compared with other ethnic entrepreneurs (Chapter 2). In other words, how were they able to make Vice President Gore and others refer to them as the torchbearers of America's ideals? Second, it explains how continued challenges within the motel owners' professional lives (Chapter 3) and personal lives (Chapter 5), reminiscent of film portrayals, take place concurrently with their integration, thus creating the paradox of high achievement along with sustained inequalities. Third, *Life Behind the Lobby* explains how Indian American motel owners respond to this paradox in ways that confront it yet, ironically, help sustain it (Chapters 3 and 4). Generally speaking, rather than trying to fully overcome economic, racial, gender, and cultural inequalities, owners took the more feasible route and worked within them. Indian American moteliers became successful and comfortable enough to make claims on the American dream, but in the process they did not fully challenge, and at times inadvertently sustained, the basis of their subordination. They lessened the inequalities they faced, but never in ways that let them move beyond them entirely. The result is practically living the American dream but within an enduring marginalization.

I am not the first to try to reconcile theories of adaptation by analyzing immigrants' experiences of both mobility and subordination. But in arguing the mutual relevance of integrationists and more critical scholars, others have duplicated the notion of mutually exclusive trajectories without retheorizing adaptation to deconstruct it. A few well-respected examples dealing with disparate groups illustrate this. Telles and Ortiz

(2008) aim to move past the dichotomy of assimilated versus racialized framings in the adaptation of Mexican Americans.[16] Assimilation is occurring in some cultural dimensions (for example, language) for Mexican Americans but not in key socioeconomic ways (for example, education), which is defined by racialization. So although both trajectories take place, they remain mutually exclusive because they apply to distinct aspects of the group.

Kibria (2002) offers the concept of racialized ethnicity (citing Tuan 1998) as a way to recognize the relevance of both assimilation and critical race (or what she refers to as "racial minority") theories in defining the adaptation of middle- and upper-class Asian Americans. For these Asian Americans, racialized ethnicity means being attentive to their treatment as racial minorities. Still, racism may not be so significant to them that they form hostilities against whites. The second generation expects to have a comfortable lifestyle. Therefore, racialization and greater integration both take place. This attempt to move beyond the either/or notion of adaptation is useful. But in contrast to assimilation theory, the racialized ethnicity perspective emphasizes how minorities experience racial marginalization despite any economic success. Race and ethnicity continue to matter; the only question is how much. The more they matter, the stronger are the ethnic and pan-ethnic boundaries, and the weaker the integration.[17]

Rather than sidestep the contradiction between reigning theories, I bring them together. *Life Behind the Lobby* does not downplay Indian Americans' achievements and challenges, nor does it suggest that they pertain to distinct parts of their life (for example, professional achievements versus personal struggles). Generally speaking, Indian American motel owners have become successful, which is applauded here. Yet this does not support the neoliberal or (segmented) assimilationist trajectory of full incorporation into the economic and social mainstream simply through integration into dominant institutions and reliance on ethnic capital. Nor does it accept the integrationists' liberal assumption of an exceptional nation-state whose immigrant minorities will be on par with whites if minor adjustments are made to key institutions. Instead, this analysis of how individuals sustain their achievements within embedded inequalities makes an epistemological point: it is possible to analyze inequalities within narratives of how a minority group has come to its achievements. At the same time, just because inequalities constrain individuals does not mean real advancement is not occurring. The assumption across theories of immigration and race continues to be that economic parity with and cultural acceptance by whites means that race is insignificant. To demonstrate racial inequalities, scholars often point to the hardships minorities face. Yet a focus on individuals' agency within constraints demonstrates how achievements and impediments occur simultaneously.

Patel Motels

Who are these ethnic entrepreneurs, and what exactly is a motel? The most significant portion of motel owners, both historically and currently, are Patels from central and southern Gujarat, although some originated from northern Gujarat and elsewhere in India. Gujarati Americans are most known for their presence in the hospitality and diamond industries, followed by their presence in engineering and the sciences (including medicine), and with relatively little representation in the high-tech industry compared with co-nationals (Sheth 2001). In fact, Gujarati Americans are significantly more likely to be self-employed than non-Gujarati Indian Americans (Kim, Hurh, and Fernandez 1989). Gujaratis are the largest segment of the Indian American population, at about 20 percent.[18]

Motels are lodging establishments with guest rooms all within the same building and with a surrounding parking lot. They typically lack the distinctions of hotels, with their extravagant lobbies, restaurants with room service, elevators connecting multiple floors, and large conference facilities. Today's motel descended from cottage courts, in which individual rooms were in their own small building or cabin, and before that, 1930s tourist camps, where rooms were attached to gas stations and general stores, and guests paid for each "amenity" separately (for example, a mattress would cost 25 cents) (Wood and Wood 2004). The cottage courts transformed into motor courts reflect the contemporary motel, or motor lodge. More and more were built along the expanding highway systems, and many developed into franchises.

Indian Americans dominate the motel industry. They are represented by AAHOA, which has more than 10,000 members, most of whom are Indian American owner-operators. Three-quarters of AAHOA members own limited-service properties, that is, motels that do not offer cooked food or drink (they lack a restaurant, a bar, room service, and so on but may have simple breakfast items).[19] Almost two-thirds of AAHOA members own a franchise motel. Among Indian Americans at large, however, this percentage is lower because owners of an independent, lower-budget motel are less likely to join the organization than are franchisees. (Although some of the owners profiled in this study do have transnational business ventures, Indian owners of luxury hotels in India or major diasporic cities are not connected.)[20]

I have been referring to lower-, middle-, and higher-budget motels. Moving forward, I also refer to more specific categories: low, low-middle, middle, higher-middle, and high (and in the industry, even more specific breakdowns are used). A low-budget motel is typically an independent, mom-and-pop establishment. Estimates are that one-third of Indian American–owned motels are independents.[21] These motels are small (generally thirty rooms or less), offer very low rates, and often serve truckers as well as long-term stays (guests staying for weeks or months at a time). They also have few amenities and cheaper-quality supplies. At a motel convention, I spoke with a towel vendor who stated that the cheapest towels, which are also the lowest quality, are more likely to be in low-budget motels because they are more easily replaced if stolen.[22] (Extended-stay motels are categorized separately from independent motels, where guests may end up staying for weeks at a time. Extended-stay motels are intentionally oriented toward those staying for longer stretches and are not inexpensive. Extended-stay units, unlike most independent motels, typically have a kitchen and supplies that longer-term guests would require, as well as the internal wiring necessary to support such stays. Few Indian Americans own extended-stay motels.[23]) Low-budget motels are less likely to be located off interstates; they are more commonly found in urban downtowns, possibly in higher-crime areas. They have very few, if any, employees.

A higher tier of motel but still lower budget is the lower-middle-budget motel. Although some independent motels fall under this category, the lower-middle-budget motels consist primarily of such franchise motels as Days Inn, EconoLodge, Motel 6, Super 8, and Travelodge. The room rates are economical, and they are often located off interstate highways. Unlike low-budget motels, they have more tourists, people on temporary work contracts for nearby companies, as well as some truckers. They tend to have more amenities and equipment that is more up-to-date. They have a small staff, such as a few housekeepers, desk clerks, and an occasional maintenance person. Like low-budget motels, however, the owner must be available and often lives on-site with her/his family if it is allowed by the motel franchise. Depending on a particular franchise's condition and location, it can be low budget rather than lower middle. For simplification, the term *lower budget* as used in this study refers to both low-budget and lower-middle-budget motels unless otherwise specified.

The middle-budget level, which consists of middle-budget motels (Best Western, Comfort Inn and Suites, Ramada Inn) and higher-middle-budget motels (Country Inn and Suites, Hampton Inn, Holiday Inn / Holiday Inn Express) are franchised. Middle-budget motels cater to business guests, not simply leisure travelers, and offer higher-end amenities and services (such as hot breakfasts, in-room coffeemakers, and Internet connections). Such motels may have meeting rooms as well. Depending on their size and revenue, they employ ten to fifteen people.

High-budget motels are very well maintained, have ample amenities, and mimic hotels. These consist of Courtyard by Marriott, Hilton Garden Inn, and the like. Although relatively few Indian Americans own such motels at this time, the numbers are slowly increasing. Owners of such motels employ numerous staff and often hire management companies to run them. Owners do not live in these motels. A few Indian Americans have been able to purchase full-scale hotels as well, such as Hyatt, Hilton, and boutique hotels.[24] To date, they represent a fraction of the Indian American motel owners.

A parent corporation in the industry typically owns multiple franchise brands at different price points. The major motel corporations in which Indian Americans are involved (Accor, Carlson, Choice, Inter-Continental, and Wyndham) operate numerous franchises (also known as brands, chains, or flags) targeted to different budgets and niches.

Research Design

To study this group of Indian Americans and how they have come to dominate the motel industry, I have conducted interviews, observed owners and their families as they work and live in the motels, and read primary materials, including ethnic and mainstream newspapers, AAHOA's monthly magazine, and other industry documents. When I was in the early stages of setting up the research design for this study, a motel owner told me to avoid conducting a quantitative survey because owners would be suspicious of a relative stranger. Formal and informal interviews and observations would work better *after* I had spent time with owners. This methodology actually suited the project goals well because owners' general stature in the industry is not in doubt. More relevant here is how they made sense of their professional and personal lives, which a conversational approach helped ascertain.

I have conducted ninety-three formal and many more informal interviews. Of those interviewed formally, fifty-three lived in Ohio. Ten owners were interviewed in Alabama, where I lived for a few months during the summer of 2002, and the rest were scattered across the country, with particular representation in the San Francisco Bay Area (the origin of Indian Americans in the hospitality industry). Geographic differences, although not the focus of this book, receive attention at various points.

The bulk of the interviews took place after 2005. They included mostly Indian American motel owners, but also a few children and employees. In addition to owners, I talked with seven representatives of AAHOA. I also interviewed some nonowners and non-Indians to flesh out the contours of Indian Americans' business and personal experiences. These included an Indian American who is an elected state official in Ohio; an Indian American community leader in Cleveland; a representative from a South Asian American television station popular in the diaspora and among moteliers in particular; a lobbyist working on behalf of AAHOA; a representative of an African American hotel owners association; and a few white owners. Less formal interviews were conducted with mostly white vendors at motel conventions. Three-quarters of the owners interviewed were men. They represent the public face of the households and the motels, often have better English skills, and are typically most available. Given the cultural context, it was difficult for me as a man to interview women, in particular recent immigrants, without a husband present, and it was difficult to find the husband and the wife available at the same time. Nearly 80 percent of the informants were first-generation immigrants who arrived in the United States as adults. The rest arrived as children (the "1.5 generation") or were second generation, as well as a couple in the third generation. Interviewees ranged in age from sixteen to seventy-something. Almost all owners were Gujarati. I have changed or deleted the names of all informants cited in this study. I also do not refer to specific motel brands except in hypothetical examples. The point of this study is not to dissect the motel industry per se but to explain the experiences of Indian American entrepreneurs. For that reason I have not interviewed franchise representatives, although I include information from meetings between representatives and Indian American owners.

Sixty percent of the interviewees own low- and lower-middle-budget establishments (both independent and franchise), as is typical for Indian American moteliers. Most of the rest own middle budget, and a couple own higher budget. Sixty percent of the interviewees own motels in nonmetropolitan areas or outer suburbs, and the remaining 40 percent own establishments in larger cities, including the inner suburbs. The main sites within Ohio were the northeast (Cleveland/Akron/Elyria areas), the northwest (Toledo area), the city of Lima, and central Ohio (Columbus area), with minor representation of the southwest part of the state (Cincinnati area). The residents of these areas vary, but for the most part they are working- and middle-class whites and some African Americans, as fitting the demographics of the state (elaborated on below).

I met owners and their families by arriving at their motels randomly, visiting Hindu temples and talking with attendees, introducing myself at AAHOA meetings and leisure events, and asking for others' recommendations. The result was a focused snowball sample that reached well beyond those most active in their area. As a non-Gujarati with no connection to the hospitality industry, I was an outsider looking in. All of the formal interviews took place in English and ranged from thirty minutes to more than two hours. Observations included working in a motel for a couple of days (assisting with housekeeping, maintenance, and desk clerk duties); attending a community's Diwali party; attending political fund-raisers; visiting temples; eating at restaurants and in homes with motel owners and their families; attending six AAHOA meetings; and attending a few volleyball games of male owners.

Indian Americans in Ohio

This book is not about Ohio, but Ohio serves as a key setting for many informants. I had access to Ohio because I live there, but that is not why I chose it as the primary location for my research. Ohio and other Midwestern sites (with the exception of Chicago) have been overlooked not only in discussions of Indian Americans and Asian Americans but also in discussions of immigration as a whole (Dhingra 2009a). There has been growing interest in "new destinations" of immigration (Zúñiga and Hernández-León 2005). These destinations are not new for immigrants—European immigrants have been settling in these areas for centuries. And they have also been destinations for Latino and Asian immigrants—a Chinatown has existed in Cleveland since the 1890s. But only recently have such destinations gained large numbers of contemporary immigrants.

Ohio also serves as a useful site for many interviews because of its ideological significance as part of America's heartland. In the contexts of the Cold War and 9/11, the Midwest has been romanticized for its purported cultural character. But the culture wars of "real America" versus "elite America" and of red states versus blue states have reduced the Midwest to a caricature. Despite these characterizations, the Midwest has important stories to tell. How have immigrant minorities been treated here? How have they succeeded here? How does this complicate the image of the heartland?

Like much of the upper Midwest Rust Belt, Ohio is undergoing an economic transition. Formerly based primarily in manufacturing, the economy is now more mixed, undergoing a slow turn to technology, health care, and revised manufacturing. The total state population in 2000 was 11,353,140.[25] In contrast to the increasing number of states that are becoming majority minority, 86 percent of Ohioans were non-Hispanic white in 2000[26] (total number 9,779,512).[27] The dominant racial minority group is African Americans, at 12 percent (total number 1,372,501), with Latinos at 2 percent (217,123). In 2000, the state's population of Asian Americans was one-third the national average, at 1.4 percent (total number 159,776).[28]

The South Asian American population in Ohio is predominantly Indian American. In fact, Indian Americans are the largest Asian ethnic group in the state. Still, the community in Ohio is typical of many across the nation, with relatively few in the state before 1965 and a large representation of professionals and entrepreneurs since. Those Indians who came to Ohio before 1965 typically did so as students, and they numbered in the low hundreds in the major cities. But after 1965, university students were joined by professionals in the medical, engineering, academic, and information technology fields, and the population increased dramatically. Relatives of immigrants have been contributing to the growth since. These relatives have diversified the employment categories into motel and other small business ownership and into working-class positions in these and other low-paying service industries.[29]

In 2000, Indian Americans made up 0.68 percent of the U.S. population (total number 1,899,599).[30] At the state level, Indian Americans comprised just 0.38 percent of the Ohio population (total number 43,119) in 2000.[31] Yet they own more than 25 percent of the hotels and motels.[32] In the state's major cities, the Indian American populations are below the national average of 0.67 percent (with the exception of Columbus, whose population is just above the national average).[33] This amounts to a few thousand in each major city. Indian American motel owners, including subjects in this study, inhabit nonmetropolitan locations as well. For instance, Lima, a small city prominent in this study, is located in Allen County, halfway between Toledo and Dayton in the western portion of the state. Allen County had a population of 108,473 in 2000, of which 199 (0.1 percent) were of Indian origin. The number of people of Indian origin in Lima itself is below the threshold of 100 people set by the U.S. Census, so the actual number cannot be calculated.[34] Still, Lima has an active Indian American population, including motel owners. In 2005 and 2006, AAHOA held its North Central United States (Indiana, Michigan, and Ohio) regional meeting in Lima.

The overall economic status of Indian Americans in Ohio is strong, as it is nationally. Their median household income nationally in 2000 was $61,322 (compared to the national average of $41,994),[35] and in Ohio was $60,344 (above the state average of $40,956).[36] Community leaders engage in charity work for local causes and causes in India. Interviews with community leaders and other Indian American service providers indicate that few are in need of social services. This is not to suggest that many Indian Americans do not face economic hardships or worry about their financial status. Some, from engineers to motel owners, face occupational discrimination. But relatively few are living in poverty or in need of multiple forms of government assistance.[37]

Indian Americans' self-employment rate in Ohio has been much higher than that of other populations in the state. In 2000, white men had a self-employment rate of 3.7 percent; white women, 1.4 percent; black men, 1.4 percent; black women, 0.7 percent. By contrast, Indian American men had a self-employment rate of 6 percent, and Indian American women had a rate of 4.6 percent (and presumably the rate for Gujarati Americans would be much higher [Fernandez and Kim 1998]).[38]

Not surprisingly, the Indian American community in Ohio is often framed as a model minority. For example, at the opening ceremony of the Indian community garden in Cleveland, local political representatives praised the community for its number of engineers and healthcare workers helping to lead the local economy. Former governor Ted

Strickland has embraced the model minority image of Indian Americans as well. He is quoted as saying at a Democratic convention honoring specifically Indian Americans in 2008:

> In Ohio, we are a diverse state and Ohioans speak more than forty different languages, and we have ethnic groups from 336 different backgrounds. Within that diversity, we are very fortunate to have a growing Indian population that brings with it the treasured traditions and a wonderful commitment to community. I am proud to say that since the last Census period, the Indian population in Ohio has grown 86 percent. . . . I am also proud to say that Indian households have the highest incomes and the highest educational attainments among all the ethnic groups in America and in Ohio.[39]

Taken as a whole, Indian Americans are considered a major asset to the state. How motel owners experience day-to-day interactions with locals, however, has been at times a different story.

The number one priority of Indian families and local Indian leaders is to pass on their culture and traditions to their children. Gujaratis, Punjabis, Bengalis, South Indians, and so on have cultural organizations throughout the state. The major cities have Hindu temples, mosques, Sikh gurduwaras, and other religious institutions. Even within Hinduism, multiple types of religious traditions exist, and certain temples appeal to certain sects.[40] One Hindu temple, dedicated to Sree Venkateswara, is currently in development (as of 2009) in Richfield, in northeast Ohio (the Cleveland/Akron area). Richfield is a rural/suburban village with a population of just over three thousand. Located halfway between Cleveland and Akron, the town has practically no local Indian population. Its selection as the site for this temple is a testament to how spread out the Indian population is in Ohio. Neither Cleveland nor Akron has enough Indians to support a temple on its own. The two communities came together to settle on this location. Leaders are hoping that the long drive for residents of each city will not deter attendance. They are also hoping that the opposition of a few locals does not become a bigger problem. Local residents have cited concerns over noise, impact on local habitat, and the exact location. One city council person said of the planned temple, "I don't think it's harmonious with the area. It's a building nobody will want to look at when buying property."[41]

Social and political interests are also bringing the Indian American community together. The Federation of Asian Indian Associations, for instance, is an umbrella group in central Ohio (Columbus region) aimed at supporting members' needs, such as helping with starting a business, nurturing transnational ties, and helping children select a college. Individuals donate to political candidates, and Indian American leaders hope that the community will play a more active and visible role in politics, especially as the second generation becomes more involved. Toward that end, in 2006, Jay Goyal (D) defeated Phillip Holloway in the 73rd District and became an Ohio state house representative, winning 63 percent of the vote. Only twenty-six years old, Goyal counted on support from Indian Americans well beyond his local district.

With such a high-status profile, it may have been inevitable that some would question whether Indian Americans are truly a minority. For instance, an editorial in *The Plain Dealer*, March 3, 2007, agreed with a lawsuit by an African American contractor in Cincinnati. The suit argued that because no discrimination in awarding state contracts in Ohio has ever been documented against them, Indian American businesses should no longer be categorized as minority business enterprises and so should no longer receive special considerations. Indian American leaders contend that economic success does not mean that they are not minorities susceptible to discriminatory actions, either intentional or unintentional. As new arrivals to the country and state, it is often difficult to prove one's capabilities or have the right connections; therefore, extra consideration is necessary. The discussion of Indian Americans' place within the state and its racial hierarchies will remain a sensitive one for the foreseeable future.

Again, although Ohio was my richest source of material, *Life Behind the Lobby* is about neither Ohio nor the Midwest. Indians own motels across the country. The dynamics between owners and with local communities can vary based on geographic setting. Informants, as noted previously, were from not only Ohio but also Alabama, California, and many points in between. So although this study is not representative of Indians nationwide, it does indeed have relevance beyond a single state or region. I now turn to how Indians entered the hospitality industry, starting with their migration from Gujarat throughout the diaspora.

1 Building the Diaspora

STUDIES IN ASIAN AMERICAN HISTORY have documented the discriminatory treatment of Asian immigrants to the United States in the early and middle 1900s. The U.S. government has denied Asian Americans citizenship, the right to own land, the right to unionize, the right to marry whom they choose, the right to sponsor relatives, and more (Glenn 2002). In daily life they encountered anti-Asian riots, workplace discrimination, low wages, residential segregation, surveillance, and cultural degradation. Indian immigrants did not have as large a presence in the United States as did Chinese, Japanese, and Filipino immigrants. Still, they faced the same racism. The "dirty Hindoos" were driven out of working-class jobs in the Pacific Northwest where many first settled in the United States (Takaki 1989). They were presumed unable to assimilate. In 1917 India was included in the Asiatic barred zone, thereby prohibiting the migration of Indian laborers. In 1923 those already in the country were categorized by the Supreme Court, in *United States v. Bhagat Singh Thind*, as nonwhites despite their designated "Caucasian" status. This barred them from attaining citizenship. More restrictions followed. In California any land they owned was taken away, along with their right to own land. The 1924 Immigration Act cut off immigration for Indians and others barred from citizenship.

With this in mind, why would Indian immigrants from Gujarat establish themselves in the United States in the mid-twentieth century rather than stay in India or go elsewhere in the diaspora? The answer requires a diasporic, postcolonial approach to Indian immigrants as racial minorities within the United States. Chapter 1 documents the migration of Gujaratis to the United States primarily from the 1940s to the 1970s—a time frame almost entirely overlooked in Indian American history—and examines their experiences in the United States that pushed them toward self-employment.

Origins of Emigration

Preindependence

The majority of Indian American motel owners are Patels. They mainly descended from the urban and rural areas of the central and southern districts of Gujarat, most notably Surat, Navsari, Baroda, Kheda, and Ahmedabad. Gujaratis are composed of numerous castes and subcastes. Of these, Leva Kanbis, also referred to as Leva Patels, are particularly represented in the U.S. motel industry. Charotar, Kadva, and Matia Patels also own motels in large numbers. Other Gujarati groups in the U.S. motel industry include Bhaktas, Desais, Nayaks, and Shahs.

Around A.D. 1100, Patels were leaders within their village communities in Gujarat, collecting land revenue for the king (*pat* means "parcel of land"). They were known as "Patlikh," which later became Patal and finally Patel.[1] They are a subcaste of the Vaishna caste, the leading caste of Gujarat (Ramji 2006). Patels are a diverse group but share a number of similarities, particularly those who became motel owners. Many of the Patels who own motels are of Kanbi and Patidar origin. To varying degrees both groups have historically been landowners and tax collectors. The cultivating caste of Kanbis, the largest agricultural caste in Gujarat, originated in the Leva and Karad districts of Punjab (Bal 2006). These Kanbis migrated to Gujarat in the eleventh and twelfth centuries, becoming known as Leva Kanbis and Karadva Kanbis (and later shortened to Kadva Kanbis). Patidars descended originally from the most "elite" of the Leva Kanbis, the dominant caste within the Charotar region of Gujarat (where a number of motel owners originate from) (Bates 1981). According to Pocock (1972), Patidars were "an upwardly mobile, middle-ranking peasant caste." Patel became the most common surname among Kanbis and Patidars. Although Patels continued to be well represented in central Gujarat, many migrated to other regions of the state. Those primarily involved in agriculture moved south to the Surat area of Gujarat in the 1820s in search of new farmland (Rutten 1995).

Together Kanbi and Patidar Patels had considerably more power and prestige than other castes within Gujarat, owing in part to British influence. As Britain gained control over Gujarat in the early 1800s, Kanbis and Patidars became favored as the main cultivators of the land (Bal 2006; Chaturvedi 2007). Along with British control came irrigation systems and easier transportation of crops on railways, and Patel farmers saw their incomes grow (Bal 2006). The British government charged them with assessing and collecting land income, and so they had a prestigious and somewhat protected role within village life.[2] By the late nineteenth century, Patel control over Kheda's rural economy and society was practically complete—they controlled the means of production by owning land and labor, and they served as moneylenders, whose transactions often resulted in the acquisition of property (Gidwani 2000).

Although of higher status in general, Kanbis and Patidars had various divisions. Kanbis were on the bottom of that hierarchy, with lesser Patidars slightly ahead, and then "authentic" Patidars on top (Gidwani 2000). Kanbis often owned small pieces of land or worked as tenant farmers on others' land. Lesser Patidars owned mid-sized farms, and the highest-class Patidars had large estates. Regardless of status, few were laborers. In the mid-1800s, lesser Patidars and Kanbis remained subordinate to higher Patidars under British rule (Bates 1981). As Streefkerk (1997) writes of Gujarat in the 1800s, "British rule meant prosperity for a small section of the peasantry. However, the condition of the majority of the peasants and tribals deteriorated. They suffered from excessive revenue demands, market fluctuations, and became uprooted" (p. M4). Patidars and Kanbis often had peasants among them (Chaturvedi 2007).

Economic upheavals took their toll on Patels in the late 1800s and early 1900s. The famine, the monsoon failure, and the plague of 1899–1902 severely weakened them. Well over a million people died in Gujarat as a result of these catastrophes (Rutten and Patel 2003). The economic basis of farmers worsened, especially in the Charotar region, where many Patidars resided (Pocock 1972). Lesser Patidars, and to a greater extent the ordinary Kanbis who farmed their own land, fared somewhat better. Many grew nonfood crops, such as cotton and tobacco, and the income from such crops rose. Also, Kanbis and lesser Patidars were receiving remittances from relatives in East Africa, and they invested these monies, often in real estate (Vishwanath 1990).

It was the higher Patidars who suffered the most as their tenant farmers left and their cattle died. It is hard to exaggerate the effects of these events. As Bates (1981) wrote:

> But in the event between 1899 and December 1900, 1,300,000 people died in British Gujarat, mostly from disease, as the price of kadbi (a principal food grain) rose from Rs 13 to Rs 36 per 1000 lbs. The Kheda district was initially among the hardest hit: the population, which had climbed from 8 lakhs in 1881 to 8 and ¾ lakhs in 1891, and possibly to nearly 10 lakhs by 1899, declined to a mere 7 lakhs by 1901.

Adding to Patels' general financial troubles, their plots of land grew smaller and smaller over successive generations. Cultural rules of inheritance called for dividing one's land equally for each son in a family. As their plots diminished in size, parents could not support their families. The ever-increasing dowries required for the marriage of daughters became more and more difficult to provide. In addition, Patels' income and status declined due to their position as village tax collectors.

These economic challenges led to shifts in how Patels planned for future economic and social gains. In particular, they looked toward education (of the men), farming different crops, moving into trade, and emigration. As Kanbi Patels began to experience more economic success, they focused less on their regional and caste distinctions—Leva, Bhakta, Matia, Kadva, and so on—and more on their unity as Patidars

(Breman 2007). Mixing between the groups took place through marriage, with Kanbis and lesser Patidars paying large dowries to marry into higher Patidar families, even as higher Patidars may have wanted to avoid such unions. Some Kanbis also changed their affiliation to Patidars in order to raise their status. The groups became more mixed than ever before, so much so that in 1931 "Patidar" became the official name of the caste. Patels still maintain regional and caste distinctions but to a much lesser extent.[3]

In addition to economic challenges, Patels faced political challenges. Despite benefiting at times from British rule, Patels in Gujarat were aware of their precarious status under colonialism and of the colonizers' exploitation of them. Following the famine, the British continued to insist upon high tax collections, even increasing their demands. This, coupled with the social and economic progress of Kanbi and Patidar peasants in the Kheda district, resulted in their becoming more militant against the British (Bates 1981), and in 1918 and 1919, Gandhi carried out his first satyagraha against tax collection in the Kheda district. A sense of unification through marriage among lesser Patidars, along with their increasing sense of entitlement and communalism following recent prosperity, also motivated the movement. In two-thirds of the villages of the district, revenue officials resigned. In one-third of the villages, revenue was not paid (Mayer 1984). Government representatives came in and confiscated property and assets, which were returned after increasing media pressure. In other words, exploitation under colonial rule created political and economic solidarity.

Postindependence Economy

Under British rule, Patels experienced economic and political ups and downs, which encouraged the emigration that ultimately led them to the United States. The natural disasters contributed to the lack of control over their financial and personal lives, which colonial rule exacerbated. Nor could Patels count on a stable economy after the 1947 independence, despite their relatively privileged economic status. In the 1950s and 1960s, the Gujarat economy, including agriculture (the ancestral profession of most motel owners in the United States), had not seen steady growth. Income and quality of life depended heavily on natural occurrences beyond one's control, such as the timing and intensity of monsoons. Rather than stable increases and decreases from year to year, the economy fluctuated strongly (Dholakia 2008; Lakdawala 1982). By the 1950s, there was already a strong history of emigration, and few incentives arose to stem the outflow.

The growth of Gujarat's economy from 1960 to 1979 was lower than the average for India as a whole (Lakdawala 1982). Furthermore, agricultural policies in the late 1950s and middle 1960s weakened Patels' economic status by assisting nonlandowners who had been disenfranchised by the British (Pocock 1972). Patels increasingly lost their agricultural standing as lower-status groups benefited from these government programs. Patels were already economically vulnerable, some even economically unstable. According to the 1961 Census of India, there were thirty (out of ninety-eight) Patidar households in Ambav village, in the Kaira district. These thirty "comprised 42% of the landholders, holding 71% of the land. They provide 70% of the village income" (Bal 2006, p. 187; see also Tambs Lyche 1982).

Gujarat remains a predominantly agricultural state. From the 1960s to at least 1980, the main crops were groundnuts (peanuts), cotton, wheat, jowar, bajri, and rice (Lakdawala 1982). But agriculture provides an unstable income. And there are few alternatives available to locals wanting to leave farming. For example, although the industrial sector has been growing at a quick pace in the Surat district (from which many motel owners originate) since the 1960s (Parekh 2008), most of those employed in this sector are from outside Gujarat. In the fastest-growing industries—cutting and polishing diamonds (mostly imported from South America and Africa) and artificial silk production—"local labor is a minority and has had to accept living and working in the shadows of aliens" (Breman 1996, p. 57). The diamond industry was especially strong in Surat postindependence, but its labor force was primarily composed of Kanbi Patels from outside Surat (only some of whom have immigrated to the United States and become owners of motels). And the growth of

industry notwithstanding, the economy in Surat remained agricultur-
ally based. Agriculture dominated the entire state, often not providing
a dependable livelihood. According to Lakdawala (1982), by 1980 only
about 35 percent of Gujarati farmers were rich, more than 50 percent were
poor, and 14 percent were landless.

Even with these challenges, the financial prospects within Gujarat
were not dismal. Nevertheless, Gujarat has had poor economic conditions compared with First World countries and inconsistent returns
compared with other states in India. As Mehta (1983) wrote:

> Gujarat is a unique economy. On the one side, it has one of the highest
> per capita incomes, and high literacy, urbanisation and industrialisa-
> tion rates [in India]. On the other side, it also has one of the highest in-
> fant, general mortality and crude birth rates, inadequate social services
> infrastructure, slow growth in per capita incomes, low agricultural
> yields, low growth in agriculture, low and highly variable rainfall, un-
> derutilisation of irrigation potential and low ultimate irrigation poten-
> tial. (p. 19)

Nor did Gujarat provide occupational security and satisfaction for
professionals, including engineers and doctors who would immigrate to
the United States post-1965 (explained below). The government under
Prime Minister Jawaharlal Nehru had invested significant money in science education following independence (Poros 2010). This led to well-
trained graduates who had few job opportunities. Indian physicians, for
instance, had few employment opportunities outside of rural India. As
early as 1967, India had sent 1,541 scientists and engineers to the United
States, second in number only to Britain (2,293), which, unlike India,
had not been subject to restricted immigration prior to 1965 (Fortney
1970). Professionals emigrate for higher salaries, more challenging work,
and an advanced infrastructure (Madhavan 1985). Sahay (2007) quotes
Usha Nayar as saying, "The Indian economy cannot absorb even the
small number of graduates from Indian universities" (p. 944). The reason to emigrate is succinctly captured in the following quote from Fortney (1970):

There is also the problem [in Asia] of underemployment, when professionals are taking jobs that are "beneath" them. The Indian Census of
1961 showed that 10.4% of persons classed in scientific and technical occupations were unemployed, this was 16.3% for science graduates, 3.7%
for engineering graduates, and 8.6% for physicians. Senator Mondale of
Minnesota in a *Saturday Review* article . . . quotes a university dean as
saying, "It is difficult to advise an Indian engineer to return home if
there is a high risk that he will be a clerk-typist for the next ten years." . . .
By far the largest part of the migration of professionals involves recruit-
ment by American industry, universities, hospitals and research organizations (many of these last three are wholly or partly financed by the
Federal Government). (pp. 230–31)

Through its immigration laws and domestic policies, the U.S. government has indirectly sponsored the migration of Indian and other foreign professionals rather than trained natives for open positions. The
Indian government has put more resources in its universities to fund
professionals. But these incubator labs have not resulted in sufficient
private industry growth (Sahay 2007). In addition, the troubles within
agriculture often impacted these professionals through family members
in the industry. So a chance to earn greater income abroad and experience more secure occupational support were major incentives to emigrate, even if one was lucky enough to find steady employment at home.

Colonial Constraints in the British Commonwealth

Before immigrating in the 1940s to the United States, in the early and
middle 1900s Patels had immigrated in large numbers to East Africa
and to Britain, where a number of Indian American moteliers originate
from. Concentrating on their experiences here is not to take away from
the role of other destination countries, such as New Zealand, Fiji, South
Africa, and the Caribbean (Brennan 1998; Leckie 1998). Nor is this an
exhaustive account of Gujaratis' immigration to the United States (see
Poros 2010). But to understand the motivations of motel owners per se,
it is useful to narrow the focus.

Indians have long favored emigration as a way to address economic insecurity. In the late 1800s, elite Patidars began leaving Gujarat to trade tobacco elsewhere in India. Emigration became even more popular in the early 1900s. As mentioned earlier, British rule, natural disasters, famines, dwindling landholdings, and the increasing size of dowries created a precarious situation for many Patels. Along with their income, their social status became threatened. As a result, Gujaratis left for Kenya, Tanzania, Uganda, and elsewhere, joining Indians who had already emigrated and connecting to a trading history with East African settlements that had been active for centuries (Pocock 1972; Rutten and Patel 2003; Tambs Lyche 1982). Although the decision to emigrate is often motivated by economic interests, the choice of destination often depends on network relations, whether through colonialism, profession, organizations, family, and so on (Poros 2010).

The immigrants to East Africa were recruited by Britain starting in the late 1800s to advance its colonial interests, in particular to fill administrative and labor jobs connected to the recently completed railway system. Punjabis had already been brought in as indentured servants to lay the tracks. The Patels who came were for the most part relatively well educated and spoke enough English to fill administrative positions. The predominance of Gujaratis who migrated to East Africa led to the nickname "Patel Railways." The British considered the Patidars to be loyal, hardworking, docile, and subservient and so wanted them to advance their colonial interests elsewhere (Tambs Lyche 1982).

Once in bureaucratic positions in East Africa, Patels helped relatives emigrate through work permits or through marriage (Rutten and Patel 2003). By the early 1900s, tens of thousands of Indians worked in the region. Migration continued to grow in the 1920s and 1930s. Men had come alone at first, but gradually wives and families joined them. After their contracts expired, 80 percent of the Patel laborers left, but most of those in white-collar positions stayed (Nair 2001).

Patels continued to do well in East Africa even after leaving their original posts. Families opened small shops and entered trade, banking, and other white-collar occupations (Tambs Lyche 1982).[4] They often became middleman minorities, serving as an intermediary between white suppliers and native black customers. They had little prior experience in business, but they strongly preferred autonomy, which business ownership allowed. Women and men worked together in the shops, at times living in them as they later would in motels in the United States (Nair 2001). As Bal (2006) wrote, "The Patidars were involved in every facet of commercial life of East Africa until they were pushed out by the regime. They had developed a diverse retail and wholesale trade and besides building a large number of factories they dominated the ginning industry" (p. 181).

The Indian immigrants' political and social status, however, was uncertain. As they gained stature and expanded into their own businesses, they saw themselves as equals to the British, in that they both were nonnatives of elevated status in Africa (Nair 2001). They framed themselves as part of not just an Indian diaspora but also a British one. They considered what was owed to them as such and often looked down on black Africans, yet their heightened successes threatened the British. As a result, they had few allies.

Furthermore, living under British rule in another group's colonized territory limited their agency to shape the discourse around their presence. In their pursuit of economic gain, they appeared to be on the one hand insensitive to black Africans and on the other hand mere pawns of the British and their colonial interests. In effect, British authorities hoped Patels would become proxy colonizers. As such, they positioned Indians between native blacks and white colonizers and racialized them to fit such a status. Gujaratis were portrayed as "civilized" and as good role models for black Africans. With the abolishment of slavery, black Africans were perceived as unwilling to work the railroads and possibly too lazy (Nair 2001). Gujaratis were "model minorities" who worked hard and did not cause problems for the ruling elite. This racial status exacerbated tensions with black Africans, who increasingly felt Indians exploited them economically. Indian settlers were also criticized for being loyal to their homeland rather than to their new home (Theroux 1967). They considered themselves Indians, not Africans. Many

in Uganda chose not to become citizens. They were criticized for send-
ing money back home rather than helping locals (Bonacich 1973). And
so on. The combination of their own approach to their diasporic setting
and their postcolonial status within the British Empire exacerbated race
relations.

As East African colonies gained their independence in the late 1960s
into the early 1970s, Gujaratis were forced or wanted out of East Africa
(and today many own motels in the United States, often starting in the
1970s). Their occupational and social status had become tenuous. For
instance, many Leva Patels in Kenya had worked in government jobs,
but such jobs were given to black East Africans by 1965 (Patel and Patel
2001). New policies were enacted that made it difficult for Indians to
open a business or attend school. In Uganda, Indians could work only
in certain industries.

The majority of Indians in East Africa immigrated to Britain in the
1960s and 1970s, first from Kenya (between December 1967 and January
1968 alone, nearly two thousand Indians arrived in Britain) and then
from Uganda (Patel and Rutten 1999). A few thousand came directly to
the United States (some of whom entered the motel industry, as explained in Chapter 2) (Pabrai 2007). Those who emigrated from Kenya
had time to plan their departure and transfer their wealth. In Tanzania,
Indians also had a smoother transition following its independence. In
contrast, the sixty thousand Indians in Uganda had only ninety days to
leave and lost much of their assets following expulsion by Idi Amin in
1972, who called them "bloodsuckers."

Going to Britain was not necessarily the preferred choice for East
African Indians, but it was the sensible choice given their other options.
Though clearly the economic possibilities in Britain were greater than
those in India, this was only one motivation for Indian migration to the
United Kingdom. According to Crewe and Kothari (1998), Indian immigrants also believed Britain represented a more "modern" civilization. Having been raised in the British school system within India, the
center of the British Empire was imagined as the ultimate destination.
Extra incentive came from the generally positive reports of Indians who

had immigrated there as seamen and professionals after World War II (Spencer 1997).

To their surprise, however, new arrivals encountered limited economic mobility, a more isolated lifestyle, racism, and xenophobia. Their "colonial" status followed them as they entered the heart of the empire. Indicative of the prejudice, a number of increasingly restrictive anti-immigration laws were enacted to limit Indian immigration. The 1962 Commonwealth Immigration Act restricted unskilled workers from entering the country, limiting immigration to highly skilled workers, with allowances for their dependents and potential spouses (Thandi 2007). In 1968, the law was changed to remove the automatic right of entry of British passport holders to enter. Now, only those born or naturalized in the United Kingdom or those whose parent or grandparent had been born in the United Kingdom could enter. This barred practically all Indians. Also in 1968, Enoch Powell, at the time a member of British Parliament, delivered his nativist and widely celebrated "river of blood" speech, in which he called for a termination of all immigration from former British colonies so as to preserve the white race of Britain. In 1971, citizenship itself was denied to British passport holders whose parent or grandparent had not been born in Britain. Indian refugees from East Africa eventually entered, but these laws created long delays and left many stateless for a time.

Many Gujaratis settled in the north and in the Midlands, where they had personal connections. There they worked in steel and textile factories. Competition for employment quickly led to tensions between locals and Indian immigrants (Thandi 2007). Stereotypes of South Asians as "natives" and as "strangers from the colonies," as opposed to being British compatriots, were the norm (Bastos and Bastos 2005). Muggings and stabbings were not uncommon. Indians, as well as black Caribbeans, also faced obstacles in finding adequate housing and employment suitable to their skills (Patel and Patel 2001). The two groups organized and took to the streets in protest of the brutality and general injustice. In the 1980s, race relations worsened as unemployment rose. Riots occurred in reaction to racist attacks (Brah 2008). Unemployment among South Asians increased as manufacturing declined, itself accelerated by

Thatcher's free-market economic policies (Thandi 2007). As the son of one of the first Gujarati motel owners said of his family's experiences there, "In England they know you only do the labor. A lot of people that came [to the United States] from other countries, they were working there and found it, you know, how difficult it is to work in, say, England or whatever."

Indians tried to make the best out of their situation in England but with limited results. Given the difficult labor market, many decided to try entrepreneurship (Basu 1998). In enclaves catering to co-ethnics, they opened small businesses, such as corner grocery stores, confectionaries, and tobacco and newspaper/magazine stores. Later, in the 1980s and 1990s, they expanded their inventory and reach to bring in the majority. Still, these were lean times for immigrants. Few preferred self-employment (Crewe and Kothari 1998). Many businesses within ethnic enclaves failed in the 1980s as ethnic items became available in mainstream stores and the overall economy remained weak. Even if successful, these businesses were very difficult to run. They depended on the exploitation of family members as employees. Another son, who also grew up in England, complained that he "got sick and tired of England. The economy, the cost of living."

In effect, rather than feeling part of a "motherland" or at least equal to the British, as they had asserted they were in East Africa, their subjugation as postcolonial immigrants continued in the colonizer's home. As one owner said:

> There was definitely less prejudice in America than in England. The British rule the world, and they really separate the Asians [Indians]. They have that superior feeling. They don't show it on the outside, but on the inside they do. There was a lot of prejudice in '60s and '70s, but they have come to realize that Indians are not low class people.

So Indians' quest for equality within a modern nation was denied. As quoted in Crewe and Kothari (1998), "When Gandhi visited Britain and a journalist asked him what he thought of modern civilization, he replied 'that would be a good idea'" (p. 13).

Migration to the United States

While Patels often found better economic opportunities in East Africa and Britain than in India, they remained within a colonial hierarchy, even after India gained independence. These experiences set the stage for Gujaratis' immigration to the United States and ultimately their interest in small business. A significant number of current motel owners arrived from Britain, and of the subjects I interviewed who own motels, about one-fifth came to the United States from a country other than India, typically Britain. About half of those had emigrated from India to another country before migrating a second time to the United States, and the other half grew up in that other country before coming to the United States. I do not analyze either group separately from immigrants who arrived straight from India. Although in some circumstance this differentiation would be valid—Bhachu (1985), for example, explains how the attitudes and skills of Sikhs in Britain who entered from another country other than India differ from the attitudes and skills of those who emigrated directly from Punjab—the communities in the United States were more comparable. For example, most informants regardless of origin had proficiency in English and emigrated with the intention of settling in the United States.

1940s–1960s

The most studied Indian immigrants to the United States were Punjabis, who settled in California in the early 1900s, with some attention now focused on those who settled in New York City and the South (Bald 2007). Many of those on the West Coast had labored for the railway and timber industries in Washington and Canada but had been driven south by the racism of anti-immigrant whites (Takaki 1989). They continued to work the railroads and also moved between fruit, rice, cotton, and other seasonal farms in northern California, often replacing Chinese and Japanese laborers (Hess 1974). By the 1920s, a small number of Punjabis had shifted from laborers to tenant farmers and even to owning their own farms (Takaki 1989). When the California Alien Land Law of 1920 prohibited aliens ineligible for citizenship from owning land, and the *United States v. Bhagat Singh Thind* court decision in 1923 prevented most Indians from attaining citizenship, they teamed up with whites who served as proxy owners of their farms. But they could not bring relatives over to help with the work because of the Asiatic Barred Zone Act of 1917, which excluded future Indian laborers from entering the United States, including relatives of those already here. As Hess (1974) wrote, "In the face of these pressures, many East Indians left the United States. Between 1920 and 1940, some 3,000 returned to India; most left voluntarily, although a few hundred were deported" (p. 590). Despite these tensions and legal restrictions, some Indians still wanted to come, and they entered illegally, often via Mexico. They were mostly laborers and had no formal schooling.

The barrier against Asian immigration remained until the Luce-Cellar Act of 1946, which allowed Filipinos and Indians to follow in the footsteps of the Chinese a few years earlier and become citizens. It also allowed a small quota of 100 Indians and 100 Filipinos to arrive per year, a quota that included Indian immigrants already living outside India. The small number was meant to limit competition with white laborers.

Practically all accounts of Indians' history in the United States make passing reference to the fact that very few persons arrived following the Luce-Cellar Act and that the "real" migration waves took place primarily before 1924 and after 1965 (Helweg and Helweg 1990; Jensen 1988; Takaki 1989). It is true that few Indians arrived in the interim. From 1931 to 1960, only 5 percent of all legal immigrants came from Asia (Daniels 1989). Before 1965, nine out of ten Asian Americans were of Japanese, Chinese, or Filipino ancestry. Between 1948 and 1965, fewer than seven thousand Indians migrated to the United States (Kitano and Daniels 1995). And a number of those returned to India, leaving a small net total. By 1965, only 1,772 Indian immigrants had become U.S. citizens (Hess 1974). Because of these small numbers, these Indian immigrants have been overlooked.

Here I write these individuals back into American history. Gujarati men during the 1940s and 1950s were the first to enter the hospitality industry, in San Francisco. As such, community members refer to them as "pioneers." Unfortunately, a history of these Gujaratis is sketchy. The experiences of Indian, including Gujarati, immigrants from 1946 to 1965 are poorly recorded. It is hard to even say exactly how many came. A couple of informants said the number of Gujuratis in San Francisco was between ten and twelve. Another said that there were eighteen. According to Jain (1989), there were twenty-two families by 1963. They arrived on tourist visas, which they later changed into permanent visas through their investments in hotels. Coming from different villages within Gujarat, they did not necessarily know one another before starting their journey from India; some met on the ship over, some met after they got here. These Patels, all Patidars, were mostly Leva Patels according to an elder informant, although some were Bhaktas Patidars and Matya Patidars (Jain 1989). As of July 2006, there were either two or three pioneers still alive, according to informants, with only one still in the United States (and in poor health). I draw from interviews with the descendants of the pioneers.

These migrants from the 1940s and 1950s were not "Midnight's Children," as Salman Rushdie famously labeled those Indians born at the time of independence, in 1947. They were young adults ready for growth and opportunities and unsure of what India might hold for them. Practically all were farmers or otherwise tied to agriculture. They regretted the challenges to mobility in Gujarat. An informant's grandfather, who immigrated to the United States in 1949, had tried to start his own business in India. He said of his grandfather:

> So he did earn some money in business before he came to the United States. But then, you know, the restrictions came upon. And then it was harder and harder for him. So he kind of felt it difficult to, kind of, get into his own business at that time in India. The general environment there was so hard. It was very bad time right after the Second World War or something.

The son of a Gujarati immigrant from the 1940s had this to say: "After independence, it was hard in Gujarat. A lot of corruption. Hard to make a good living." Some of these Patels emigrated before India's independence. Others waited to see what opportunities a new India would offer, because with independence and sovereignty came a sense of possibility, of new opportunities. Another informant's father postponed his departure until after independence:

> Actually, my father, he could have gotten the visas back in 1948, or '49, you know at that time, but India would just [have] turned independent. He decided to . . . you know, jump on, you know, coming over here a little bit later. He just said, you know what, let's just wait and see. But, India at that time was also very tough, you know. Um, you have to work on the fields, you do it on your own.

The reasons to emigrate were clear. The reason for Gujaratis choosing the United States was less clear, given their lack of presence here. The immigrants were still within a colonial or nascent postcolonial hierarchy, which defined their understanding of nations. In fact, information on the West was limited except for Britain. According to informants, there was an "American fever" after World War II. This American fever stemmed from the nation's status as independent and as a global military, economic, political, and social leader after the war. Indians read this through a postcolonial lens. According to the grandson, the colonial status of India and other diasporic destinations, in contrast to the self-governing United States, made a significant impression on his grandfather. This informant spoke of the impression an Indian relative living in the United States, Kanjibhai Desai (discussed more in the next chapter), gave to his grandfather in Gujarat:[5]

> Even back in the village, that uncle, very smart. So these letters used to encourage my grandfather, that if I [the grandfather] do go to a foreign country, I'd go to America—Kanjibhai wrote two letters back home, explaining how [the United States] was. First of all, he was emphasizing it is an independent country. [India] was not independent that time. So . . . opportunity is there if you work hard.

To these Indians, with their postcolonial mentality, independence from colonial rule meant opportunity.

The postcolonial condition of the pioneers motivated them to move to San Francisco in particular. They arrived at Ellis Island and then continued on to San Francisco and the surrounding area. This was partly because the immigrants knew of San Francisco's role in the anticolonial movement by Indian Americans, namely the Ghadar Party. But they also moved to San Francisco because they knew more about that city through connections there, including Desai. As one informant said of the pioneers' first settlement:

> And I remember talking to a couple of [the pioneers] about that journey, and you know, they only had a few dollars in their pocket, which was essentially their entire asset, clothes on their back and maybe a bag to have some extra clothes. But they ended up in San Francisco. And the reason they ended up in San Francisco is that San Francisco is known in India because there was a freedom movement that originated in San Francisco, it's called the Ghadar movement—it was the newsletter that was published in North America that was distributed to the Indian community at large to push for independence. And you know the weather in San Francisco was a little more conducive to, uh, from where they came from, you know, those kinds of things.

For these immigrants, San Francisco was the epicenter of the freedoms, anticolonial ideology, and economic possibilities that the United States represented. And it was this overall perception that drew these immigrants to the United States at a time when few made, indeed were allowed to make, the trip.

Post-1965

The next and by far largest wave of Indian immigrants to the United States arrived after 1965. Because this migration wave has been well documented in many texts and in popular media, I provide only brief coverage of it here. The Immigration and Nationality Act of 1965 eradicated the limited quotas against Asians. This raised the quota to 20,000 visas per country, with no preference based strictly on national origin. In other words, each country was to have equal representation, at least in theory. Migrants from India came in mostly under the act's preference for professionals in the science and medical fields; they arrived as doctors, engineers, professors, students, or managers, with a relatively equal number of women and men. Since the 1990s, a growing number now enter under the H-1B visa program, which allows work visas for white-collar professionals in technology fields.[6] Gujaratis and Punjabis make up the largest percentage of post-1965 Indian Americans.

Others arrived as sponsored kin of Patels already in the United States. The Luce-Cellar Act allowed Indians to become naturalized citizens, and as naturalized citizens they could sponsor relatives. An informant in California boasted of how his father, a pioneer, "called in over 100 people. Just by him being [a] citizen, there are over 100 people [who] came." In time, many professionals who arrived post-1965 also became citizens and sponsored their relatives. A majority of the post-1965 immigrants arrived as families. And although many settled in major urban areas, there were also some who ended up elsewhere because of job placement. Rather than frame 1965 as a dividing year in the history of Indian immigration, as the beginning of contemporary migration, it should serve as a milestone that shaped Indian migration.

The image of the United States as a country of modernity and freedom continued to grow in the middle to late twentieth century. Even relative to other Western countries, the United States represented freedom to these immigrants. Those from Britain came to the United States because of a perceived lack of discrimination and less restrictive immigration laws (Rutten and Patel 2003). Many came as sponsored relatives, hoping the United States would offer more economic opportunities (Crewe and Kothari 1998). A 1.5-generation informant who grew up in Britain explained his family's reasons for immigrating:

> For a better standard of living and better environment. India had its independence at that time, but it was still a Third World [country]. Wanted to go to a country with more resources. At that time immigrating was a chance to have a better future. My dad was a chemist and did his graduate work in London. And we moved to England. And then we

moved to America since the opportunity to bring your family [to Britain] was slim. In America you can bring your brothers and sisters and parents.

So the United States represented a confluence of desired factors: a sense of independence, economic resources, and family reunification.

From Freedom to Subordination

The notion of the United States as symbolizing freedom had given immigrants hope, but it was soon felt to be a false one. The pioneers did gain some footing in agriculture. The son of a pioneer claimed that in the early 1950s, his father found farming in the United States to be easier than in India:

> You know, the weather in San Francisco is very mild. And you go in India and you work on the fields, it's, it's pretty hot and in the summer, you know. They felt like why they decided to stay here was, you know what, we can earn a little bit more money because of the dollar-rupee you know, valuation or whatever. Um, they felt like the work was not as hard as like working on, in India and on the farms.

Given these conditions in Gujarat, it is not surprising that pioneers' visits back to the homeland affirmed their decision to stay in the United States. As the descendant of a pioneer said of his father and his father's peers, "So [the pioneers] didn't figure in those times to stay here long. And so what happened was that, every time they went back [to India] they thought, you know what, it's better over here."

These immigrants viewed their experiences not only through a transnational lens but also through a broader diasporic lens. The son of a separate pioneer expressed, "You work [in the United States], you have opportunity. Other countries there is a prejudice. There is prejudice here, but not like what's in Africa and other countries. Here, you do hard work, you get the return at the end of the day. That was a big deal."

Agricultural work, however, was economically insufficient. Often the pioneers migrated between farm and city as the seasons changed. It was when competing for jobs in the city that Indians became more clearly racialized. This discrimination is not surprising. Immigration laws already framed them more as extensions of India than as potential contributions to U.S. citizenry. For example, the Luce-Cellar Act did not represent a simple increased tolerance of these ethnicities (Chandras 1978). In fact, even some who supported the law voiced racist attitudes toward Indians, maintaining that their quota needed to remain so low to avoid competition with native whites even as the ban had to be lifted somewhat in order to signal some openness to India and non-whites generally (Chandrasekhar 1982). The United States was worried that Japan would push into India and that India would ultimately join Germany. India was a strategic place geographically and was hostile toward the British already, all of which would make the eastern segment of the country amenable to Japanese entrance (Takaki 1989). In addition, the United States' calls for racial equality within Nazi Germany were made hollow by its own racism in forbidding even limited immigration from Asian countries. In other words, the law changed in order to promote U.S. interests abroad rather than because of a commitment to racial equality at home.

Economic preferences of employers also motivated the changes. Allowing more Indian and Filipino Americans to enter the United States served Californian landowners dealing with labor shortages. During World War II, the United States had been recruiting immigrant labor to work its agriculture industry, and bringing in more made sense (Posadas 1999). But urban residents were not so open to immigration. The pioneer's son who spoke of farming in the United States being easier compared with India talked about his father and his uncle trying to get work:

> They weren't able to get jobs. They used to stand on union lines and what not, and they said as soon [as] our turn gets right near the window, they would close the window down.

Q: *What kind of jobs were they trying to get?*

Oh, whatever. My father was working for a few months at, I don't know, at [a] department store. My uncle, I think, he was working at [a] hotel doing laundry. And some, you know, people were doing like this, and then on the weekends they would go and pick fruits. Then a lot of people started to think, you know what, let's just open up our own, if we can get into this type of business. And so this was back in the early, you know, 1951, 1952. And so they used to say, you know, there's no jobs for Hindus or whatever. Just open discrimination. And so people thought, man, you know, if you can get into this type of business, it may not be so bad.

In other words, the colonized status of Indians within the British Empire translated into a racial subjugation akin to other minorities in the United States. As another informant said of Gujaratis who migrated in the 1940s and early 1950s, "So, anyway, they settled in San Francisco, and they ended up working as laborers, you know, Goodwill, the Salvation Army, farm workers."

In Gujaratis' search for freedom from colonialism and postcolonialism, they instead found the racialization of the United States—a standard pathway of realization for Asian immigrants (Okihiro 1994). They were framed as foreigners competing against "natives" for work.

Professionals who arrived post-1965 had an easier time finding employment but still faced obstacles to mobility. Much like the Luce-Cellar Act of 1946, the Immigration and Nationality Act of 1965 was meant to resolve the hypocritical image of the United States espousing equality and democracy to other nations while exhibiting hostility to people of color within its own borders. Also, those endorsing the passage of the Immigration and Nationality Act predicted that the racial makeup of the nation would remain unchanged. Instead, immigrants of color arrived. As for the pioneers, the labor market did not offer the "freedom" the professionals had sought. Complaints about employment discrimination were widespread in the 1970s (Chandras 1978). Immigrant professionals often took jobs for which they were substantially overqualified or were denied jobs outright because of their Indian heritage. Only a few of my informants expressed frustration at not having their educational degrees from India recognized in the United States.

Mostly they believed that hidden, if not open, discrimination has restricted their upward mobility. As I sat in the house of one informant, a middle-aged man who emigrated from Mumbai, his son walked in and out of the living room. The father spoke uneasily about the obstacles he faced that contributed to his move out of a job despite its six-figure salary:

> If you're class of '80 from Ohio State, you're on the board. But you know, I am not a class of '80, I graduated in Mumbai. I am not from Ohio State. I never been from Ohio State. So I'm never going to make—the secret handshake I cannot.

Discriminatory treatment resulted partly from designs by the federal government. It can work through indirect and unintended facilitation (Light and Bonacich 1991). Through visa programs it privileges highly skilled migrants who expect strong returns and professional opportunities but instead often end up in lower-status jobs. Indians who found work in their chosen professions often complained of a glass ceiling or of low compensation compared with that of whites with similar qualifications. As Barringer and Kassebaum (1989) write, "The bottom line of this analysis is that Asian Indians are an ethnic minority, paid well but paid less than their education and occupational concentration would produce if they were not a minority in the United States" (p. 517).

Many of the Gujaratis of the post-1965 immigration wave, who later turned to motels, arrived in the United States as engineers, yet were unable to find jobs. One informant said in a resigned tone, "I applied to jobs in Georgia. All positions were filled by less qualified persons than me, by blacks or whites. It was my guess that it was prejudice." Parlin (1976) explains in his case study comparing Western and non-Western citizens and noncitizens, in which Indians comprised almost half of the non-Western noncitizen sample, "In summary, it is evident that the non-Western noncitizen realizes considerably more discrimination in employment opportunities than the Western noncitizen. However, when compared to citizens, the immigrant professionals' prospects of employment in this company are nothing short of dismal" (p. 25). Non-western non-citizens were the least likely to get called in for interviews and the least likely to receive job offers. As others have found regarding Asian American professionals turned entrepreneurs, "the most educated populations perceive the most intense blocked mobility" (Raijman and Tienda 2000, p. 697).

Not all Indians arrived as professionals, obviously. Immigrants who arrived as sponsored relatives of professionals, whether from India or the diaspora, on average had less education and poorer English skills than their sponsors. This left them more vulnerable to fluctuations in the job market. Sometimes their positions were eliminated or downgraded because of the exportation of jobs to other countries in the increasingly service-based economy of the United States. For example, an informant came to the United States with a bachelor's degree in commerce from India. He worked as an electronics technician in the Boston area for six and a half years, soldering components to printed circuit boards:

> In Massachusetts. Got laid off. Was making fifteen dollars per hour. Wife making eleven dollars per hour. All our friends and relatives owned motel. We decided have to go motel too.

Some informants blamed President Reagan, others the North American Free Trade Agreement signed by President Clinton. Some felt pushed out of the labor market; others simply felt discouraged.

To understand why Indians across different eras have migrated to the United States to enter the motel industry, it is necessary to place that choice within the context of other options. Patels have a long history of migration throughout India and the world, both for seeking economic security and for seeking greater personal opportunities. The story of Patel motel owners is not simply a transnational one between India and the United States but a diasporic one that involves various destinations, most notably the United Kingdom and East Africa. The United States did not represent the same totalizing colonial hierarchy that had marred Gujaratis in the British Commonwealth. Nor did the racism and job instability they encountered in the United States mean they lacked economic security in their jobs. Still, immigrants from both before and after 1965 became disenchanted with the labor market as the freedom promised in this "land of opportunity" proved elusive. This history is a missing part of the Asian American, and American, story and not only offers a fuller picture of an immigrant group but also provides a necessary backdrop to their entrance into the motel industry, explained next.

2 Reaching for the American Dream

ACCORDING TO AN ARTICLE PUBLISHED in the *New York Times* in 1999, "the first Indian motel owner in the United States is said to have been an illegal immigrant named Kanjibhai Desai, who managed to buy the Goldfield Hotel in downtown San Francisco in the early 1940s."[1] Desai made his way to the United States without documents from the West Indies through Mexico. It was 1922 San Francisco. Years later Desai came to the Goldfield Hotel, a residential hotel that was then owned and managed by a Japanese American. The internment of Japanese Americans by the U.S. government created the opening for Desai to take over the hotel. A son of a Gujarati pioneer, one who immigrated in the 1940s or 1950s and was of the first set to enter the motel industry soon after Desai, said:

> You know, this was at the time of World War II, but Japan attacked Pearl Harbor. He was staying at this hotel, and I guess there [was] a Japanese lessee or Japanese owner. And um, he had leased it. So, [Desai] bought this lease for, I don't know, whatever, for a couple of hundred bucks. I don't know what it was.

> Q: *Because the Japanese were put in internment camps?*

> Yeah, they were put into those prison camps. And so and that's how he ended up getting this. That's how he ended up renting this hotel.

"This hotel" was on Fourth Street, just south of Market Street in downtown San Francisco. As is common for residential hotels, rooms lacked individual bathrooms and private kitchens, and people often lived in them for months at a time or longer. No one can visit it today. In its place stands the upscale Moscone convention center.

Fast-forward almost seventy years and in some respects little has changed for other Indian American residential hotels. In August 2008, I took a tour of downtown San Francisco's lower-budget residential hotels. My guide was the son of another Patel pioneer who had migrated in the 1940s. Near the corner of Mission and Sixth streets, we approached a hotel and pressed the doorbell. When buzzed in, we entered through a heavy, red metal security gate. We stepped up to a check-in desk shielded behind a glass wall. There was no lobby, no furniture, and nowhere to congregate. Stairs to the right of the desk led up to private rooms. Posted on the wall were various notices to guests. One read, "No Rats, No Cats, No Dogs."

The guests, walking in and out through the relatively dark entryway, some standing outside to smoke a cigarette, were all men, typically unshaven and somewhat unkempt. A couple were physically handicapped, most were middle age or elderly, some were white, others were black, and all appeared poor. Many were on government subsidies, according to the manager. He was young and a recent immigrant from Nepal. Wearing a blue short-sleeved shirt, wrinkled gray pants, and tennis shoes, he described the guests as generally seeking long-term accommodations. Few cause problems, but drinking and possibly drugs were not uncommon. Surrounding the hotel were a couple of adult XXX stores, a launderette, a community service center, and other lower-status establishments. For at least this hotel, little has changed since the 1940s, when Gujarati immigrants started in the industry. Many residential hotels in this area are still owned by Indian Americans, including this one. I found one hotel that was purchased by a pioneer in the early 1950s, and is still owned by that pioneer, who is now elderly and in ill health.

Yet in other respects, much has changed from the days of Desai and the other pioneers. Some Indian immigrant owners of middle- and upper-budget motels have earned leadership positions in the main-stream motel industry. For example, at the national level, in 1999, H. P. Rama became chairperson of the American Hotel and Lodging Association, the first minority to hold that post.[2] At the state level, Amar Pandey, an owner of a higher-middle-budget motel, was chair of the Ohio Hospitality and Lodging Association in 2006, an advocacy organization representing hotels, motels, resorts, and other hospitality establishments in the state.[3]

Indian Americans in middle- and upper-budget motels enjoy a setting quite distant from those of the immigrant pioneers. When I visited an owner at his upper-middle-budget franchise near Toledo, Ohio, I waited for him in an expansive lobby. The floor was polished clean, and it had comfortable, muted-colored chairs and couches. Behind the front desk stood a white desk clerk. Guests were short-term tourists and business travelers and for the most part were white. They wore casual clothes or professional attire, and all seemed relatively relaxed as they made their way through the lobby, some rolling their luggage behind them.

The owner was a second-generation Gujarati American who had grown up in a small, independent motel in Pennsylvania. He walked through the lobby wearing khaki pants, a gray dress shirt, and black dress shoes. His hair was short, and he was clean-shaven. He spoke to his maintenance person about an air conditioner in a room. The maintenance person walked off, and the owner told a housekeeper that the air-conditioning unit that she had reported broken actually worked fine. He wore no tool belt and did not inspect the unit on his own. Then he came over to greet me, and we began our interview.

Between the two extremes of residential hotels and upscale motels lie most of today's Indian American–owned establishments. They are predominantly at the lower- and middle-budget levels (Bhakta 2002), both independent and franchise, and carried on through multiple generations. How did Indian Americans become such a presence in the motel industry from the humble beginnings of Desai? How did they achieve national dominance in this industry?

Other ethnic entrepreneurs have achieved recognition but have not had such a broad presence. For example, Jewish Americans have an entrepreneurial history in the garment industry in New York City and a few other cities, but their descendants have not often continued in the industry, nor has this niche spread nationwide (Steinberg 1986). The small businesses of Korean Americans also are found only in select cities and have not been maintained by their children, who typically move into white-collar professions (Kim 2006). Chinese Americans are well known for their small businesses, but these are primarily located within ethnic enclaves of major cities ("Chinatown"). And in San Francisco in the early 1900s, Japanese Americans were well positioned in hotels and in agriculture. But they did not expand to other parts of the country or across multiple generations (owing in part, of course, to internment during World War II). Even other Indian American niches, such as fast food chains, lack the geographic dispersion or multigenerational nature as found within the motel industry (Rangaswamy 2007).

Indian American motel owners across generations encountered many of the same factors leading other groups to ethnic entrepreneurship, primarily (1) disadvantages in the labor market, (2) opportunities in the business field (including franchises), and (3) the ability to take advantage of those opportunities because of personal, family, and community resources (Yoon 1997). Yet domestic and global inequalities joined with these factors to fuel Indian Americans' dramatic growth compared to other groups (Abelmann and Lie 1995; Valdez 2010).

Disadvantages and Optimism in Motivating Entrepreneurship

As explained in Chapter 1, Indian immigrants encountered an unstable and at times discriminatory labor market, which motivated an interest in self-employment (Portes and Rumbaut 2006). Pioneers saw running a hotel as one of the very few ways—if not the only way—to make a living, given their economic challenges in the city and farms. The grandson of a pioneer spoke with pride of the pioneers' dedication: "It was not that it was extremely lucrative or anything. But, it was their hard effort. They used to do everything [in] the hotel, 24 hours a day. And they made some [money]. So, it was hard effort, and the margins were not that great. At least there was something there." Another informant emphasized the desperation of the pioneers, saying, "Once they came out here . . . [they] just do business to survive."

The son of a pioneer recounted his father's and uncle's need for employment:

> My uncle when he got here, he got a job at a hotel. Basically, as like a laundry person, like his younger brother [my father]. And then on their off times, they used to work in the fields, you know, pick roots and what not. And um, but what happened was that when they came here they were staying at this hotel, the Goldfield Hotel.

As a fellow Gujarati, Desai most likely attracted the Gujarati immigrant laborers of the 1940s and 1950s who also needed to stay in residential hotels when in San Francisco. Staying at Desai's hotel created a link for them to jobs in the industry.

In the 1960s and 1970s, when more Indians (from India, Britain, East Africa, and elsewhere in the diaspora) arrived and strengthened their foothold in the hospitality industry, occupational mobility within established organizations continued to be a challenge. In fact, disadvantages in the labor market remain a motivating factor for contemporary entrepreneurs. One owner of an independent motel near Toledo echoed the popular theme of turning to small business as an alternative to unstable employment. "I've been in and out of motel business last ten years. I saw some opportunity [in motels]. Job is shaky ground, especially when started motel." Some, especially professionals, had not encountered job instability but complained of their low income compared with peers who owned motels. An informant spoke of her brother-in-law and those in general who came on a student visa, a common mode of entry for Indians.

And once he graduates, then he get a good job. And after they save the money, they go into the motel business. They thought motel is making more money, so he quit the job. He go in motel business. They came here as a student visa, because they want to come to USA. You know, no matter what they want to work. Study was not the goal. Dollar was the goal. And then, they thought that, you know, motel business is good. Better than the job.

Discrimination and a tough labor market were not the only motivating factors to enter the motel industry. Patels claimed a latent interest in self-employment. Barriers at work served as a catalyst. This helps explain Patels' quick entrance into entrepreneurship compared with other immigrants (Sanders and Nee 1996). For example, an elderly but energetic immigrant engineer turned to motels after seeing his brother's impressive financial returns. He said with a stern voice,

> Job is a job. If you are highly educated, doctorate degree, I think you can advance quite a bit. If you don't have that degree, it is hard to advance. . . . Business can take you wherever you want to go. . . . Whatever business will be successful for you, you go for it. It's not that you like it. Wherever opportunity you can make, you go for it.

His decision to switch to motels certainly involved the possibility of more money, but it symbolized something larger: the ability to be in control of one's own destiny. In effect, business ownership lets you decide your own future, whereas a job decides your future for you. And that future may be dim. An owner in Kentucky summarized this frame of mind very succinctly: "What's to say that you walk into the office today and see a pink slip on your table." This attitude turns on its head the prevalent view that self-employment is too risky and that working for someone else in an established business makes more sense (Pabrai 2007).

This belief in self-employment stems from Gujaratis' class culture, that is, the resources and values gathered from their occupational background (Light and Bonacich 1991). The son of a pioneer said, "We haven't been working for anybody else since for many, I don't know, generations . . . because we own our own land [in Gujarat]." Similarly in East Africa many Patels owned stores. The same preference for working for oneself rather than for someone else continues for Leva Patels in Gujarat. As Gidwani (2000) wrote, "A Patel who engages in manual work on his own plot of land is far less likely to invite derision from members of his caste than a Patel who toils on someone else's land" (p. 152). In general, those familiar with entrepreneurship before immigrating, even if they had not owned their own business, are more likely to start a business (Aldrich, Jones, and McEvoy 1984; Yoon 1997). Furthermore, owning a motel meant owning property, which, from their history as farmers, Patels valued as representing self-control and a safe investment.

So although Patel motel owners are referred to as "accidental owners" because they fell into the hospitality industry by default rather than by design, it was not a total coincidence. The pioneers' motivation to own a business, which continued with later immigrant waves, was not simply the hope of greater income. It also stemmed from their class culture.

Franchising Middleman Minority Opportunities

An interest in self-employment must be joined with profitable opportunities in order to come to fruition. Indian Americans became so prolific as owners compared with other ethnic entrepreneurs because of an increasing number of available motels, especially as franchising took off in the 1980s. Before this the pioneers started as middleman minorities, akin to other ethnic groups.

When entering an industry, immigrants have limited resources and typically choose businesses that more established groups either avoid or cannot access (Waldinger, Aldrich, and Ward 1990). Businesses that cater to co-ethnics within enclaves provide protected markets that nonethnic capitalists have difficulty entering because of language differences, cultural dissimilarities, and lack of access to particular goods.

When ethnic entrepreneurs start businesses outside the realm of co-ethnic enclaves, they often do so as middleman minorities (Zhou 2004). Middleman minorities run lower-status businesses with low profit margins, few staff, and nonelite (possibly poor) clientele within a stratified society (Bonacich 1973; Cobas 1989; Duany 1989; Min 1996; Zhou 2004). Simultaneously, their businesses are at the mercy of big capital, including their suppliers, franchisors, and corporate clients (Kim, Hurh, and Fernandez 1989; Yoon 1997). A final characteristic of middleman minorities is racial hostility from outsiders. Customers and locals frustrated with oppressive economic conditions may scapegoat owners for these troubles (Abelmann and Lie 1995; Duany 1989; Light and Bonacich 1991; Min 1996).[4] The middleman minority concept serves as a useful heuristic device to understand lower-budget Indian Americans' opportunities and challenges.

The first residential hotels Indian Americans ran fit the middleman minority profile well. There was a stable customer base near the bottom of a domestic stratification. Customers were poor, minorities, reliant on social security, seasonal laborers, and the like (Groth 1999). A son of a pioneer said, "When the pioneer was here, they were owning those in a downtown slum area. Any place in a downtown is always a problem area. There's always, what you call winos. You know, those alcoholics." The hotels served a dependent population that other hospitality segments had abandoned. The grandson of a pioneer said of the clientele:

> I feel that it was probably more the lower end . . . where it was probably easier to get into the leases. Locations are very mediocre. These people that stay are more from the city. Welfare people and stuff like that. You know, it's not real travelers.

As Kim (2000) argues, standard theories of entrepreneurship emphasize a group's resourcefulness and business opportunities but overlook the inequalities that facilitate those opportunities. In this case the disenfranchisement of poor residents proved essential to Gujaratis' business development.

This type of clientele translated into little hotel revenue, with rooms rented at "fifty cents a day. Really cheap. And two dollars a week or two dollars and fifty cents a week," according to one informant. So competition with other ethnic groups was not a problem in acquiring the hotels, which meant more opportunities for the Indian pioneer entrepreneurs.

European immigrant owners were ready to move out of the business, creating ample opportunities for Indians.[5] A grandson said of his grandfather pioneer's opportunity:

> At that time these hotels used to be owned by Frenchmen. Now with the Frenchmen, their second generation, they became professionals. There was nobody to operate these hotels. [The owners] kind of wanted to lease them or sell them. Mostly in the beginning [Indian pioneers] used to lease them.

Pioneers typically leased rather than purchased their hotels. Purchasing was too expensive and too risky. The pioneers' hotels ranged in size from 32 to 160 rooms (Jain 1989).

Furthermore, as the Progressive Era gained strength during the first quarter of the twentieth century, residential hotels were criticized as public nuisances, which drove away other potential investors (Groth 1999). In the late 1940s and early 1950s, when Gujaratis began buying hotels, these establishments were slowly in decline. Zoning and housing laws were put in place targeting residential hotels. Their construction slowed in the 1950s, and by the 1960s some were being torn down. Between 1975 and 1980 alone, almost one in five of San Francisco's residential hotels closed (Groth 1999). In fact, the first hotel owned by an informant's parents in the Bay Area was condemned by the city six months after it was purchased in the early 1950s. They struggled for a while before acquiring another one. As I toured Fourth and Fifth streets of downtown San Francisco with the son of a pioneer, he pointed out where hotels used to line the streets. Gujarati immigrants had leased or owned many of them. Today they are gone. He reminisced about his family's old hotel, which he lived in after arriving from India at age eleven in 1955. It was a ninety-two-room, two-story hotel on Fourth Street:

> When I first came from India, my hotel was right at the end of this block. . . . There was a bar on the corner. . . . My father leased [the hotel]. . . . My father paid $400 per month rent. So he made good money on it. . . . The owners sold it [in 1969] to the city for redevelopment. . . . We

had an apartment in this hotel, my mother, my father, myself. Living room, kitchen, and office. Anybody rings the bell—we go from our apartment to office!

In its place now stands an apartment complex with commercial properties at the ground level, including a Whole Foods grocery store. Quite a different clientele walks these streets today.

Whereas other entrepreneurs would avoid such clientele and low profits, Gujaratis considered the opportunity a good fit. Customers did not expect highly attentive service, which meant owners did not need to be well acculturated to serve them.[6] An owner who emigrated in 1968 smirked as she explained the fortuitous fit between early Indian migrants and the motel business:

> Many [Indian immigants] don't speak English. That's how it started. They came from India, and you can't operate [most businesses] without speaking English. So these people didn't know [English]. So in a hotel they don't have to speak English. In the room they do laundry and they do that. And they hire the front desk person and that's how the whole thing started.

Owners could serve their locality without sticking out too much culturally. In addition, although physically demanding, running a hotel did not require advanced training.

Hotels also seemed appealing given the lack of other suitable business sectors. Some Patels avoided restaurants because of a religious aversion to handling meat. Other industries had too much strong competition backed by large capital. For instance, clothing stores had been popular among Patels in East Africa. Upon migrating to the United States in the 1960s and 1970s, it became clear that selling everyday clothes would be too challenging. Following the precedent of motels started by the pioneers, which they did in large numbers, made more sense. One informant explained:

> [Indians in Africa] used to run very small stores—clothing, shoes, or knickknack and like that. Here they come, they see Target, Sears. They

realize they cannot compete with this thing. Sears buys one item and says, I want five trucks of it. [The small business owner] cannot even afford five boxes.

Also, hotels allowed owners and their families to live rent free, a major incentive.

The pioneers compared their opportunities not only with other opportunities in their vicinity but also with opportunities in India and elsewhere in the diaspora. The son of a pioneer said of his father's generation:

In 1960, [my parents] went back [to India]. You know, they still at that time sent a lot of money from here back to help out the old family. . . . If they got [home and] saw the economy really improved . . . [but] every time they visited back to India, they just felt like it was much more better here. . . . But like I said, you know, when they were working in India in the farms, they felt like this was still a lot easier to do than to sit and working in the heat, in the fields. [*laughs*] Big crops with everything. The heat and everything.

An elder immigrant noted similar challenges facing immigrants in Britain:

[In Britain] you can work all day—even today—they work and they don't save anything. And they already knew of this [motel business in the United States], and they saw [that] a lot of people were here with their own business. So, I guess they were patient enough to try to find their own business.

And Gujaratis from East Africa compared the opportunities in the United States in the 1960s and 1970s with the political and economic turmoil they were experiencing.

So early Indian American immigrants found worth in the hospitality industry. The businesses made even more sense as spouses joined them. Many male owners had returned home to Gujarat after a few years in the United States in order to get married or to bring over their wife and family. Most wives arrived after 1956 and assisted in the hotels (Jain 1989). One informant explained the decision of pioneers like his father to emigrate alone for only a limited time:

> My father got married in 1950. And um, when he took the visa in 1951, . . . [all the pioneering men] came alone because he says they don't know what they're gonna get into here. And, how can we afford to have an extra person live here? . . . They all went back to pick, you know, get their wives after three, four years later. . . . They used to . . . um . . . do everything by themselves. We didn't have room cleaners; [wives] had to clean rooms, vacuum the floors, clean the public rooms twice or three times a day. I mean, it was still very demanding at that time.

As wives labored in the hotels, the prospects for staying increased. Most often wives took charge of housekeeping duties and also worked the front desk. Some even ran the hotels as their husbands worked elsewhere. One such pioneering woman who arrived in the 1950s commented that she and her husband did all of the hotel work themselves with no hired help. The work was exhausting, but the hotel turned a profit and made her proud to live in the United States.

Expanding into Motels and Franchises

Over time the pioneers shifted to motels, which provided a foothold in an expanding industry. The first step up from the lower-end residential hotels was into slightly higher-end hotels just north of Market Street (Jain 1989). The first *motel* owned by an Indian immigrant was purchased in the 1960s in downtown San Francisco. There is disagreement over the exact date of purchase. The nephew of the original owner put it around "the late '60s, '66 [or] '67. I don't know the exact year." Another descendant of an "old-timer" offered an earlier date. He also explained the shift to motels as a way of seeking a slightly higher-income clientele:

> Everybody had a hotel, and there was only one [Indian-owned] motel back in 1963. Was the Ninth and Mission, Mart Motel. Small in size, and the quality of customer are better. Because all the time they had a hotel,

it was all the residential hotel. And they all are senior citizen, or very low working class, or government-aided or people on welfare. That kind of hotel they started at the beginning in 1949. And so maybe this guy probably want to go in little better in a motel. And just get a little bit better clientele.

I visited the Mart Motel in 2009, now a Rodeway Inn franchise. The motel sits above a street-level parking lot, which was full of cars.[7] The person behind the desk was a young male Indian immigrant, unaware of the motel's history. In the small, nondescript lobby, there is no sign of the role it played within the Indian community. Instead, like practically any motel lobby, there was a set of tourist brochures, a large check-in counter, a mural of a blue sky with puffy, white clouds, and other generic accoutrements. Its history is being lost.

Increased opportunities to purchase motels at discounted prices allowed Indian immigrants to expand nationally rather than remain in select locations or fade out, as was prevalent for other ethnic niches. There were only sixty or seventy Indian American–owned establishments during the 1960s.[8] These were run mostly by the pioneers and the relatives they had sponsored. Then a number of rundown motels became available in the 1960s and 1970s. With as little as $5,000 down, one could purchase a motel (Pabrai 2007). The buildup of motels in the United States had stemmed more from government and corporate interventions than from customer demand. The interstate highway system developed in 1956 through federal assistance. Banks relaxed lending requirements, which increased construction of homes and businesses. Leisure became its own industry. Nevertheless, motels had a difficult time earning money. Construction of contemporary hotels increased because of urban renewal programs. Some motels were situated in out-of-the-way rural areas, where there was little demand. Also, lower-budget establishments came to be seen as havens for prostitution and illicit sexual affairs. Even as early as the 1950s, the supply of motels was greater than the demand. "By 1956 it was estimated that about one-half of all motels earned no more than a modest income from their twenty or fewer rooms" (Jakle, Sculle, and Rogers 2002, p. 85).

An increase in the number of business openings along with the native labor force's loss of interest in working for those businesses is essential for immigrant groups to take over a niche (Waldinger 1994). As for residential hotels in the 1940s and 1950s, few other groups sought these motels in the 1960s and 1970s, given their precarious stature and unsupported growth. As more Indians arrived post-1965 from India, Britain, East Africa, and elsewhere, they valued self-employment just as their predecessors did, worried about mobility within their occupations, and knew of other Patels in the industry, so they took advantage of opportunities in motels. In fact, Indian Americans are credited with turning around many failing buildings. As an informant noted for the independent sector:

> [Indian Americans] were kind of the strongest force penetrating into the economy sector, the mid-tier sector of the lodging industry. . . . The old, tired independent motels that are probably not maintained well and everything. At least with them buying it, they would maintain and then fix up the motels back to a good condition.

Franchising created even more chances for individuals to open a motel. It began in the 1950s, but really gathered speed in the late 1970s and the 1980s, at a time when many immigrants were seeking opportunities outside the labor market (Jakle, Sculle, and Rogers 2002). Many current major motel brands started in the 1960s, 1970s, and later (for example, EconoLodge, Hampton Inn, Embassy Suites, Days Inn, and Super 8) (Jakle, Sculle, and Rogers 2002). Some have been around for much longer (for example, Holiday Inn, Howard Johnson, and Ramada Inn) (Morgan 1964). And, of course, many brands failed during this time as well.[9] During the 1970s and 1980s, more attention was placed by franchisors on monitoring individual franchisees to ensure compliance with guidelines. Franchised and corporate-owned motels could more easily keep up their physical appearances, which customers valued, while holding down costs with sophisticated accounting procedures and employee training (Morgan 1964). Still, the growth of franchises was slow. According to Jakle,

Sculle, and Rogers (2002), "Mom and Pop still owned 54 percent of all motels, according to the 1987 federal census" (p. 85). Only since the latter part of the 1980s has franchising become the dominant force in the industry.

The growth of the franchise motel industry enabled Indian Americans to develop a national presence as owners rather than remain in select areas. Immigrants who arrived during or after the 1970s entered both the independent and the franchise motel industry. They gradually purchased run-down motels and motels in oversaturated markets cheaply—some independent, some already franchised—and then remodeled them to fit the expectations of a franchise that was looking to expand. The sought-after franchise was typically in the lower-budget range. One proprietor detailed the process:

> They buy the existing rundown hotel. And he called a franchise, Comfort Inn, or Days Inn. Okay, I want to make a Days Inn, give me your PIP List. . . . That means, what I should do in a room. Carpet, furniture, painting, wallpaper, whatever. So just tell me exactly what I need. . . . I think it's been . . . between '80 and '85. . . . First of all you get a good deal in any motel. Then you convert.

I heard numerous stories of walls that had been torn down, new carpeting that had been installed, wiring that had been redone, and so on. Owners made a point to comment on such work as they showed me around their places. In this manner, Indian Americans rejuvenated the economy franchise sector. The *New York Times* reported, "Many of the older Indian-owned motels were long ago refurbished, if only to measure up as franchises—a method the Indians quickly saw as a route to financial independence."[10]

An increasing number of motels in the 1980s were foreclosed and then available for purchase at discount prices. Factors external to motels contributed to this, namely the weak financial market of the 1980s that followed high gas prices in the 1970s. I met a co-owner of a few motels near Toledo at his volleyball game, where he took time out to explain the rise of Indian franchise ownership across the country:

We pushed it really hard in '80s, between the 1980s and '90s, when there was a lot of property bankruptcy. We started gearing up to buy those properties from the bank. All franchise.

Q: *Which franchises?*

Cardinal Knights Inn, those are the properties that went into bankruptcy. Because of the management. A lot of people bought properties from banks. And then they did really good on their properties.

Knights Inn is one example of a franchise that lost market share during the 1980s as new owners rebranded them into more popular brands, such as Days Inn and Motel 6. Indians also purchased motels that were not necessarily bankrupt but whose owner was looking to sell for whatever reason (retiring, found a better motel, and so on). The timing worked well for Indian immigrants, who were arriving and growing frustrated with the labor market.

So Indian immigrants purchased failing motels and updated them to fit desired brands, which gave them pride in assisting local communities. An owner in California carried a chip on his shoulder, for he believed Indian Americans deserve more credit than they receive for assisting the hospitality industry and neighborhoods:

If there was no Indian buying any hotels, half of the buildings would have been torn down. Be closed. Nobody would run it. I mean, imagine if the Mexicans weren't here—we're not gonna get all the farming done. We're gonna have half the crops rotten in the field. Same way in San Francisco. If there was no Indian in the hotel. . . . And same thing with the franchise outside. If there is no Indian, they will not remodel it or they will not spend money. But [the motel] will be all boarded down, and somebody has to put the new building.

Once franchises recognized Indians' commitment to the industry in the 1980s, they began to target the eager group with more opportunities. The racialization of Indian Americans as a "model" group to work with began to take hold, signifying that more than just motivation, opportunity, and resources shape entrepreneurship (discussed in Chapter 3) (Valdez 2010).

Over time Indian Americans came to dominate the lower-budget level of the motel industry. Not surprisingly, these would-be abandoned buildings often relied on a clientele not too distinct from those in residential hotels. Many of the motels of the 1980s and still today—including franchises—continue to fit a general middleman minority profile, even if not to the same degree as the residential hotel. Lower-budget motels rely on a customer base with few resources and so have low economic returns that more privileged investors avoid. It is still common for those too poor to afford the security deposit and first month's rent on an apartment to stay in a cheap motel for weeks or months at a time (Ehrenreich 2001). Conservative government policies have contributed to the growth of this otherwise homeless segment. Reductions in welfare and public housing, lack of universal health insurance that in turn keeps many poor people sick, insufficient mental health care and rehabilitation programs in prisons, and underfunded and segregated public schools have left many people, even people who are working, without sufficient resources to afford an apartment or a home. The mortgage and unemployment crises that began in the mid-2000s have created a whole new pool of people unable to afford "normal" living quarters, and many have turned to motels. Cities and nonprofit organizations have partnered with motels to subsidize this use of motels because homeless shelters are filled to capacity.[11] Some motels work directly with local governments to serve state-subsidized clients. As real estate developers sought to maximize their own interests, owners of independent and lower-end franchise motels stepped in and attended to those left behind.[12]

By the 1990s, many Indian American motel owners had established themselves financially, and some decided to take risks on new, more-upscale franchise brands, and franchises approached clients already in their portfolio for new acquisitions. One owner gave an example of how indebted certain franchises were to Indian Americans for trying out unproven brands: "Because imagine, Holiday [Inn] Express. They are 1,200

Indian Americans, like these in Ohio, have started constructing new hotels in large measure.

[motels in the country]. Bet you 500 are owned by Indians. Five or six hundred." The construction of new motels also created opportunities, thereby continuing the growth of the industry.[13] This is not to suggest that cheaper, independent motels do not remain popular. As Kalnins and Chung (2006) state, "The unbranded motel retains a niche in these markets typically overlooked by the large branded chains" (p. 244).[14] It is increasingly common for Indian Americans to own more than one motel, whether as the main shareholder or by investing in a colleague's property.

Taking advantage of motel opportunities was not easy for Gujarati immigrants at first. Despite the need for such establishments, Patels encountered discrimination in entering and insuring their motels in the 1970s, framed as foreigners trying to enter a native-oriented industry instead of staying within an ethnic enclave. A quote from a hotel consultant is useful:

As investment and ownership expanded, the Patels were accused of a wide variety of crimes: arson, laundering stolen travel checks, circumventing immigration laws. In an unpleasant burst of xenophobia, *Frequent Flyer* magazine (Summer 1981) declared, "Foreign investment has come to the motel industry . . . causing grave problems for American buyers and brokers. Those Americans in turn are grumbling about unfair, perhaps illegal business practices: there is even talk of conspiracy." . . . The article concluded with an unmistakable racist remark, "Comments are passed about motels smelling like curry and dark hints about immigrants who hire Caucasians to work the front desk."[15]

Institutional racism against Indian American moteliers also existed in other media. The American Automobile Association was sued for discriminatory motel ratings.[16] Newspaper articles critiqued the growing trend of "foreigners" buying up American motels just to stay in the country legally.[17] The message was clear: Indian Americans are not trustworthy and are non-American.

Racist targeting led to collective actions on the part of Indian Americans. They founded the Midsouth Indemnity Association in Nashville, Tennessee, in 1985, which became the Indo American Hospitality Association. The Asian American Hotel Owners Association (AAHOA) began with twelve members in 1989 in Atlanta. In 1994 the two organizations merged as AAHOA.[18] (AAHOA's efforts receive attention in Chapter 4.)

Global Networks Within a Global Inequality

An interest in entrepreneurship and the opportunity for it are not sufficient for a group to enter small business. The last major set of factors informing ethnic entrepreneurship includes immigrants' family, class, and ethnic resources (Portes and Rumbaut 2006; Sanders and Nee 1996; Yoon 1997). Indians emigrated mostly as families, particularly those who came after 1965. Extended family also proved an invaluable resource of information and inspiration. Anecdotal stories about Patels' rise in the industry emphasize the role of family assistance, and for good reason. A first-generation engineer mentioned his brother's motel business as motivating him to start one as well:

A lot of people own franchises, like Burger King, Dunkin' Donuts, Subway sandwich. But when I went into business, few Indian people, less than 1 percent had that kind of business. I didn't know if successful or not. I have a brother who was in hotel business since 1964. I see that he has [been] successful in business.

One informant of the second generation considered various kinds of businesses before deciding on motels. In fact, his parents had not owned motels. He said,

At the end of the day I have the real estate. If the business drops, there is still the value of new construction and the assets sitting there. That's what got us into the motel business. And obviously everyone knows at least one or two Indians in the motel business. Talking to them got us more attracted to it.

Even the pioneers relied on networks to draw them into motels. Desai was the first in the industry, and he attracted other pioneers to the industry.

Yet beyond the family ties immigrant entrepreneurs generally have access to, Indian Americans benefited greatly from transnational kin. The family reunification strategies of U.S. immigration trends have created a pool of low-wage workers to sustain the U.S. economy (Reddy 2005). Extended-family members willing to emigrate for low-wage employment proved essential for Indian Americans' expansive growth. Siblings and their spouses were commonly brought over, often with men being the main negotiators even if one's direct relationship was with a woman (e.g., sister). A lower-budget franchise owner, formerly an engineer, emphasized his reliance on family members as he related his unplanned entrance into motels:

I lost the job—unemployed. I bought the motel and thought, let me try. I didn't want to. I was looking for a job. I knew my brother-in-law was available. So I took the motel and I hired him. I was coming in every day also, because his English at that time was a problem. . . . Then I saw the money was much more than I was making [as an engineer]. If I would have found a job, I would have gone back. . . . I had the power of labor, our own people. In this way a lot of motel people went into motel too. Joint family work. . . . Then he buys his own. It goes into the family.

Numerous informants told a similar story of Gujaratis coming to domi-nate motels by drawing from the "power of labor, our own people." The networks included owners' nuclear family, extended family, and other Indian Americans either already in the United States or who came here specifically to work and live in motels. The availability of such labor made investing in motels less risky for the owners, especially for those owners in which one spouse continued to work at a paid job, which was a common occurrence.

As more and more owners sponsored relatives to come to the United States and assist in their motels, the number of future moteliers in-creased and so helps explain Indian Americans' national presence in the field. One informant said:

> If I'm new to this country, you're gonna find the best possible way for you to succeed. And for the Indians, one of the things that they suc-ceeded in is that they had families that mind the hotel business. . . . For example my mother-in law's brother . . . had a hotel. So he put [his rela-tives] at the hotel, and taught them the basics. And then they run the hotel. . . . So they went and bought a small hotel in Arizona, okay. Now, what happened when they moved [to Arizona]: they opened up that hotel for another family member to come and get educated.

This is an extreme version of the classic story of networks offering appren-ticeships that then extend into business ownership through industry-specific training and access to business openings (Portes and Bach 1985; Raijman and Tienda 2000; Waldinger, Aldrich, and Ward 1990). The spon-soring family typically helped pay for the relative's motel and so earned money back on the investment.

This process—sponsoring family members to come to work in the motel who then go on to purchase their own motel—became self-sustaining. Indian migration grew based on its own labor creation. Those who migrated and entered the motel industry through this route did not experience a disadvantage in the labor market—in fact, they may not have experienced any labor market other than that of the motel industry.[19]

Owners' kin could find work given the particular characteristics of the motel. Based on how informants spoke, one would think motels were designed for groups like Indians. For instance, one informant chuckled with amusement as he explained practically any Indian's ability to run a motel:

> [In] the motel business, you don't need to be an educated person or anything like that. As long as [you] can say thirty-nine dollars, ninety-nine cents plus tax, here is the key, and that's the room. . . . It's a service industry where you don't come into much contact with the person.

In addition, most of the work takes place behind the scenes. A longtime AAHOA member explained,

> [The motel] served multiple purposes. You can live in your own motel. Because you have an apartment in your own motel, you don't have to pay rent. The other thing is that the whole family can work in the hotel. From making beds to laundry to maintenance . . . everything. So you really didn't need to go out and find work because the motel could keep the whole family busy.

Ethnic groups can form a niche when their networks extend to multiple parts of an industry rather than simply one aspect of it (Poros 2010). An elderly woman recognized her and many other Indians' limitations, which motel life compensated for. "In our community most people own motels when we come here, because we got a problem with the English. And this—this will give everybody work."

In addition, the free accommodations to sponsored relatives helped them save enough money to possibly buy their own establishment. This distinguishes the motel from other common immigrant-owned businesses. Green grocers, dry cleaners, convenience store owners, and the like may have an attached apartment where the owner and nuclear family can live, but such quarters can rarely accommodate other families for long periods of time (Jung 2008).[20]

"I Didn't Pick This Country"

It makes sense that Gujarati owners would want relatives to emigrate, live near them, and assist in their motels. But why would these relatives want to leave their home and homeland to labor in motels scattered across the country, with only the possibility—not the guarantee—of eventually owning a low-budget establishment? Understanding this is essential to explaining how networks are enabled and why Patels came to dominate the industry. The standard framing within immigrant entrepreneurship literature of a local reliance on ethnic networks would not fully capture the broader dynamic at play (Portes and Rumbaut 2006). Instead, a sustained global hierarchy between a recently postcolonial nation and the hypercapitalist First World joins with the connection of family to explain how motel owners' networks were so ready to emigrate and serve as resources (Abelmann and Lie 1995).

Given that the standard of living between India and the United States has been so disproportionate for so long, family members needed neither an understanding of the U.S. labor market nor an expectation of what they would be doing before agreeing to migrate. And although India has developed considerably over the past twenty years, a desire to immigrate to the West, even for a low-status position, still has appeal. Such a backdrop joins with the stories shared among family members of opportunities, of personal needs, and of the desire for reunification.

The impact of this hierarchy is evident in how immigrants spoke of their emigration. I was struck by the matter-of-fact way that many informants explained their motivations for emigrating. They came simply because they were sponsored by someone already in the United States, even if motels and entrepreneurship were disconnected from their previous line of work. For instance, a proprietor of an independent motel near Toledo, which caters to truck drivers, had married an Indian woman already living in the United States and then migrated here in 1989, and his motel life began. His practically unemotional tone revealed the resigned approach so many immigrants had to working in motels. He shrugged his shoulders a little in response to my first question:

Q: *What were you doing in India before [migrating]?*

In college, studying.

Q: *You didn't plan on coming to the U.S.?*

No. And as soon as I came, my wife—her family, they were managing a motel and it was too hard to manage. So I just joined in the next day.

Q: *So you didn't know about managing motels before you came?*

No. I learned by doing.

The turn to working in a motel represented a "contradictory class mobility" for many immigrants, that is, earning more wages and/or having greater security upon migration but with a lower-status job (Parreñas 2001).

The prospect of residing in the United States offered enough reason to change one's life plans. A lower-budget owner in rural Ohio prepared to work as an engineer when he arrived, sponsored by his brother. His brother wanted him to work in his motel:

I come [to] find out, he had a plan, he's changed everything around. The very first day I came in here, he told me, he said, "[The motel] is what my plans are." I said, "Okay."

An elderly woman in an isolated, independent motel similarly referred dispassionately to factors beyond her control as leading her and her husband to the United States:

I didn't pick this country, but my sister-in-law applied for us. And we came here. She is a motel owner too. . . . It's a hard life there [in India]. And this is an advanced country.

The question of why to immigrate was absurd to her; she and her husband came because they could.[21]

The fact that newer immigrants entered the motel industry so readily signifies how dependent they were on their sponsors. As one informant explained,

> Whoever sponsored [the new immigrant], if they are in motel business,
> definitely you are going to go in motel business too. Because that's all
> you're going to see when you come here.[22]

By the late 1970s, the promise of motels had spread throughout Patel
communities in Gujarat, making the United States a preferred destination (Breman 2007). An owner of an independent motel said that before
he emigrated, he heard about the U.S. motel industry: "Village people.
All my neighbors owned motels. They said it was good business." Emigration out of Surat has been especially dramatic. An elder immigrant
said:

> Our district, our village, you'll find a little [emigration], fifty years ago,
> sixty years ago. You know, there might have been like twenty people
> out of the village, you know, [in] England or America or whatever.
> Now there's like 75 percent, or probably more than 75 percent are in,
> you know, England, whatever, South Africa, America. . . . Surat city
> [a major district of Patel emigration] is like 30 miles from where we
> live.

According to Breman (2007), "of all the 107 households of the dominant caste in [a village within the Surat district] . . . 115 Kanbi Patel men
and/or their adult sons live and work abroad, nearly all in the USA" and
in the motel business (p. 355). About 30 percent of the houses in the district he studied were empty. Even villages in central Gujarat not known
for emigration have begun to send residents to the United States to run
motels. It is not uncommon for Patels in Gujarat to wait ten years or
more for a visa to come to the United States, and they will not even visit
on a tourist visa for fear of hurting their chances (Breman 2007). This is
despite a rising standard of living among wealthier Patels in the Surat
district, a result of increasing sugarcane profits.

The strength of transnational networks has altered how some Gujaratis approach even their education in India. They feel that spending
more time in school in India can block rather than open up opportunities. One immigrant who arrived at age twenty wanted to come as a young
teenager:

When I come, I thought I want to buy motels. I don't want to think about anything else. Just buy motels. Easy. . . . Knew of motels for long time [in India]. Wanted to come to America at age fifteen. If I come early, I have to go to school. Between thirteen and eighteen you come, that's good future since learn better English.

From the point of view of the immigrants, the prospects of behind-the-scenes work and modest pay were tolerable given the guarantee of employment in the United States, the training received, and the ability to live for free. Would-be employees often trust a co-ethnic firm more than a non–co-ethnic firm for its training and likelihood for mobility (Bailey and Waldinger 1991). Although friction among family members does occur, informants reported mostly harmonious relations (but see Chapters 4 and 5). Because of family or other connections between them, workers and owners feel solidarity with one another and can keep track of one another more easily (Portes and Zhou 1993).

Owning a motel appealed to new immigrants for legal reasons as well. The government has created incentives for immigrant self-employment, namely, the possibility of legal, permanent residency if the business meets certain criteria. This policy is currently known as Green Card Through Investment.[23] Sponsoring relatives could guarantee employment of the immigrant, which facilitated entry, a technique other ethnic groups have used as well (Sengstock 1982). According to an elder motel owner, Indian immigrants from Britain often arrived as tourists or as relatives sponsored by current U.S. citizens, rather than on student or work visas. Such immigrants gained legal status to stay in the United States after working for a few months in someone else's motel and then buying their own:

[Immigrants] just came here has a visitor visa and buy a business. Buy a hotel. Then they go back. Okay they buy the hotel, then they just write the letter with some hotel deal. . . . And government . . . says okay, you want to invest $30,000 here, fine, and your experience is there, fine, you get the green card. You're giving a job to four, five people, bingo. And that's a lot of people got a green card. . . . And *lots* of people from '73 to '78, lot of Indians from Gujarat [used this], same relatives of all those pioneers came. . . . [The] biggest chunk came after '72, '73 . . . from England, mainly.

Q: *They bought motels right away?*

Uh, within six months . . . they had to buy right away because that's the only way they can get the green card.

Highly represented among these British immigrants were Indians originally in East Africa (Sheth 2001). According to informants, these were mostly legal immigrants who arrived with their families and who had the resources to take advantage of this opportunity. They rarely purchased very low-budget motels.

Overall, Indian American motel owners fit a common trajectory, that of increased upward mobility and integration partly because of strong ethnic networks across a variety of group members. They were in the right place at the right time, and they took advantage of the opportunities that arose. But the larger story of Indian Americans' rise in the industry is a diasporic one. A global inequality made relatives abroad want to come to the United States notwithstanding the lack of clear prospects or connections to previous interests. Transnational enterprises are normally perceived as run by elites who import goods and money from their homeland to the diaspora, or vice versa, for businesses mostly targeting co-ethnic customers (Landolt, Autler, and Baires 1999; Portes, Guarnizo, and Haller 2003). Here we see a different type of transnational enterprise, one that depends not on products but on transnational relations.

Money

Family resources combined with class and ethnic resources to enable immigrants to afford to purchase a motel. How much a motel costs depends on a variety of factors, including number of rooms, gross income history, physical condition, built-in amenities, strength of the local economy, future prospects, number of competitors, and current franchise (if applicable). Putting a number on a hypothetical motel is impossible, but prices in Ohio in 2007 ranged from $700,000 for an independent motel to a few million for a middle-budget franchise. According to informants in Ohio, motels in the first decade of the twenty-first century sold on average for three or four times annual gross sales, again depending on contextual factors (location, maintenance, and so on).

Indian immigrants accrued money for the motels from a variety of sources, including money they had saved before emigrating and money they had saved from earnings while employed in the United States. Rarely, though, was this enough for a down payment. They borrowed money from relatives and close friends, often other motel owners. Because the lenders know how to run motels, they felt comfortable lending money based on a handshake to someone buying a motel. It was not uncommon for twenty or more people to lend $2,000 each.[24] Even family members in India sent money to relatives in the United States to help them purchase motels. Those who lent money became investors who could see a return on their loan.

Many informants highlighted the significant degree of trust involved in lending money. Lenders had to be relatively confident in not only the borrower's character but also that of his/her family. An independent owner near Toledo borrowed money from relatives and friends to purchase his motel. He had this to say:

[Lenders] know I'm working hard. They trust people. [They] never ask [me] to show books. If you want to give, you give. I'm not going to show books. My dad's credit in India is main thing. How the family works hard, make money. Not my credit. That shows good family.

Q: *If business goes bankrupt?*

Have to work somewhere else and get money back and pay them back. Don't want to lose my credit.

Q: *By credit you mean reputation?*

Yah, reputation.

Borrowers rarely put timelines on when the money was due. Few charged interest, but it did happen. Informants claimed that money was nearly always paid back, if not by the borrower then by someone in the family. Given how intertwined their social networks were, it was difficult for borrowers to cheat their lenders.

Despite the common use of networks among ethnic groups, informants view their heavy use of networks as particular to their ethnic culture (as do most ethnic groups) (Gold 2010). For example, an elder immigrant avidly stated:

> Now what happens is that this is a very, very unique thing about this community, which you don't even find in even other Gujarati communities. You only find this in the Patels. And that is helping each other out. . . . In our community, especially in this Patel and Gujarati community, it's [a] very herd mentality. That once some of them are in this business, the others would come. . . . If I were to use a vendor, if I did something, other people just knowing, okay [I'll do the same]. They would not think twice. . . . Patels are the only group to help one another out in lending money. . . . Trust that will get the money back because [you] know the family for generations.

Cultural theories of entrepreneurship, while prominent in popular discourse, are critiqued by many academics for their tautological nature. The components of an "entrepreneurial culture" have not been established, especially as pertaining to particular ethnic groups (Portes and Rumbaut 2006). I recognize the role of ethnic culture. But culture must interact with social conditions to become actionable (Light and Bonacich 1991; Waldinger 1986). To whatever extent a use of social ties is culturally driven for Gujarati Patels, it is strongly facilitated by their mode of incorporation, namely, their employment opportunities, community oversight of one another, and legal status (Portes and Rumbaut 2006).

Even as networks played a considerable role, many buyers also relied on loans from banks. The turn to more institutionalized financial capital took place gradually and allowed immigrants to expand beyond "mom and pop" shops (Yoon 1997). As one informant said, "Now people have credit from the bank, get 100,000, $200,000 credit from the bank, based on your motel."[25] It is easier to secure a loan from a bank when buying a franchise, which is partly why franchises have become so attractive to owners.

Before bank loans became more commonplace, Indian Americans purchased motels through owner financing. Under this arrangement, the owner keeps the title while the person running the motel makes payments to the owner until the business is purchased. This saves the buyer the high cost of interest on loans, and if the person cannot pay the owner, the owner retains the business. This process remains common for newer immigrants, now buying their motels from fellow Indian Americans and even at times utilizing Indian American–owned banks.[26]

Like many businesses, the amount of money a motel brings in fluctuates from one year to the next. After accounting for fixed expenses, a lower- to middle-budget motel may bring in from $90,000 to $140,000 per year (in 2007 dollars). From this, one must then set aside how much will be reinvested into the motel for upgrades (such as carpeting, roofing, and amenities) and how much for the family's salary, which can range from $20,000 to $60,000. Owners often have one adult family member work at a minimum wage job to earn needed income. The wealth accumulated from the motel itself creates a greater financial incentive than does the salary.

Those running higher-middle- and higher-budget motels obviously take in more money but also have to put aside much more for upkeep. So although their take-home pay is higher than those running lower- and middle-budget establishments, it is not substantially so. According to a second-generation owner, his higher-middle-budget motel earned him, his father, and his brother (all three are partners in the motel) a combined total of between $200,000 and $250,000 per year.[27] His personal take-home pay is less than the $100,000 he used to make as an engineer. But he still felt the motel was offering a higher quality of life:

It's more money in the long run, the wealth that you build. You're not going to get that from a job, even if my job paid me more money to live on. Let's say I make $100,000 at the job, but only $50,000 here. . . . But, the thing is that by the time that I retire the value, even in like five years, [with] the equity [from the motel], I could get another [motel].

He also earned more money than in his previous occupation because he pooled money with his brother and father. This was a common strategy of families that had multiple generations in the motel business and/or multiple motels. Income was shared to a certain extent. The first generation typically spent less of their disposable income than did their children and so could use their money to assist the children. The father of this informant, for example, helped him pay the down payment on a condominium.

For most owners, especially at the lower-budget level, money was tight and had to be prioritized for the motel. In the owners' living quarters that I visited, I saw little furniture (often a dining table, a coffee table, and a couch or a few chairs), few amenities (except large flat-screen television sets), and generic dishes and kitchenware (discussed in Chapter 5). People's clothes were rarely designer brands (which would not be conducive to the physical labor required to run a motel without much staff). By saving money on leisure activities, rent, eating out, and other expenses, owners were able to earn money over time (Pabrai 2007).

Children of Immigrants Expand Ownership

Further explaining the remarkable presence of Indian Americans in the hospitality industry has been its continuance across generations. No definitive data exist on how many children of Indian immigrant owners stay in the motel industry or in small businesses generally. Based on my interviews, it appears that their rate of entrepreneurship is lower than that of their parents but probably higher than that of whites. This does not include those who invest in a relative's or friend's motel as a silent partner. Also, the number of younger-generation motel owners appears to be increasing. AAHOA has created a "young moteliers" group within its organization to speak to this demographic. I see more and more young owners and prospective owners at AAHOA conventions. In fact, the newly elected secretary of AAHOA is a thirty-one-year-old, second-

generation motelier (and the AAHOA secretary becomes the organization's chairperson within four years).[28] A representative of a hotel management school noted to me an increasing presence of Indian American
students. Most of these young moteliers are male. The second generation typically owns economy franchises, although some are breaking into
middle-budget and higher-budget establishments and even full-service
and boutique hotels.

The standard assumption has been that the grandchildren, if not the
children, of immigrant business owners will move into the standard labor market as they become college educated and more job opportunities
present themselves. Evidence has supported this argument, in particular for older waves of European immigrants during the late 1800s and
early 1900s. But similar trends apply to contemporary immigrant communities. U.S.-raised Korean, Vietnamese, and Chinese Americans of
entrepreneurial parents typically leave their parents' business and enter
careers (Kasinitz et al. 2008). Children of Indian Americans in other
businesses, such as Dunkin' Donuts, also leave the industry (Rangaswamy
2007). Such children saw these stores as too small and too low-status to
be worth their time.

Yet generational decline is not always the norm. In fact, the second
generation may increase the small business activity over that of their
parents, as found for Iranian Americans (Min and Bozorgmehr 2000).
And as I stated above, although the second generation's rate of entrepreneurship is generally lower than that of the first generation, it is likely
still higher than that of whites (Gold, Light, and Johnston 2006). This
should not be surprising. According to Hout (1984; Hout and Rosen 2000),
the children of self-employed fathers are more likely to enter self-
employment or other autonomous professions compared with those of
their ethnic group whose fathers are not self-employed. Often, the second
generation stays in small business when they have few other opportunities, such as if they did not do well in school and cannot enter the white-
collar labor market (Portes and Rumbaut 2006). Some of those who stay
in small business change industries in search of safer and more profitable
sectors (Min 2008). Less frequently, others move up in the same industry

as their parents, such as Iraqi Chaldean Americans moving from small stores in urban areas to larger stores in the suburbs over a generation. This final trend, of moving up within the same industry, applies to Indian Americans. This includes the 1.5, second, and recently even third generations. My comments concentrate on the 1.5 and second generation.

Why have so many Indian Americans stayed in the motel business across generations? It is not because of a lack of other options. All of my 1.5- and second-generation informants had graduated from four-year colleges or universities, majoring in engineering, computer science, finance, and the like. A few went on to get their MBA. One informant pursued a degree in hotel management. Nor did they romanticize the rough years of their parents. Most saw white-collar employment as a "professional" lifestyle in contrast to the lifestyle they grew up in of running a low-budget motel (Park 2005). Practically all had had or planned on having a career outside the motel industry.

Yet once in such jobs, most sensed a very different reality, one not of rewards but of barriers to full economic rights because of their race. As one owner who had previously worked as an environmental engineer said,

> [Regarding my previous job,] if you want to move up more, it's who you know not what you know, unfortunately. And unfortunately when there're not a lot of Indians in higher positions yet. And especially in the same field. . . . I know doctors that quit practicing because of insurance and stuff and went into running hotels. I know lawyers that have trained as lawyers, once again, couldn't break the barriers to get ahead. . . . Well the thing that you have is that they get bypassed for promotions and things like that . . . and that's aggravatin'.

Another owner conveyed slight embarrassment as he relayed his unanticipated trajectory into motels:

> Well, I promised myself after high school, I'm going to go get a good education, and I'm gonna go work for a national company and never get into the hotel business. . . . And I got a great college degree, I got a degree in

physics. . . . I worked for a few years, and what I noticed was, I'm working thirteen, fourteen hours a day just like my dad was [in his motel]. However, in my case, somebody else is getting fat. . . . And then I saw my dad and his cousins who were not working as many hours any more, but they're making three, four times my pay.

Although a disadvantaged labor market explains the motivation of many young owners to enter small business, it was coupled with the same quest for autonomy found among the first generation.[29]

One owner grew more animated—twisting in his chair—as he predicted his exploits in the motel industry. He left his job as an engineer at a global automobile firm that, he believed, relegated Indian Americans to niche positions.

[Careers at the firm] kind of tiered off in two directions—one is administrative and one is more technical. The Indian always excels with the technical. I mean, they will be head of the research groups, head of the engineering, stuff like that, and they will get those positions. But they won't get vice president of the division or vice president—that's more of a rarity. . . . [Motel ownership] blows [my previous job] right out of the water. See if you think about it, when I was an engineer, I had a boss and his boss and his boss, and all the way to the top of the company. I'm like nothing. And all of a sudden, being in this business—this one business—my boss at that job means nothing now. And when I get two, three, four, five hotels down the line, the guy who was the vice president of the division—I don't care, I own ten hotels. Screw you! The cash flow is two and a half million dollars a year, and with ten hotels that are worth fifty million dollars, what does your V.P. of whatever mean? . . . I don't want to answer to nobody. It's my own, it's my way.

During these final comments he jabbed an index finger into the air. He was on a vengeful path toward freedom—expressed in sexually dominant terms—previously denied to him by the "V.P. of whatever."[30]

The children of immigrant owners also were motivated by a desire for personal freedom. While the previous informant hints at it, a peer near Toledo stressed it explicitly. He turned down a job offer at the famous Waldorf Astoria Hotel in New York City to run an economy motel outside Toledo:

> [The Waldorf Astoria] offered me a position. But the bottom line is, what am I going to do there? I can work there, I can go there and work there fifteen years if I really wanted, but I'm never going to own that. So the bottom line is ownership, that was the only persuading thing. As an owner you have more freedom. Freedom is a big thing. I can do whatever I want to [this motel]. If I run it down to the ground, then I run it down to the ground. If I make it successful, then I make it successful. That was my only difference, or I would have gone there. . . . All of my American friends have no idea in hotels. They would all say man, you're making a mistake [turning down the Waldorf Astoria]. . . . But all the hotel people, believe it or not, they all said, dude, what are you doing? Why are you going over there? You know, your parents own motels, you got a chance to run them, you have a chance to grow with them, to grow with yourself.

As is fitting with neoliberal ideology, the second generation believed in being self-sufficient. Staying in the same bureaucratic career would counter that goal. For example, one owner had liked her job as a chemist. She said,

> I mean, it was a great company to work for. But then, I guess owning your own business, it's hard work, it's seven days a week, and the areas that we bought our properties were rural areas, so help was difficult to get. So we did almost every aspect of running a hotel. At the end of five to six years, when you turn around and sell the property, you can see "oh it was worth it when we did that."

Motel ownership allowed for the combination of personal growth and familial growth. Children built on their parents' success, affirming a trajectory of gradual integration. An owner in Chicago said,

> The history of why people got into a mom and pop motels, when we arrived to the America, [is that] we didn't have the communication skills to get jobs. You could live there and make money, and it didn't take

much education or skills. We could educate our children. And the children want to take it to the next level. And the second generation is comparing itself to the Hiltons and Marriotts. Once you see something bigger, why would you come back to a twenty-room?

By entering motels, the children of immigrants fulfilled their parents' goals and also their own. It is common in India for children to take on the same profession as their parents (typically father to son).

The industry allowed them the best of both worlds: they could distinguish themselves from their parents and still build off their parents' success and benefit from their community's collective knowledge (see also Sengstock 1982). A number of them inherit motels from their parents, which they then use to acquire newer ones. Because franchises exist at a variety of budget levels, they offered the second generation a means of working in the industry at a higher level than that of their parents. This is different from other kinds of ethnic niches, such as gas stations and donut shops. So the second generation did not feel that they were simply replicating their parents by staying in the motel industry and therefore not growing as individuals.

Other Indian Americans have begun pursuing fields connected to the motel industry, which similarly allows them individuality while using their parents' capital. One informant said it would be ludicrous for her to walk away from her father's miniature motel "empire":

> My dad didn't build this empire for no reason. Building eleven properties and managing it the way he has over twenty-five years is no easy task. I think it's fun. The biggest thing is that it's entrepreneurial. I don't have to start from ground zero. . . . I am getting my JD, MBA degree. Utilizing my law degree as the general counsel of the business. I can manage the legal matters of eleven properties. That's something that would be very cool, to incorporate my education, my experience, and interests.

Another descendant of motel parents planned to start in the furniture business with her father, specializing in motel furniture. Indian Americans have also opted to become real estate brokers and loan managers and have started furniture manufacturing companies and motel management companies (Sheth 2001).

As seen here, children of immigrants chose motels because of their community's presence in the industry, because of their personal motivations in line with neoliberal ideology, and because of the nature of the motel industry and their opportunities within that industry. The sense from the younger generation and more successful moteliers is that the sky is the limit, even if their current holdings are cheaper properties. Challenges in breaking into elite properties (for example, resorts and five-star hotels) are viewed not as racial but as a function of Indian Americans still being relatively new in the market. It is not surprising, then, that Indian Americans represent a successful trajectory for others. For instance, leaders of the National Association of Black Hotel Owners, Operators and Developers have turned to AAHOA for guidance.[31] So although Indian Americans still have a ways to go, that they are now serving as a model minority for others is testament to how far they have come.

Indian American moteliers fit the standard theories of ethnic entrepreneurship—of encountering troubles in the labor market, finding opportunities in labor-intensive businesses, and relying on group resources. Their dramatic occupational presence compared with other ethnic niches stems from other factors as well: their subjective approach to small business, the development of franchises coming at a time when they were seeking business opportunities, and the availability of transnational social capital. Given Gujaratis' belief in self-employment, owning a motel served as much more than just a job; it symbolized freedom and justified having left the Commonwealth. The increased opportunities and franchising in the motel industry coincided with the sustained immigration of Indians pre- and post-1965. And, as the community became grounded in the industry, motels became a reason to come here rather than only a path toward sustainability once already here. The second generation then followed suit. In effect, ownership symbolizes a neoliberal freedom and the American dream sought after in the diaspora.

Owners' transnational ties deserve particular mention in explaining Indian Americans' rise in the motel industry. Beyond their reliance on transnational labor, they measured the worth of their businesses, however meager, relative to options elsewhere in the diaspora. And now they are expanding into transnational markets (see Chapter 4). This transnational component broadens the domestic focus of standard theories of entrepreneurship, such as middleman minority theory and its attention to the domestic disadvantages of clientele. It adds another type of transnational business, beyond those of transnational goods. Yet as discussed in Chapter 3, Indian Americans faced problems running their businesses partly because of the transnational and domestic disparities that shaped their entrance into the industry.

3 Business Hardships and Immigrant Realities

INDIAN AMERICANS' IMPRESSIVE PRESENCE in the hospitality industry has led to claims in the media and in political speeches that they no longer face disadvantages. Elite moteliers make this claim themselves. For instance, at the 1999 annual conference, H. P. Rama, an Asian American Hotel Owners Association (AAHOA) founder and its first chairman, remarked:

> Each one of us has had to confront the institutional barriers that attempted to deny us a place in this industry. Each one of us has faced and overcome the discrimination and prejudice that threatened to hold us back. And each one of us has successfully met these challenges with dignity and courage.[1]

At that same conference the keynote speaker was then Republican presidential candidate Steve Forbes. He told the audience, "All of you here exemplify the American dream" (Sheth 2001, p. 293). As a wealthy white male conservative candidate, his presence augmented Indian Americans' claim on national belonging.

Without a doubt, outright resentment toward Indian American moteliers has decreased since they became embedded in the motel industry. Yet as compelling as this linear narrative is, economic, social, and cultural challenges continue across budget levels partly because of owners' immigrant minority background. I address these challenges not because they necessarily dominate owners' concerns but because they illuminate the continued role of racial, cultural, and gendered privileges within dominant institutions and client expectations. As a young woman whose parents and even grandparents owned motels explained,

> I think that there will probably be [racial] tensions for a while. . . . I can definitely see how [being known as an Indian-owned establishment] would veer people away. Maybe because we have this stigma that we may be cheap, or, you know, something there is turning [customers] away from it.

Such impressions do not take away from Rama's claim that institutional barriers tied to race and immigration have decreased, especially compared with when he started out. And owners have shown dignity and courage. Still, real-life experiences complicate any generalization, especially for the vast number of Indian Americans who own lower-budget motels.

I focus on the influence of race and other social hierarchies on owners' economic security. Economic security was their main concern. Race, immigration, and other hierarchies often indirectly and sometimes directly complicated their pursuit of profits, thereby adding to the challenges they faced in running their business. Because of this, these marginalizing hierarchies deserve scrutiny, even if their effects appear to be dissipating.

To appreciate how owners can experience inequalities side-by-side with major accomplishments, it helps to look at the two distinct but related ways that racialization impacts Indian and other Asian Americans (Ancheta 1998; Kim 1999). On the one hand, they are measured along the standard black-white paradigm, as either lazy/poor/threatening (black) or hardworking/successful/accommodating (white). On the other hand, they are framed in a distinctly immigrant fashion, whether as part of the nation or as foreigners. When Indian Americans are characterized as being similar to blacks, it typically also involves framing them as non-American. But even being characterized as similar to whites can imply a foreign culture. The model minority stereotype illustrates this, for it honors Indian Americans as "out-whiting" whites educationally and economically but assigns their success to their inherently "Asian" makeup (Prashad 2000).

In Indian Americans' dealings with franchisors, government representatives, and individuals, they felt they experienced both types of racialization. This is because of the historic racialization of Indian Americans and their rise to dominance in the motel industry. Race both facilitated their accomplishments and created hurdles, creating a two steps forward, one step back situation. How does this paradox of inequality and impressive dominance of an industry come about, and how do owners defuse inequalities even as they complain about them?

Evaluating Franchises

Indian Americans found much to appreciate in franchises. They knew that the brand name attracted customers, and they recognized that franchisors took risks in accepting them as franchisees. They also believed that franchisor expectations improved their motel operations, through streamlined procedures and more attention to customer service. And owner-franchisor relationships have ameliorated somewhat over the years. At the 2006 AAHOA convention, most owners responded on a survey that they were content with their particular franchise, which was reported as a shift from previous years. Still, owners were quick to critique franchises for limiting their freedoms and profits. (Such complaints apply to franchising generally, beyond motels.) One summed up a common sentiment when he said franchisees and franchisors are engaged in "an adversarial relationship." As befitting neoliberal practices, individual owners carry more of the financial burden during the tougher times while theoretically being able to attain more profit during the good times.

Informants frequently complained about the high cost of running a franchise in the manner dictated by the corporation. They felt strongly that the required adherence limited potential revenue and resulted in a lack of autonomy. Informants particularly objected to the seemingly constant need to upgrade their motels by adding new amenities and improving existing ones, without the freedom to choose where to purchase the supplies and with no guarantee of increased revenue.[2] And as one motel chain upgrades its amenities, others must do so to remain competitive. Even the lower-budget chain Motel 6 underwent significant upgrades in amenities and styles starting in 2008. As the upgrade progresses, rooms are now featuring flat-screen TVs, granite furniture in bathrooms, new flooring and bedspreads, wireless Internet, and so on. An article in *USA Today* stated that travelers appear split on the plan and went on to quote a traveler who uses Motel 6: "'I don't think they'd get a new following,' says David Conerly of Boston, an occasional guest. 'Motel 6's appeal is based upon price.'"[3] Rates have generally stayed the same, however, because of brand constraints, and market share of the renovated motels has risen, although this is in part due to the poor economy that leads customers to lower-budget rather than mid-budget motels.[4] Independent motels also must respond to the rise of amenities, since they compete with lower-budget franchises. One owner of an independent motel west of Cleveland showed off to me the recently installed microwaves and mini-refrigerators in her rooms. She cited competition with lower-budget franchises as the reason.

Franchise corporations claim that they are responding to customer preferences and the market with their push for upgrades. They also state that they want to be sensitive to owners' financial needs and so introduce upgrades gradually. An owner I spoke with saw it differently:

> Now the mid-scale economy, I try to give them better service and better amenities for less price basically. . . . We are caught in the middle [between higher- and lower-budget motels]. And yet we lose on the demand generator, which is revenue. We lose on that aspect because it costs just as much as the other hotels to upkeep the expense of the amenities, but we don't get that back in revenue.[5]

I went back to his motel a month later to conduct observations. On my second day there, he received a phone call from a potential customer. He listed the amenities that his motel offers. He gave the price of a room

An owner of an independent motel shows off a microwave, a refrigerator, and other amenities, which she added to all of her rooms. She cited competition with franchises as a reason for the upgrades.

and then raised his voice a notch to say that yes, an independent motel in town does offer a lower price but that it does not offer his level of service. He hung up exasperated and launched into an often-voiced critique of the customers and the industry at the lower- and middle-budget level. These complaints are not to suggest that Indian American owners do not want to spend money on upgrades—some owners even go beyond franchise expectations.[6] They just want more control over that process.

The numerous fees charged by franchisors also contribute to owners' costs and sense of lacking control. Franchise fees are meant to facilitate operations, which in turn benefit the franchisees. Still, the fees can take up a considerable amount of a motel's revenue (Culbertson et al. 1993). One informant listed just some of the fees: "You have your franchise fee, marketing fee, reservation fee, royalty fee—their profit."[7] Owners did not mind paying fees but resented the overall total and the number of different fees. Also, the fees represent an agreement for the franchisor and franchisee to partner with each other, but franchisees rarely felt treated as complete equals. An informant of the second generation stated in no uncertain terms,

> The franchisor is the parasite living on the entrepreneur. If [a franchise corporation] filed bankruptcy, I would still have my place and could find a new flag. If all the franchisees went bankrupt, the franchise wouldn't exist. . . . If you have progressive board, they partner with the franchisee. And there are companies like that. And there are others that are short sighted.

Another owner stated simply, "Fees are too much. I do all the work and they get the gain." Mathew (2005) argues that the comparable dynamic found among New York City taxi cab drivers—paying fees to an owner to run one's business—represents the shift of financial risk from corporations to individual owners and lessees. This is part of a larger neoliberal trend, one that applauds individuals for being entrepreneurial but also takes away their protections.

Franchisors differ in their fees and procedures, with some taking pride in the ease by which contracts can be terminated and the amount of liquidated damages expected, the ability to transfer ownership of the motel to family members, their efforts to assist franchisees during troubled economic times, and more. Still, owners' complaints continue. These become especially vocal during difficult economic times. At a panel session at the 2010 AAHOA annual convention, franchise executives representing the major hospitality corporations in the country were asked if they would lower fees during this grave recession. They all said no. They argued that fees did not rise during good economic times and so should not decrease during bad economic times. Audience members buzzed with resentment, even as they recognized the executives' logic.[8] In effect, owners resented corporations' refusal to bend on the neoliberal logic that individuals, in this case owner-operators, must bear significant risk as compared to the risk borne by the corporations.

Owners found franchisors burdensome not only when business was poor but also when it was strong. When an owner's business does well, its franchise corporation may open up another brand within its portfolio right next to one's motel, which could drive down the existing owner's business. Within a franchise agreement, an owner is guaranteed that the same brand of motel will not be opened up within a specified radius of his/her motel. The franchise can, however, open one of its other brands within that radius. This can be a brand with a comparable name to the existing franchise or a brand that targets a similar demographic. An informant explained this:

> For instance, if there is an exit on an interstate, a [franchise corporation] will tell you to put [one of its] hotels near the exit. You cannot license [that motel brand] within a certain number of miles near it. But to maximize their income, [the franchise corporation] will solicit someone to put a [comparable brand] there, which they also own. And that directly hurts the [first motel]. And there is a guy who put his life savings in this, and the corporation puts a [comparable brand] there. This guy's investment in jeopardy there. And the corporation is laughing since they are getting more income. That's totally absurd. They should say that we will drop our royalty fees for both [owners] since their incomes will drop. They will actually put someone there. Hey, this [one motel] is doing well, so let's get a [comparable brand] there.

Those outside the motel business have criticized this practice. The moderator of the aforementioned panel of franchise executives was a Fox Business News correspondent with no connections to the industry. During the panel she questioned the fairness to the franchisees of having parallel brands owned by the same parent company placed so close together, given that she and so many others do not know the difference between them. Audience applause echoed in the convention hall in response to the question.[9] In response, franchise representatives assured the crowd that they paid attention to the marketing and segmentation of their brands. They said that they wished to avoid this problem as much as did the franchisees and that they would continue to monitor and address such complaints.

Within this industry, however, brand competition is almost inherent in the business expansion model. Baum and Haveman (1997) find that for hotel owners in New York City, the optimal strategy is to open a hotel next to competitors but to offer a slightly different product so as to draw in customers. For motel franchise corporations, the market strategy is similar. A single corporation will open up more than one brand in the same location, each of which theoretically serves a distinct segment of the market. Yet distinctions between a franchise's brands are often lost on customers, and at the lower-budget level where Indian Americans predominate, brand loyalty may be less important than price, distance from interstate exit/entrance ramps, proximity to a gas station or restaurant, and so on. This is not to suggest that Indian American owners do not like to be near one another. In fact, Indian American owners of independent motels benefit from being near co-ethnic owners of franchises, from whom they can gain resources (Kalnins and Chung 2006). But they regret the competition partly encouraged by franchises' incentives.

As one would expect, an oversaturation of motels in a given locality lowers average occupancy rates. An independent owner in Lima, Ohio, explained in 2007,

> Ten years ago, motel business was good. But there are more rooms available everywhere. . . . In Lima need only 1,000 rooms for refineries. But now they have 2,400 rooms. Nineteen motels in Lima. So what is happening, hotel occupancy is going down to 50 percent. Sixty percent occupancy is good for motel profits. . . . Hotel business—whatever make in business, 50 percent goes to expenses and 50 percent goes in hand. That was ten years ago. If have 50 percent or higher occupancy, then make good money. But with less than 50 percent occupancy, then you are only working to pay for the building.

An owner of a lower-budget franchise explained the problem in Lima this way:

The Asian [i.e. lower-budget] market is saturated, and [owners] basically try to compete with each other. The individual hotel here does not benefit from [this] because the only people [who] benefit is the franchisor. So in a nutshell, too much competition.

To further complicate matters, many of the strategies entrepreneurs can use to limit competition do not apply to moteliers. For example, business owners try to keep secret their business ideas (Shane 2003), but franchisees' ideas often come from the parent corporation. Independent moteliers face other challenges: they lack the resources or local power to consolidate a popularity among customers and suppliers, another common business technique.

Ethnic Effects on Franchise Challenges

Despite the appearance of these troubles as completely generic, they were exacerbated at times by owners' immigrant minority status. On the surface, the problems of amenities creep (as the ongoing requirement for upgrades is often called), fees, and intense competition lack an immigrant or racial connection. Franchisors' goal is to grow, regardless of the ethnicity of their franchisees. Also, franchisees seek out franchises to purchase and so enter any agreement voluntarily. And all motel owners, not just Indian Americans, have these generic complaints.

In the literature on ethnic entrepreneurship, "racial" issues refer to explicit confrontations, such as boycotts and riots, between black and Latino inner-city residents and business owners (Abelmann and Lie 1995; Lee 2002). Other "ethnic" problems include hostilities by suppliers with immigrant owners, cultural conflicts with employees, and intra-ethnic competition (Kim 1981; Min 2008; Yoon 1997). On the other hand, problems of long work hours, risk of failure, possibility of robbery, and the like are read as generic and endemic in small business, even as they can be pronounced among ethnic entrepreneurs given their mode of entry into small businesses (for example, reliant on social capital and few financial resources) (Bonacich and Modell 1980; Gold 1995). These are viewed as simply economic troubles and as a result are not generally included in discussions of *ethnic* entrepreneurs' difficulties.

Such a perspective on "generic problems," however, overlooks the veiled roles that owners' background as Third World immigrants played in furthering them, and so how they connect to more explicit ethnic and racial problems. For example, the frequent framing of Indian Americans as the model minority, rather than as everyday owners, both benefited and potentially limited them when it came to franchises. At AAHOA national conventions, franchise representatives—mostly white—occasionally speak a few words of Gujarati or Hindi to the audience when they come on stage to introduce a speaker or kick off an event that their company has sponsored. One white male vendor even dressed up in an elaborate royal red sherwani long coat and turban.[10] The goal is to show respect for Indian culture. In fact, the word *respect* is constantly used by vendors when they speak to an audience at conventions. Franchisors have echoed this model minority narrative. For example, a commercial real estate lender told me he valued the immigrants' work ethic and culture of mutual assistance that allowed for a strong repayment record.[11] A representative of a major franchise corporation (which operates a number of franchises) told a couple of second-generation owners at a convention in Lima, "Your parents came and you guys worked really hard to get what you have today. That's great."[12] In other words, ethnic narratives can facilitate industry insiders' respect of Indian Americans, which in turn can facilitate their growth in the motel industry.

The flip side of this model minority rhetoric is the expectation that Indian Americans will take on extra burdens and not complain. One Indian American owner of a middle-budget motel, active in AAHOA leadership, argued passionately that franchisors, not the economic crisis that began in 2007, caused extreme financial instability for owners. According to her, franchisors took advantage of Indian immigrants' reputation for being hardworking:

But as [franchises] saw the Indians coming in, and this community coming in, they knew that we were going to own the majority portion of this industry. What they did was like, "Oh well, you know what? Who cares? They are building hotels left and right here, and this is what they know, and this is what they're going to do, and this is what they are going to do forever." . . . And that's what's killing us. It's not the economy itself. If we didn't have this surplus of hotels, I think we'd make it in this industry. . . . Who cares if [one] hotel does not succeed because, you know, [the corporation] made their money, and they're getting royalty fees. They'll just give some other Indian that's ready to build because the other one is out of the system.

Franchisors see Indian Americans as worthwhile owners, otherwise they would not sell properties to them. And yet, in her opinion, compliments of Indians' work ethic and rags-to-riches dedication can become the basis for manipulation.

In addition, although Indians' immigrant-based eagerness to own motels contributed to their strong presence in the industry, that eagerness indirectly benefited franchisors at the possible expense of motel owners as a whole. A politically active owner who by and large defended franchises from other owners' criticisms had this to say about the oversaturation that he feels is in part encouraged by franchises:

> Some of the things some of the franchises do have hurt the Indian owners. . . . There's a lot of Indians that have built those brands. . . . Right now as we speak they have a sales team, the franchises. They know when there's a site [of available land] available or even becoming available, probably a year or two years before. They're going around to these developers that they know. If they know me or someone else that builds hotels, they'll approach them before the contracts even expire and try to line something up.

Franchises will pursue buyers regardless of ethnicity. Their interest in Indians made sense, given the group's motivation to be moteliers and their track record in the industry. The result, however, was viewed by some as ultimately handicapping Indian American owners.

Owners' immigrant status also weakened their ability to negotiate contracts with franchisors, which further marks their troubles as tied to their ethnicity rather than as simply generic. As immigrants desperate for a sense of permanence and stability, they rarely took the time to properly understand, much less negotiate the terms of, their franchise contract, which AAHOA representatives recommend. Many owners lack the cultural and human capital, such as fluency in English, to negotiate confidently with major corporations both before signing an agreement and afterward in their continuing relationship. An elder motelier believed Indian immigrants benefited from franchising overall but spoke of their disadvantages as a group that migrated here just to own motels:

> We do have a problem because those guys are unable to read [the contract] or don't know too much about signing the contract. . . . But they got more advantage by that sign saying [a franchise brand]. I know the franchises are taking advantage of [owners by demanding more amenities]. . . . The franchise know that if you want to get out of [the contract,] that [other] guy wants it.

Immigrant owners can have proficiency but not fluency in English. As this informant stated, "I got language problem. English is pretty good. But hard to read papers, lawyers' papers. Sometimes [a nearby owner] reads for me."

Informants generally believed that franchises were aware of their vulnerability relative to the corporation. This belief may have been justified to the extent that franchises took a distinctive approach to immigrants with limited cultural capital compared with the approach they took with those raised in the United States or with an accomplished motel record. The average immigrant owner was respected more for his/her hard work and cost-saving strategies than for his/her accounting or marketing sophistication. For example, at one session at the 2006 AAHOA convention in Las Vegas, representatives of major hotel and motel franchise corporations spoke to a predominantly second-generation audience. In remarking on the differences between working with immigrants versus working with Indian Americans raised in the United States, one representative said,

> Every day I hear more and more about more business school type driven equations. It makes it a little more difficult on us, but it also makes the game, it makes the whole process a better process. . . . Whereas [with the immigrant generation] the conversation is a little more murky.

Another representative similarly said about the second generation,

> You guys are pushing us to be better. . . . You guys are pushing us to have the latest technology, to have the sexy lobbies, to have the stuff that makes these hotels, really nice, be showplaces.

The immigrant generation was respected as hardworking and sought after to grow the motel industry but also possibly afforded less credibility, given their lack of formal business education and dependence on motels for their livelihood.

In addition to being characterized as the eager yet cautious model minority, Indian Americans at times felt they were characterized as lazy and incompetent. Sometimes this treatment was indirect, sometimes it was direct. Most times it targeted first-generation immigrants, but sometimes it targeted those who were born and raised here. A second-generation motelier encountered the dual racialization of being characterized both as a foreigner and as incompetent. He owned three franchise motels and sat on various franchise boards. He recalled a phone call from a franchise corporation regarding an already extant billboard sign for a motel he recently bought:

> [The representative] said, "You have a billboard on the highway, and do you realize that there is an [American] flag [on it]?" I said, "I never thought about it, but now that you point it out, yah. Is there a problem?" She kind of hesitantly said, "Well, you are not American." It was the twenty-first century, I couldn't believe I was listening to this conversation. The flag denotes that it was American owned. I said, "I have an American passport, what are you trying to tell me?" "Well, you're Asian." I just cut the conversation short. And that's a franchise! . . . And sitting on a lot of franchise boards, I can see that when they walk into an Indian versus American-owned establishment, their inspections are different. Their impressions and mind-set are different; they expect Indians to fail.

The assumption that Indian Americans mismanage their properties was made explicit at a Choice Hotels Owners' Council (CHOC) meeting. This is an organization of elected franchisees of Choice properties (Comfort Inn, EconoLodge, Quality Inn, Rodeway Inn, Sleep Inn, and others) who advocate on behalf of franchisees' interests to the Choice corporation; it is not made up of Choice corporate employees. More than 60 percent of Choice Hotels properties are owned by Indian Americans. At a March 23, 2010, meeting, the CHOC chairman complained about the increasing number of Indian American AAHOA members on the CHOC board, indicating that they bring down the quality of both the organization and the franchise corporation:

> It [having AAHOA members lead Choice motel owners] is just like sending your child to school, to college. Do you want to send them to the best college? Do you want them to be taught by the best professors? Or do you want them to be taught by the worst?[13]

Suggestions also were made at the meeting to alter the bylaws defining who can serve on the elected board in ways that would limit Indian Americans, including requiring a longer motel ownership period for candidates.

In response to pressure from AAHOA and others, the CHOC chairman who had made the comments stepped down. The vice president of communications at Choice Hotels International issued a statement emphasizing the corporation's appreciation of Indian Americans:

> It concerns all of us at Choice a great deal that remarks made at a recent meeting, without Choice representatives in attendance, are being reported, misrepresenting Choice's views and the facts. We take great pride in the relationships that we have built with leaders and organizations within the industry, including . . . groups such as AAHOA and its board.[14]

Overall, race and immigration do not have a singular effect. They join with the factors listed in the previous chapter, such as transnational networks, ethnic financial capital, the rise of discounted motels to purchase, and motivation for entrepreneurship, as the context for explaining Indian Americans' rise in the industry. Franchisors sought out the model minority, and owners benefited in some ways. Their success allowed them to meet directly with franchise representatives at AAHOA conferences. The franchisor-franchisee relationship served the latter to a significant degree. Most owners appreciated the brand recognition that a franchise offers. They also recognized franchisors' efforts to listen to them, especially as franchised outlets have come to make up more of a company's revenue than the motels owned by the company (Culbertson et al. 1993). Franchisors provide guidelines, trainings, regulations, updates on amenities, and a social network of fellow franchisees. Having a franchise also makes qualifying for a loan easier, whether for the purpose of building a new motel or renovating an existing one. Ethnicity did have helpful effects.

Nonetheless, just as their immigrant minority status facilitated their successes, it also contributed to obstacles. Corporations or their representatives are not "racist" toward Indian Americans, although examples of explicit differential treatment do exist. Instead, owners became susceptible to burdens within standard corporate procedures mostly through indirect means. The same transnational and domestic factors that encouraged Indian Americans' presence in the industry exacerbated their oversaturation and poorly negotiated contracts, which their racialization as hardworking immigrants likely facilitated. In other words, inequalities will not dissipate as more Indians move into the business and move up in the business. Instead, the factors leading to their prolific achievements and public applause could simultaneously be the basis of their challenges.

Pressures on Lower-Budget Owners

The other major entity owners complained about was local governments. Although these problems primarily affect owners of independent motels, owners of franchise motels are also affected. Indian Americans' troubles with the government stemmed from their mode of entry into motels along with their racialization. In an examination of owners' problems with local governments, it is important to recognize their financial constraints.

The costs associated with running an independent motel have increased, even as the price per room remained low and choices for potential customers increased. Although some such owners earned a middle-class income, most struggled to get by. One owner outlined the costs for his fifty-room motel in Ohio, along with the benefits involved:

> I'm paying $5,000 per month for mortgage. One day is a $150 for mortgage. . . . Per day my hotel costing is $400. No matter how busy. Minimum expense. $1,200 utilities. $1,000 for the maintenance. $1,000 for the supplies. $1,000 for salary. $1,000 for my mom's salary. $600 for phone system. $500 for cable system. Minimum $12,000 fees per month.

Another owner elaborated on her twenty-two-room independent motel's expenses, part of which stemmed from the actions of unthinking guests:

> Property tax, state tax, you know. Your insurance is heavy. Your parking lot to clean. Maintenance lawn. Snowplowing, all that thing. [Guests] stay here. They don't care, they waste water, electricity, everything. Air condition, all that thing, you know.

As mentioned earlier, independent motels also deal with the amenities creep in response to franchises.

Adding to owners' frustrations are possible crackdowns by local governments on both independents and franchises. As is common for middleman minorities, such owners often serve a more disenfranchised population. As local, state, and federal governments cut public assistance funding under the auspices of "tough love" and other neoliberal slogans, the burden for individuals' well-being falls into the private market. Motels pick up the slack by housing otherwise homeless individuals and those priced out of the rental market, as referred to in the previous chapter. If such individuals engage in criminal activity, the owner can be held responsible. Mayors and city councils rush to shut down these places or, alternatively, must defend them against public criticism when their city needs them to house their otherwise homeless population (Jain 1989).

Furthermore, all hotels and motels—regardless of ethnicity of owners or budget level—have their share of prostitution and other illegal activities, for there is a room, a bed, and privacy. As one owner of a middle-budget franchise noted to me over dinner at an AAHOA convention, some customers wear suits and ties or nice dresses, and others do not, but they all engage in the same activities. Still, independent motels have become associated with this problem.

None of the motels I visited catered to prostitution in an extreme way, such as by having an attached club or bar known as a "pickup" site (Prus and Irini 1980). Nor did owners report knowing any prostitutes or going out of their way to protect them more than other guests. Some owners turn a blind eye to the "quickie" business of prostitution, and others actively reject it when suspected. A maintenance man who did some work for an independent motel mentioned that if the owner knew illegal activity was taking place in a room, he would open up the room and kick the customers out. An owner of an economy franchise used this as well as a less confrontational tactic to keep out presumed drug dealers:

> You serve all kinds of people. So [drug dealers will] stay here. I can stop them if I know. I can kick them out. I've done that tons of times.

> Q: *How do you know if it's going on?*

> I know. There's lots of traffic [in and out of rooms]. I say I cannot rent you room. Or do you want to pay $100/night? And they cannot afford that. They know that I know. They leave. Never had a problem.

Another common technique was calling a room upon seeing a guest (not a guest of the motel) entering and asking the customer how long the person would be staying. Many leave at that point.

Other owners would stop prostitution in their rooms when obvious but recognized that it took place regardless. One informant said,

> Everybody wants to fuck, you know. [laughs] Lots of business. . . . If police see prostitute coming in, [the owner] cannot get arrested. You get warning. If you don't listen, then you can get arrested.

Other owners were philosophical on the issue of prostitution. As one said,

Prostitutes is human nature. You cannot control. Somebody asks me, I'm going to his room, he's my friend. You cannot stop them. He can say this girl is my friend. Why do you stop them? Also, I'm renting the room and the bed. I cannot control what they do in that room.

These activities have framed owners as inviting nefarious elements. Local governments across the country have targeted owners of small motels, forcing changes that will hurt their business revenue. With these changes, the presumption is that either the illegal activity will stop or the motel will be run out of business, or both.[15] Numerous examples exist (Jain 1989). In one case, a motel in a poor, predominantly black inner-city neighborhood of Cleveland had been severely criticized by parents, city council members, and a school board for the types of customers who rented rooms. At one meeting at a nearby school, the conversation between the owner and local residents ended with the residents charging up to the motel, as reported in the *Plain Dealer*:

> But after a half hour of shouting yesterday, the meeting with Champak Patel, owner of the Crosstown Motel, fell apart. A disgusted Patel left, scurrying through the halls, then the gymnasium, followed by a pack of reporters and screaming residents. . . . The group surrounded Patel's van, then charged up to the motel, where they shouted at hotel employees and residents. . . . "I tried to work with them. I just bought the place in January. I cannot say much right now," were Patel's last words, as he left the school with about 25 parents on his heels. . . . "You're just trying to get paid," Aretha Tucker shouted at him. "But my babies are out there with the prostitutes, not yours."[16]

As is common for middleman minorities, owners felt trapped between trying to run a legitimate business and the desperate conditions in city areas. Owners felt that governing authorities unfairly punished them as a result, with a double standard relative to affluent businesses. A previous chairman of AAHOA elaborated:

> I'll give you an example. There is an ordinance being considered, where if the desk clerk doesn't check the ID of the person checking in, that

desk clerk can be arrested. Think about, do you really think that cop is going to go to a Hyatt Regency and arrest the desk clerk if Donald Trump walked in and he didn't check his ID? Now the target is mom and pop shops who sells motels to the use of clientele who has issues with the law. . . . I think it's actually very common. Um. You know, always target the guy that caters to that clientele right. I mean, who doesn't want a Hyatt developed in their city, right? But if you've got two rundown properties next to each other, then of course you're going to criticize those—attracting those, you know the bad element, that's the phrase I guess.

In this equation, Hyatt owners are good citizens, and independent owners damage local areas. Other crackdown efforts elsewhere in the country involve police cars being stationed in motel parking lots, requiring set visiting hours for guests of customers, demanding owners to check the identity of any guest of a customer, requiring one security officer outside a motel for every fifteen rooms, police confronting guests leaving motels, and more, all of which lower occupancy and revenue.[17] Owners tried to befriend local police, politicians, and business leaders so as to counter these trends, but with varying success. There is no official data on the number of such ordinances or their impact on moteliers. Suffice it to say, AAHOA representatives from across the country had anecdotes to share.[18]

Ethnic Effects on Lower-Budget Owners

Local governments often view lower-budget motels, regardless of owner ethnicity, as catering to prostitutes and drug dealers. Indian Americans' mode of entry into the industry, the factors of which are explained in Chapter 2, was frequently through the purchase of a lower-budget motel, a type of motel that other entrepreneurial groups avoided. And because they owned more of the lower-budget motels than did other groups, Indians more often experienced these problems with local governments.

A direct racialization of Indian Americans may also be at play. Long-time residents of economically struggling towns have been known to specifically blame Indian motel owners for their town's conditions.[19] Some owners also cite racial profiling. On occasion owners have been fined and even had their property confiscated for allegedly being aware of prostitution and drug dealing taking place in their rooms.[20] The possibility of racial profiling in such cases led to a lawsuit by owners. As reported in *India West*:

> "The actions [to punish motel owners] were . . . in violation of the Equal Protection Clause since the actions (were) improperly motivated with the intent to drive plaintiff's members out of business and also primarily targets hotel/motel owners and operators of Asian-Indian origin," the lawsuit says. . . . [The motel association's attorney] said Oakland's action is "a microcosm of the issues facing Indian American" motel and hotel owners in the inner cities of California. The cities need help from the hospitality industry for the homeless in high-crime areas, but the motel owners are blamed when drugs and prostitution take place on or near their properties.[21]

As this article pointed out (and as discussed in Chapter 2), motels are expected to take the place of government housing and shelters. The paradox is that they become targets of the government when the types of problems often associated with the homeless arise.

Informants also complained occasionally of direct discrimination. For example, an owner of an independent motel in the Akron/Canton area said,

> So we are brown. [If] we are white from inside, like Americans, they [still] will not accept us. So if we have to keep our own ways, we would rather be Indian, living life. It's much better. . . . The government agencies—sometimes they treat you differently. . . . If we cannot change the people, we have to improve ourselves. We have to learn the ways. We come here to make money and we go the route, they treat us differently.

This interviewee speaks of direct discrimination from "government agencies" rather than from random individuals. He was wary of elaborating further, except that he felt that he received less respect from government employees charged with serving him because they saw him as a foreigner

with a low-budget establishment. When I inquired if other Indian owners had similar encounters, he replied, "Probably, yes." I mentioned this
to an Indian American who has dealt with a variety of owners in the
Midwest, and he agreed that such discrimination was not rare: "Yeah,
I'm sure there's stuff like that goes on."

Nor is racial profiling limited to motel owners. The crackdown on Indian American moteliers is part of a larger trend in their being denied a
full belonging (Maira 2009). The U.S. Drug Enforcement Agency's Operation Meth Merchant was a crackdown on convenience stores in northwest
Georgia. Although most stores in the area are white owned, Operation
Meth Merchant started in 2003 and targeted stores run by people of color,
primarily Patels, in part because of their presumed limited English skills.[22]
They were accused of selling common household items, such as Sudafed,
aluminum foil, and matches, whose ingredients can be used to formulate
methamphetamine. Deportations resulted from this operation. And after
9/11, government profiling of South Asian and Arab Americans rose from
what was already a high rate.[23]

Even if owners did not have run-ins with government authorities,
they still faced cultural challenges in communicating with elected officials. People lacking fluency in English or an awareness of government
bureaucracy can feel overwhelmed by the prospect of confronting officials. AAHOA assisted owners in this regard. So did the National Association of Black Hotel Owners, Operators and Developers (NABHOOD).
A representative from NABHOOD had this to say:

> Talk to any Indian from any small town, they will tell you they feel a
> kinship with us [black owners], that they are treated with the same sort
> of discriminatory behavior as other African Americans. The unfortu-
> nate part, there is not a synergy between these Indians and African
> Americans. . . . I've talked to several [AAHOA] members who said,
> "Hey, man, will you come to my city and talk to our mayor or a black
> elected official? I don't know how to do it, I don't know the process."
> And we don't mind doing it. That's part of our relationship with AAHOA
> and with Indian moteliers.

An inability to trust government agencies created potentially danger-ous situations for owners. They depended on police not only to investi-gate crimes in their motel rooms but also to protect their safety. Many motels, in particular at the independent level, rely on cash as a form of payment. One woman said that she had been robbed a few times at her franchise. An owner of an independent motel near Toledo told a tragic story that serves as a reminder of how dangerous such work can be:

> I got robbed in '99. I was doing the work here for about a month and my partner was the manager and he didn't shut the bathroom. I just hired him. Business was busy [in] '98 and '99. It was crowded. . . . The guy came to rob this place, and he killed my partner and his son. Twenty-year-old son. And then after, [no staff] wanted to stay here. I stayed after that. He was gone . . . he was not caught. I was by myself all night. . . . I had no choice.

More generally, the perception of lacking support from local agen-cies encouraged the population to further withdraw into itself. Inde-pendent owners restricted their interaction with the public because of fears of anti-immigrant criticisms. One owner said that I would have a hard time interviewing people because they would not want their name showing up in the newspaper (even as I assured this would not happen). One evening after a volleyball game, I was with a group of owners at one's home (in his motel), and we were cooking dinner. The proprietor said half jokingly not to write about what we were doing (even though we were simply cooking, drinking, and chatting). Another said that I should because it shows that we are enjoying ourselves and that nothing is wrong. Many informants were nervous about publicity of any kind and wanted to keep a low profile.

Overall, Indian Americans' historical reliance on disenfranchised customers and their eagerness to own motels contributed to both their successes and their challenges. Their means of engaging in the industry combined with their racialization resulted in their being framed some-times as hardworking and eager and sometimes as cheap, substandard, and a bit too foreign.

Challenges Arising from Customers, Non-Indian Motel Owners, and Paid Labor

Owners also encountered tensions at the individual level from various constituencies. Although significant, the problems described in this section do not mirror the extreme tensions facing other ethnic entrepreneurs, such as widespread boycotts and violence (Gold 2010). Instead, owners endured racist slurs and depressed business, most notably when business-related disagreements arose.

Customers

Indian American–owned motels have a reputation as being dirtier and less well kept than those owned by whites. In the 1970s, when the majority of owners were getting started in the industry and learning the trade, this reputation may have had some merit, but no longer (Sheth 2001). Owners did not dwell on current discrimination. They consider racism to be ubiquitous worldwide and beyond their control, and they found ways of dealing with it (discussed in Chapters 4 and 5). Most informants also said that the number of racist incidents has decreased over time. Moreover, they did not think that prejudiced customers made the difference between being profitable and unprofitable. In addition, customers are slowly realizing that with so many motels owned by Indians, it is of little use to try to avoid them. Some owners reported friendly relations with customers. In fact, customers who practically live in lower-budget motels sometimes take on front-desk duties in exchange for free accommodations or cash payment.

Yet racist practices did not go away, and owners had many stories to tell. Some customers would leave a motel upon learning that it was run by a person of Indian origin. Some would drive into the parking lot slowly, notice an Indian American behind the desk, and then drive off. A second-generation owner viewed this as a pan-ethnic Asian critique: "If they get the impression that the property is owned by an Indian, they don't expect it to be as good. It was like a Japan[ese car] impression—we tended to think that they were cheap. And now we think they are better made."

Indian Americans would encounter racist comments more often when customers had complaints because they were no longer perceived as the supportive, compliant minority but as conniving foreigners. For example, an owner of an independent establishment near Toledo said,

Indians are seen everywhere in the Unites States as a minority, as a foreigner. When you treat [non-Indians] good, they so, oh, you are good. When you tell them you cannot do this, then they tell you, you are a foreigner. Somebody come for a room and it's a busy time, so it's a higher rate. And they [say] no, I don't have that much money. And they say go back to your country! You tell them you guys are also foreigners. Nobody's from America. They say, their grandfather was here. . . . It happens all the time.

Nor was it only the owners of lower-budget motels who had such troubles. Owners across budget levels reported similar experiences, even as lower-budget owners stood out as more "foreign" and representative of the "Third World." As a middle-budget franchise owner near Cleveland said, "Customers come in, see us and a white person behind the desk and assume we are the cleaning staff and don't even look at us. Look at the white person. Then, [if] they find out we're the owners, [they] leave. Say, you just want my money." An owner of a middle-higher-budget franchise had this to say about racial slurs:

Generally what we find, when our rates are high, especially in summer season, people are not looking to pay for that. . . . As far as what the rate is, that's the rate. But that's how people tend to come up with a lot of different excuses. And then that's when that type of stuff really gets into the thing, and you just have to kinda bite your teeth and really just kinda bear with it. Bite your tongue and just kinda sit back and listen to it and just go on, go on with it and do whatever you can.

Although most owners bit their tongues in response, some spoke back to the verbal attackers. At an AAHOA convention in Chicago, one male owner said that whenever customers said anything racist, he told them to leave and that he did not want their business. A female motelier's mouth dropped open in disbelief, and she responded, "Can we say that?!"

Racist resentment stemmed not only from stereotypes but also from a perceived status discrepancy between immigrants and natives. As an independent owner said,

> I'm here for twenty-five years and own my own business. Within twelve years have the business. Some people here working whole life, they don't have money, they don't have a house. That's jealousy. . . . [I] tell them, I worked twelve years in factory job. Worked hard. We don't spend a lot of money. We save. After that apply for business. Friends help me out. Still jealous but they can't do anything about it.

Another source of resentment from customers stemmed from the misperception that Indian Americans received special loans to start motels. As one owner said, "A lot of them don't know how we started. They think that we got interest-free loans from the government. . . . You tell them the facts." Recent immigrants owning their own business violates the "proper" order of upward mobility, in which natives would have first opportunity at entrepreneurship (Lee 2002).

Even with all of their anecdotes, owners likely underestimated how often their ethnicity was questioned by potential guests. A couple of white front desk clerks (one franchised, one independent) reported that it was not uncommon for customers to ask them if the owners were "Arabs or Iraqis." This happened more often than owners realized. The workers assuaged the customers' fears. One explained to a customer that while Indian food has a different smell, so does Mexican food (which is generally accepted), and so the motel should not be turned down. Some customers were more curious about Indian ethnic differences than they were antagonistic—Indian Americans appeared less threatening and problematic than the current "enemy," Arabs and Muslims in general and Iraqis in particular. I interviewed a middle-aged white front desk clerk at an independent motel. She and her son lived in the motel, and she performed other duties in addition to those of desk clerk. A heavy-set woman with brownish blonde hair, she spoke with a no-nonsense, almost irritable tone when talking about customers' racism. She felt indebted to the owner for the job, housing, and assistance he had provided and so was quick to defend the motel when she encountered racist customers. Upon entering the motel one can see part of a Hindu symbol behind the front desk. She said that upon seeing that, people asked her "every day" if the place was Indian owned. She would answer in the affirmative. Customers would respond,

> "Oh, really?" And I say, "Yeah, he's like a second father to me." I tell everybody that.
>
> Q: *Do they leave or do they stay?*
>
> No, they stay. They just find it remarkable that so many Indians own motels. People look at Indian like, different than Iraqi or Arab. They differentiate a lot.

The enmity toward Muslims has helped make Hindus into a docile novelty for the time being. Post-9/11, only a few owners commented that they were mistaken for Muslim or Pakistani and criticized for "attacking us," as one owner recounted.

Non-Indian Motel Owners

The prejudice displayed by some customers could be an asset to non-Indian motel owners. Whites make up the bulk of non-Indian motel owners. Many Indian Americans reported cordial relations with white peers when at franchise and chamber of commerce meetings. And owners have worked together across racial lines—for example, within motel associations—for local or national initiatives. Still, tensions existed at times below and above the surface. The image of Indian American motels as being dirty is sometimes perpetuated by white owners. For example, a white owner in Ohio gave an implied critique of Indian-run establishments during an interview. When asked if he knew any Indian American owners, he replied, "Couple. I'll just say, I'm sure you have bad American operators [too]."

The above-the-surface discrimination from non-Indian owners has been even more severe. As they face competition from Indian Americans, a reaction has been to attack the loyalty of the "foreign" presence. Some white owners, including owners of franchises, capitalize on—and exacerbate—prejudice against Indian American "curry palaces" by posting "American-owned" on their properties and including it in their advertisements. As noted earlier, other markers of non-Indian-owned motels include having an American flag or other patriotic symbol on billboards for a motel. Such displays signal a politics of exclusion based on Indian Americans' presumed foreign status, in effect associating the ability to own property with white privilege. Although these practices have subsided over the past twenty years, they have not gone away.[24] In fact, and not surprisingly, they increased after 9/11.[25] Indian American owners have told me they choose not to use such practices even if they are U.S. citizens not only because of their questionable effectiveness in luring guests but also because of their clear xenophobic intent.

Racism has not been the only response by native-born owners, however. By purchasing first run-down residential hotels and later run-down motels, Indian Americans proved themselves to be decent owners, good businesspeople. Although this entrepreneurship has not eradicated the old images, it has led some whites to defend Indian Americans to other whites. Jim Conkle, executive director of the California Route 66 Preservation Foundation, wrote in *Route 66 Pulse*,

> While some travelers might prefer to support only American-run lodging establishments, one must consider what would have happened to these motels if these folks from other countries had not bought and kept them open. Most would have gone the way of so many others that were abandoned after Route 66 was decommissioned; in ruins, demolished or worse. . . . You can stay wherever [you] choose and can afford; that is your right. But please be open minded and courteous to our non-native motel owners along Route 66 and everywhere else you travel in the United States. They may not have all been born on American soil, but they all share the American Dream.[26]

Indian immigrant motel owners are central players in maintaining classic American icons like Route 66.[27] Indians' success in the industry is praised as signaling the durability of the American dream. But those who represent the roots of that dream and therefore those who best defend it has not changed.

Paid Labor

Most non-Indian laborers said that they quickly got used to working with Indian immigrant owners. They judged their employers by how straightforward and fair they were rather than by their background. As a Latina housekeeper said of working for Indian Americans, "It's fine, I don't see a difference really, you know what I mean. You know, everything's pretty fair to me." Similarly, an African American maintenance man said of his Indian American boss, "Get along with 'em, easy to get along with, you know. . . . They don't ride your back every five minutes and be all over you."

Workers appreciated when owners provided health insurance and other similar benefits, but this was not the norm in the industry (Zuberi 2006), so its lack did not cause employees to feel particularly mistreated. When employees did feel mistreated, however, race and immigration sometimes came to the surface. A franchise owner in a Cleveland suburb referred to his white and black staff:

> Some employees don't like to work for immigrants. I tell them that there is a dollar limit to what I can pay you. They say you want to take this money home, and then they leave. There is always resentment to us.

Employers, for their part, criticized employees for what they viewed as lack of dependability (Min 2008). But most staff positions earn little over minimum wage, rarely include health insurance, and offer little, if any, possibility of advancement. Under such conditions, many employees are not as dedicated as they otherwise would be. As a result, owners' most common complaint regarding employees was that they did not always show up, which meant that a family member had to pick up the slack. A proprietor of a lower-budget franchise motel outside Cleveland said,

> Hotel owners cannot afford to pay much. . . . Can't afford to pay more than six dollars and fifty cents per hour. And reliability is most important.

> Get calls in the morning saying I can't come in. . . . You can find people to work and not reliable. They get their paycheck and are happy, won't be back for seven days.

As if on cue he received a phone call from an employee who said that she could not come to work that evening because the class she was taking had been moved from the day before to that day. The owner became upset, expressing disbelief. He raised his voice and challenged her, saying that classes are never changed like that. The conversation ended there, and she was not going to be coming in. He felt he could not count on her anymore but still had to because he was going to India soon and could not find a replacement worker. A standard business-owner problem becomes magnified for immigrant owners whose visits "home" entail significant time away and expense. For this reason, owners often ask relatives (siblings, cousins, nephews) to assist in their motel when they leave for India. (Chapter 4 provides more information both on employee perspectives and on how owners treated employees, in particular co-ethnic employees.)

In their everyday encounters with customers, other owners, and workers, Indian Americans had to be ready for racist stereotypes. Such mistreatment arose mostly during business-related disputes. The stereotypes give the perpetrators moral and possibly economic advantages (when used by white owners) and so serve a function for them as they struggle to make sense of recent immigration and cultural diversity.

The Challenge of the Midwest Economy

The everyday, micro-level prejudices that owners encountered bothered them. But they also stressed over macro-level economic challenges. According to an AAHOA representative, since the recession that started in 2007, members are facing foreclosures at an unprecedented level. To provide a fuller appreciation of the problems facing motel owners, I turn to the Ohio economy and its impact on the motel business. The Ohio economy has historically depended on manufacturing, with health care, advanced electronics and related industries, food processing, aerospace and defense, and other industries also contributing. The decline of manufacturing jobs (not necessarily productivity) across the Midwest has contributed to unemployment rates on par with or often above the national average, especially since the recession of 2001.[28] For example, in 1992, the national unemployment rate was 7.4 percent, and in Ohio the unemployment rate was 7.2 percent. In 2002, the national rate was 5.8 percent, in Ohio 5.7 percent. A couple of years later, in 2004, the national rate was 5.5 percent, in Ohio 6.1 percent. By 2007, Ohio's rate (5.6 percent) was a full percentage above the national rate (4.6 percent). The Ohio Department of Jobs and Family Services' analysis of the state economy, published in 2009, stated:

> Employment growth [in Ohio] has lagged the national trend since the mid-1990s. Ohio employment never fully recovered from the 2001 recession. The current recession is hitting Ohio hard. Employment is declining farther in Ohio than in the nation as a whole. . . . Ohio's per capita real GDP in 2007 was $34,040, well below the national average of $38,020 and 33rd among the states. Ohio dropped from 23rd in 1997.[29]

The U.S. postindustrial global economy has created some benefits for Ohio but has also created some fundamental problems. Ohio has not been a center of global or national economic innovation. As of 2007, Ohio had the second-weakest economy in the nation, just behind Michigan. The tangible result is that people travel less, businesses bring in fewer people, and a weaker tax base must compensate for a lack of economic growth. As an owner in Lima said,

> Most people in the Midwest want to get out. See, in the early 1990s business was good in Ohio. You could buy a hotel for two times revenue, stuff like that. And the economy was good, the business was good. But ten years down the road there are more hotels built here. Also so you are paying top dollar here too. So why would you pay top dollar, live in the Midwest, only have six months worth of business out of the year, and then have trouble with the weather! It doesn't make sense. . . . I think a Midwest crisis can happen. Because a lot of companies here [are]

moving their industries to Mexico, Canada or whatever. NAFTA, you know? There's a manufacturing company here in Lima that's moving a hundred jobs. They are moving to Mexico. There's another company on the next exit. They closed the plant down. They moved the whole plant and equipment to Canada. . . . Yeah I think there is definitely a Midwest crisis.

Tourism has not declined, but business travel has, which lowers motel occupancy.[30] Most of the tourism has come from state and regional travelers looking for bargains and staying local because of economic troubles. When gas prices rise, owners note a decline in travelers. As an independent owner said in 2005,

American economy is worse now. People don't have that much money. Everything is getting expensive. Before they were spending money. Also gas is expensive. Some don't even have enough to feed family, so how can you do entertainment? Gas was ninety cents a gallon, now is three dollars a gallon.

Motel occupancy rates across the state have fallen and are below the national average. In November 2009, the year-to-date average occupancy rate was 56.1 percent nationally and 50.9 percent in Ohio.[31] The average daily rate (ADR) of rooms sold was $97.8 nationally and $77.1 for Ohio. The room revenue based on the number of rooms available (RevPAR) was $54.9 nationally and $39.2 for Ohio. All of these numbers reflect declines from the previous year. For Ohio, occupancy fell 7.6 percent from 2008, ADR fell 4.4 percent, and RevPAR fell 11.7 percent. The national figures showed slightly higher declines. The number of rooms available to rent increased over the same time period.

The overall sense of crisis did not mean that there were not bright spots to doing business in the state. Owners stated that there was less competition among owners and a lower density of motels than in the South, a region envied for its weather and increasing population. One needed to be strategic in the type of business one opened and where. Budget-oriented motels were maxed out; higher-budget places that catered to those in more affluent geographic areas would pay off, according to a few owners. In addition, Ohio offered an advantage over other states, according to an owner near Cleveland:

> I liked the fact that Ohio is a unique state. [O]ther states have, like say Chicago, and then there is no second-level city. While here you've got Cleveland, Columbus, Cincinnati, Dayton, Toledo, I mean you've got . . . Youngstown. A lot of small second-level cities there are. There is no Chicago here, there is no New York here but there is a lot of activities. . . . And if someone is going to Chicago they'll go to Chicago through Indiana and get out. They won't go south through Springfield. Here you will go to Columbus, one hour from Cleveland, one hour from Cincinnati, you might want to stop by and see for a couple of days. You know, so it's like there are lots of things to do in the small towns. . . . There is a lot of trucking companies and there are offices all over.

Ohio, like all states, has begun to market itself for tourism in the region. Motel owners may benefit from that. In the meantime, owners continued to worry about the area's prospects.

Bankruptcy

With all of the problems that owners encounter, it is hard to imagine that so many make a profit. In fact, just over 50 percent of all new businesses fail within the first five years. Self-employed immigrants do not necessarily earn much in the first place (Logan and Alba 1999). The competition and the weakened regional economy have led to a number of defaults by motel owners in Ohio, though few reported bankruptcies. According to the area's AAHOA representative, the lower-budget franchise owners are the most likely to face financial problems:

> There's a lot of people who aren't doing well these days any more. . . . And the business has really decreased. Because the guests are upscale, and they don't want to stay at places like that, with those sort of budget chains. And their businesses have gone down because so many new properties came up. So the supply for new rooms is much greater

than the old supply. . . . [Some owners] haven't paid their royalties, or [the franchises are] doing their inspections and they've told [the owners] to do certain work. And really some of them, they just can't afford it. So if the place isn't making money and their franchise wants them to pump in thousands of dollars, which they know they're not going to get back.

Business failure is common even in strong tourist areas. As an informant in Florida said of her friends,

I mean, I have some friends that are in some areas that are destination areas, and [they] are really struggling. [I'll ask,] "What are you doing?" And they'll say, "Nothing." And I'll say, "Nothing!? Well why don't you get out of that property?"

Each part of the country has its own circumstances and events that can financially threaten a region's tourism industry. These consist of natural disasters, local recessions, violent incidents, and more. Unless owners have set aside a good amount of cash or have highly liquid assets, they face bankruptcy when downturns lengthen. Many Indian Americans are now entering nonmotel franchises whose royalty fees are much lower.[32]

Despite all of these challenges, the number of Indian Americans declaring bankruptcy has been low. The son of a pioneer explained,

Very few times bankruptcy happens and you turn over to the bank. Even if the business is not making money, you can sell it to someone else at a loss. The property is always earning money. You may owe the bank three million, and your property is worth six million. You may take an offer of four million, knowing that it's less than what your property is worth. The bank will get its money.

In the 1970s and 1980s, Indian Americans bought motels cheaply from owners who never had to declare bankruptcy but were struggling. The same trend continues today, with Indian Americans now the ones selling, often to co-ethnics.

Ironically, the factors that explained Indian Americans' rise to dominance in the industry—their transnational capital, eagerness to immigrate and purchase motels, access to middleman minority opportunities, access to franchising, and model minority racialization—contributed to their dilemmas. This, in turn, negates the simple American dream narrative. Similar to Filipino Americans (Espiritu 2003), Indian American moteliers experience some degree of a differential inclusion. At times they endure explicit racist treatment, and their efforts uplift corporate and political elites. Yet rather than argue that their sustained inequalities belie a narrative of success and respect, it is necessary to recognize that the burdens they bear are part of their general mobility trajectory. Owners' successes are real, yet how owners interact with reigning institutions and key players remains influenced by their immigrant minority background. To appreciate the effects of race and ethnicity, more attention should be directed toward owners' critiques of the entities, groups, and individuals with whom they interact and profit from, rather than simply pointing to racially explosive episodes (boycotts, slurs, and the like).

Despite these challenges, owners generally downplayed their disadvantages. This was partly to justify their immigration and their own commitment to the industry (such as after leaving a corporate career), for if they conceded that discrimination constituted a problem, it could lead to questioning major life decisions. It is also common for minority entrepreneurs, and Americans generally, to believe in the power of individual effort even while recognizing obstacles (Valdez 2010). But also, Indian immigrants had reasons to be optimistic. As small business owners, they have become part of the nation. Furthermore, the most pressing problems they faced were tied to the economy, franchises, government, labor relations, and the like. As such they were mostly generic and mostly indirect, making it easier to discount the role of race, immigration, class, and gender. At the same time informants view prejudice on the part of individuals—whether employees, vendors, customers, or other owners—as inherent in being an immigrant or a minority and so not worth dwelling on. Owners had achieved a meaningful level of success—some more than others—despite these problems, and so they chose to accentuate the positives. Yet their simultaneous success and embedded hierarchies raise a fundamental question: how do Indian Americans find ways to succeed in their businesses yet continue to face a marginalization at the same time? I turn to that in Chapter 4.

4 Professional Appearances and Backstage Hierarchies

HOW CAN AN ETHNIC GROUP simultaneously be honored as representing the American dream yet experience sustained hierarchies? How did owners address their disadvantages when running their businesses, and what impact did this have on the hierarchies constraining them? In Chapter 4, I address this paradox and examine the ways in which Indian American motel owners have been managing their motels, both from the perspective of the owners' daily on-site operations and from the perspective of the Asian American Hotel Owners Association (AAHOA).

How ethnic entrepreneurs manage their businesses has received far less attention than how they start them (Zhou 2004). When done so, research on business operations has not addressed how ethnic groups handle embedded hierarchies in running their businesses (Kang 2010). Instead, it concentrates on how immigrant owners negotiate "cultural" or "ethnic" differences from mostly black customers in daily interactions or through community outreach (Gold 2010; Lee 2002; Min 1996; Yoon 1997). The literature on ethnic entrepreneurs portrays the United States as a country that can reward "savvy" immigrants who have sufficient resources. Entrenched inequalities based on race, culture, or gender that handicap owners are overlooked. The bulk of the chapter shows how owners deployed labor and cultural symbols to develop their motels into worthwhile establishments for customers.

Efforts to advance moteliers in the face of external challenges also took place at the organizational level. In the last section of the chapter, I turn to AAHOA. Collective-action organizations like AAHOA represent the voice of ethnic owners in their interactions with more powerful establishments (Light and Bonacich 1991; Min 2008; Waldinger, Aldrich, and Ward 1990). AAHOA is one of the most developed ethnic organizations in existence today in terms of membership base, operational structure, and effectiveness, according to industry insiders.[1] In effect, AAHOA engaged in a process similar to that of individual owners, that is, pushing against and also working within existing hierarchies.

Individual Owners' Day-to-Day Operations

Individual owners could not alter franchise or government practices, much less shift an economy out of recession, so they focused on daily issues. Owners' primary concerns were to keep expenses down, manage employees effectively, adhere to regulations, and draw in customers. For their motel to be a viable business, owners needed quality furnishings in the rooms and public areas, desired amenities, well-maintained buildings and grounds, a clean environment, efficient operations, good workers, and affordable prices. And although owners did not dwell on racial, cultural, or gender inequalities, they had to be mindful of them in their day-to-day operations. I attend to these latter issues, within owners' broader economic priorities, so as to better understand the roles of race, gender, and class within small business.

A key component of a motel's image is its entrance and lobby, the "front stage." Owners paid special attention to creating an assimilated front stage so as to attract guests, including those who may not initially want to stay at an Indian-owned motel. When the interactions that take place between guests and staff in the motel entrance and lobby are viewed as an "interaction ritual," the efforts involved in creating a desired sense of place follow a clear logic (Goffman 2005). Rituals create a pattern of social relations and meaning for individuals. According to Goffman, every standardized interaction is a ritual that offers members of social groups an opportunity to affirm or contest their status in relation to each other. During the interactions that take place in the front stage, individuals present themselves within social roles that they hope will gain them deference from the other participants. As Collins (1994) writes, "Attempts are made to present an 'idealized' version of the front, more consistent with the norms, mores, and laws of society than the behavior of the actor when not before an audience" (p. 35). Successfully engaging in the interaction produces "a momentarily shared reality, which thereby generates solidarity and symbols of group membership" (p. 30). When this happens, the actor may "win" in the interaction and achieve a goal tied to her/his social role.

The role the motel owner seeks in this interaction is that of proprietor of a nonforeign (that is, "American") motel, so as to affirm a "fictive kinship" with the customer, typically a white native (Lee 2002). Ethnic entrepreneurs encounter problems when they appear too distinct from their customers (Waldinger, Aldrich, and Ward 1990). So owners hoped to keep their ethnicity backstage. The shared public reality becomes that of a non-Indian customer checking into an ethnically ambiguous motel.

I now turn to how Indian American owners and employees tried to present an appealing front stage while dealing with racial, cultural, gender, and class hierarchies. Rather than only contest or complain about overwhelming hierarchies, male and female owners and laborers worked within them. In the process, they advanced their business and their goals but ultimately also reinforced the challenges facing them. I break down this process into three parts: (1) how owners dealt with their own minority status in relation to guests and employees; (2) their constant workload and the gendered ways they handled it; and (3) owners' racial preference ladder for paid labor, and how co-ethnic employees viewed this.

Whitening the Lobby

In order to accomplish a front stage that would appeal to their primary customer, owners monitored their bodies and choice of physical objects in the motels. As Foucault (1977) argues, the body is disciplined within regimes that in turn advance nationalist and capitalist aims. In this case owners disciplined their own bodies in order to satisfy a corporate and culturally normative model of the "proper" motel. Such efforts could be controlled by owners (unlike macro economic trends or oversaturation) and could help their business, even if only to a minor degree.

This disciplining took place often through the selective use of labor. Most owners hired white women as their desk clerks—particularly for the afternoon and evening shifts, when most check-ins occur—if they could afford to do so and had access to the demographic. This practice was more prevalent among franchise owners, who had to uphold the reputation of the franchise and who more often had the resources to have a paid staff. One owner of a middle-higher-budget franchise outside Cleveland connected customers' intolerance for Indian American motel owners to the intolerance of Indian Americans in corporate America:

> I think you have to [have whites as desk clerks], and some of that kinda goes back to the glass ceiling as well. If you're running an upscale hotel with an Indian at the front desk, you know, unfortunately we still live in a society that uh, doesn't look upon us kindly at times.

More than simply being the same race as the typical customer, white desk clerks bestowed Indian American–owned motels with acceptance. A white desk clerk's front-stage presence symbolized that a place was worth the customer's money. Complaints about room prices would not take on a racial charge (Park 1997; Yoon 1997). Customers would not wonder if the motel was owned by a foreigner who did not give back to the area. Of course, not all owners employed whites as their desk clerks. Worker selection depended on the available labor force, wage rates at comparable jobs, and so on. A few owners insisted that as the operator of the motel, they could bring in more customers than a white labor force. Still, most referred to race as an important consideration in employment choices.

In predominantly African American urban neighborhoods, immigrant store owners hire African Americans to work as "cultural brokers" with their customers (Lee 2002). Such employees help defuse racial tensions between customers and owners. For most motel owners serving primarily white customers, a similar dynamic is at play but with a different consequence. Motel owners, in effect, reinforce their own racial subordination to whites by privileging the white body. Even wealthy owners with multiple properties, who did not worry about discrimination against themselves, privileged whiteness. One owner, wearing a crisp navy blue suit, told me over hors d'oeuvres and cocktails at a motel convention:

> I want all non-Indians. Women are preferable. If you walk in there and you see a Sidharji [a Sikh man wearing a turban], you might not like. At the end of the day, you have to please your customers. I have seen the comments they will pass. . . . My property is near a Marine base where all these young kids come for the training. [The soldiers] are going to face those similar-looking people over there [in Iraq and Afghanistan]. . . . That [Sidharji] will be target practice! . . . When you are upset already when you walk in, you are going to find something wrong with the property. [They may stay] but then they complain. Their mind-set is already gone. They may say the carpet is dirty or there was a hair in the bathroom, and that is not 100 percent satisfaction and need money back. To avoid all these possible problems, I am of the opinion to have the young, average-looking [person.] When in Rome.

In spaces of heightened national loyalty and citizenship, South Asian (and Arab) Americans became stand-ins for the "enemy."

Similarly, a young third-generation motelier whose parents owned a major *hotel* franchise did not worry about discrimination personally. She believed she lived the American dream. She distinguished between the model minority stereotype and the incompetent Third World stereotype:

> If you want to look professional, you have a non-Indian at the door, you know? Um, otherwise it sort of looks like you have a mom and pop operation. . . . You're not gonna see a want ad for an Indian face or whatever. Unless it's like a CEO role, something a little higher up. Not on a flier or not at the front desk.

The racialization of minorities takes place differently across class levels. Indian Americans remain defined by their foreign nature, as inherently intelligent when in the corner office or culturally inferior when behind the check-in desk.

Gender joined with race to define the preferred front-stage staff. In upscale hotels, employers prioritize workers' ability to attend to customer details because that distinguishes one hotel from another in the eyes of discerning guests (Jones, Taylor, and Nickson 1997; Sherman 2007). Employers look to hire people who appear eager to help others, are hardworking, and the like. Because women are read as naturally empathetic, they bear the brunt of such "emotional labor" (Hochschild 1983). Employing white women was a very conscious use of gender, relying on the sexist binary of women as both alluring and nurturing. One male informant near Toledo commented crudely on the sexist preference for women at the front desk for the presumed male heterosexual guest. "Hire a woman. You come in, you're looking at her tits, and you don't walk out. That's fact! I'm telling you, that's fact." The motel owners' goal was to create an enticing interaction ritual for "him."

In addition to racial and gender attributes, these employees also possessed valuable cultural resources, for example, an ability to speak fluent, standard English and a comprehensive knowledge of the local area. An owner of a lower-budget franchise in Lima, Ohio, commented, "Sometimes language is problem. If you can't give directions to Walmart, the customer doesn't like it. If you are not telling the right answer, that's not right." To properly accomplish the ritual of greeting and serving the standard customer, one must appear as American as possible. The employees' style of interacting matter (Whyte 1946), but so do their physical and cultural characteristics. This is not to say, however, that clerks always had to appear colloquial. For instance, a young, professional Indian American motelier remarked,

> Even foreign is not a bad thing. I was just at a hotel a few weekends ago, and there was a French lady at the front desk. It sort of, not enhances the experience in a way, it's just sort of nice. I liked her accent, and I like the fact that she's from somewhere else, you know? It gives some, you know, flavor to the place; it's cool to me. . . . You're not going to get that [impression] from an Indian, no way.

Clearly, the kind of foreigner one was mattered, with Indian laborers as the wrong kind.

Not all owners who hired U.S.-born desk clerks were trying to suggest to customers that their motel was not Indian owned. They simply considered it advantageous to have employees who mirrored the customers. An owner of a higher-middle-budget motel in a Cleveland suburb thought American employees could better understand and so better serve customers. She said, "[I'm] not hiding the fact that we're Indian. Americans can do the job better because we're catering to Americans. Americans are the ones who spend money; immigrants don't." Owners recognize that they cannot describe themselves as "regular" Americans.

Many independent motel owners cannot afford to hire any staff, and so family members or other co-ethnics usually work behind the desk. With a much cheaper price, owners needed to work less to earn the acceptance of the customer within front-stage interactions. As a result, the interaction ritual when guests enter is less structured. Upon stepping into an independent motel, it is not uncommon to have to wait a minute or so until an owner shows up to the front desk, typically from his/her attached home in the back. Owners often present a less formal body—they wear casual clothes, such as shorts, T-shirts, sweatshirts, and jeans. On one occasion I showed up to a motel without realizing it was too early in the morning for an interview. It became apparent when the owner came to the front desk in his pajamas. On another occasion, as I waited for an owner, his mother, wearing a faded cotton salvar kameez, wiped water from the lobby floor with a rag while her two grandchildren walked with her. On yet another occasion an owner came to the front desk with one hand held purposefully away from her clothes. She had been eating a lunch of Indian cuisine with her hands when I rang. It is such presentations of the body, especially of racialized brown bodies, that have given independent motels the unfair image of being unkempt.

Creating a professional (that is, white) front stage so as to fit into the local environment and accrue more money required not only privileging white bodies but also presenting other mainstream symbols, which further marginalized owners' ethnic background. One strategy was changing their names when front stage. Chris Patel, Mike Patel, Sarah Gandhi, Sara Patel, Tom Desai, and the like are how employees, guests, and business colleagues referred to owners (while backstage, close family members referred to one another in their given names). Even business cards contained the commonly American, and often short, names. Other owners would go by the initials of their first and middle name.[2] And although families took great pride in their children's ability to speak Gujarati, when front stage, owners would speak in English, even to co-ethnics.

Owners felt it necessary to actively create an Americanized public role, distinguishable from their more sincere backstage persona; this required keeping their ethnic culture hidden backstage. Those who lack social power—in this case, ironically, business *owners*—must make an even greater switch between front-stage and backstage identities. This affected how owners, in particular those who lived on-site, ran their home lives. A top priority was to avoid the smell of Indian food at the entrance, which was difficult if their apartment was near the front desk. Those whose apartment did not enable them to have their kitchen located far from the front desk would cook when fewer check-ins were expected and/or would install an exhaust system to drive the smell away. As one owner of an independent motel in Lima said, "Cooking [is] not good for the business. We cook but no one can smell it. Kitchen is on back side [of the apartment, away from the front desk]. Business is business. Need to fit in." As immigrants who not only had moved from another country but also frequently had left family and friends elsewhere in the United States to find a business, blending in was the goal.

Creating a proper front stage required hiding not only ethnic symbols but also even certain ethnic people, namely, one's children. Children helped in the housekeeping and other tasks, but I rarely saw young children at the front desk or in lobbies of franchises. Owners of independent motels worried less about customers seeing one's children. As one owner explained,

> If I make a Best Western here [in place of my independent motel], will cost me $700,000 to do that. Guests [would] pay seventy dollars. They don't like noise. They need respect, hi, hello, door keeper, and everything. You are paying twenty-nine dollars [here now]. What do you expect from the owner? . . . We try to minimize the noises. Sometimes I don't rent the rooms next to where me and my kids are staying. I give distance from them. Mostly I rent the rooms at the end of the building or the upstairs. I have a lot of people working midnight and sleeping daytime. All those people [sleep] on top of the lobby. So if my kids crying downstairs, they don't hear.

Few owners forbid their children from public spaces. But the extent to which they were visible became part of the economic calculation of what a room was worth.

Some owners went further than just hiding ethnic representations. They carefully chose cultural references for their lobbies that would preempt "un-American" perceptions. Above the check-in desk at one franchise motel in Ohio was a copper plaque of two hands almost flat together, emblematic of the Christian prayer. I asked the Indian American manager why that was on the wall. He smirked and responded that it helped with customers by suggesting (falsely) that the establishment was Christian owned. Other places had Christmas trees despite the owners being Hindu. There was rarely any visible reference to Diwali or other Hindu celebrations. An owner of an economy franchise explained why: "Because 99 percent of customers are Christian people. You will answer every day, what is that? And people might not like it too." Through such presentations of Christian images, owners met customer expectations and possibly avoided losing business.

Owners did not mind displaying a sign in the lobby that showed their name and indicated they were the owner, for they thought it created credibility and status. But they rarely drew attention to their ethnic ownership. In this way the motel differs from businesses for which ethnicity serves as a selling point. For example, having Irish or Chinese paraphernalia in an Irish bar or a Chinese restaurant is not just tolerable but desirable—it lends authenticity. Consumers expect a motel to be a certain way, free of any signs of the owner's private life and of personal tastes generally. Owners often kept ethnic symbols backstage. During an interview with one owner in his office, for example, he opened a cabinet door to show me his miniature temple.[3] Post-9/11, it could actually help owners to be seen as both Indian and Hindu, as opposed to Arab or Muslim.

Overall, owners' efforts to create a nonethnic front-stage interaction ritual have had a complicated effect on race and ethnic relations. On the one hand, owners have inadvertently exacerbated their own racial and cultural subordination. Despite being business owners, they lacked full prestige even in relation to some employees. On the other hand, owners' tactics simultaneously subverted racial issues by resulting in the accrual of money and, as their employers, some power over whites. Of course, straightforward business factors, such as the quality and price of the room, helped shape customer impressions. Still, in recognizing their own racial and cultural subordination, owners were able to somewhat disrupt it even as they affirmed its existence. In this way, a differential inclusion and the American dream go hand in hand.

The Family Doing It All Themselves

The paid-labor front stage played a crucial role in the presentation of the motel. Yet family members performed much of the work in running motels, especially the lower-budget franchises and independents. A key reason for Indian Americans' success has been their reliance on family labor. Many owners, in particular those of low-budget motels, could not afford any paid labor. Working in a twenty-four-hour-per-day occupation became a source of both pain and pride. Owners described motel ownership as a "twenty-four-hour headache" (elaborated on in Chapter 5). As one owner of an independent motel in Alabama said of the manual labor that's required, "If you think, 'Oh, it's too dirty for me to do,' you ain't shit." Owners looked down on motels, stereotyped as white-owned, that employed separate persons for each set of responsibilities, such as a manager, distinct from an assistant manager, distinct from a desk clerk, and so on. The owner of a middle-lower-budget franchise near Toledo said, "If I have to run with American staff, you won't meet costs. . . . If you have titles [for employees], then get into money. Only title you get here is front desk. That person earns six dollars an hour."[4]

As an example, while assisting in a lower-middle-budget motel, I sat with the male owner in the morning at the front desk as he went over paperwork, checked out guests, and instructed his three housekeepers. Around noon, his wife arrived from the laundry room, where she had been folding sheets and monitoring some of the same housekeeping staff. Upon her arrival, the husband donned the tool belt sitting in his office, and we went off to do minor repairs in the rooms, including changing light bulbs, fixing door hinges, replacing television sets, and the like. Later at lunch at a local Chinese restaurant, he commented that he should leave a stack of fliers of his hotel here. In effect, he had served as desk clerk, accountant, manager (along with his wife), repairman, and marketing director, all by two in the afternoon.

Within family labor a gender division was evident, often—although not only—with the same purpose as that of the racial division of labor: to present "professional" motels.[5] Wives typically worked backstage and husbands up front, as is common for immigrant families engaged in hands-on businesses (Lee 2005). Although having Indian female owners work backstage is a gender reversal from having white women working up front, it advanced the goal of having more acculturated persons interacting with customers. This division of labor also fits a gendered hierarchy commonly found when immigrant communities engage the mainstream. Women generally have their freedoms curtailed in the diaspora so as to create "proper" appearances for outsiders (Espiritu 2003). So female owners remaining backstage fits a trend within immigrant adaptation. The result is having the patriarchy of the domestic sphere reinforced in the family business (Baines and Wheelock 1998; Bonacich 1987; Lee 2005; Westwood and Bhachu 1988).

But female moteliers also asserted agency and accrued power from the backstage, as fitting integration theories. Immigrant women gradually seek a domestic equality as they are exposed to more mainstream institutions, such as the workplace, even if they have weak economic prospects (Foner 1998). Ethnic enterprises in particular offer a comfortable working space for family members (Portes and Bach 1985). Women may encounter patriarchy, but gender relations gradually improve (Park 1997). In line with these findings, female owners assisted in decision making, took on an increasing amount of the responsibilities, and felt proud of their achievements.

I frame female owners as being between the two poles of subjugation by outsiders and co-ethnic males on the one hand and increasing equality and integration on the other. I do not simply mean that they achieved "some" equality. I am speaking also to the manner in which they asserted their agency. As for front-stage race relations, women gave in to hierarchies in order to, ironically, promote their equality and the motel's profits.

The gendered division of labor   As an unexpected visitor to smaller motels, I often found men behind the front desk or sitting nearby while women were doing the housekeeping. Female owners were often responsible for cleaning the rooms and bathrooms, doing the laundry, and pos-

A male motel owner in Indiana folds laundry while his wife is out.

sibly helping with the financial books and banking. Male owners were responsible for the front desk, for maintenance, for representing the motel to third parties (banks, vendors, the franchisor, and so on), and for the major decisions of the motels.[6] In larger motels with paid staff, women oversaw the housekeeping, sometimes chipping in, and occasionally assisted with the accounts.

Husbands did not refuse to perform backstage tasks. They often did. But typically it was when the wife could not. For example, a male owner of an independent motel gave a common response when asked who cleaned the motel rooms:

> We both. Whatever is required, someone does it. If someone is out, other person does it. Cannot wait until that person gets back.

Although both front-stage and backstage work are essential to running a business, the former carried more status. Husbands appreciated their wives' contributions but occasionally downplayed their role in the motels. For example, one immigrant owner subconsciously compared his wife with a maid when discussing her role in the motel:

> She gives suggestions. She says things about the room. We have to re-place this, replace that. Bed sheets are torn; pillows are flattened; light is out. The maid also tells. I make the decisions regarding the motel. The decision is mine. My wife is more involved with the house.

The fact that women's labor was seen as an extension of their domestic duties limited husbands' impressions of them as equals. Nor did women bring home a separate paycheck.[7]

Even when women played active roles in running the business, they rarely had the same level of responsibility as men (Dhaliwal 1998).[8] This is a trend AAHOA has sought to change. According to the organization, wives need to know how to run the business in case their husbands no longer can. (In discussions of female moteliers within AAHOA and else-where, they are assumed to have husbands rather than work independently or have female partners.) One female immigrant motelier active in AAHOA pushed for more education-oriented sessions for women rather than women's speakers on fashion or cooking, as has been common at the conventions. She noted the difference between the management side and the entrepreneurial side of motels. The former involves the day-to-day tasks of the motel, such as scheduling staff, attending to the rooms, and checking inventory. The latter involves investigating new businesses, considering major changes, thinking more broadly of the market, and so on. She said,

> I think a lot of women probably do have an input into larger decisions that are being made. It's not like they're totally out of it, but, I don't know, maybe that's not the focus right now. . . . You know, right now it's still a man's world when it comes to that, I think. . . . Give [women] the skills to become entrepreneurs. Give them the skills to read a PNL state-ment, to read a Star Report. If you want to build a hotel, how do you do it, where do you start, what is the process? You know, that kind of infor-

mation, so that the women can become involved in being entrepreneurs and developing a business.

One owner of a higher-middle-budget franchise had a larger role in her business than most women I interviewed. She said, "If I don't know the housekeeping, the laundry, the front desk, how can I tell my employees if they are doing right or wrong? I take pride in working each and every department." Nevertheless, her justified pride remained within the daily business side of her motel. The entrepreneurial side belonged to her husband.

When women proved highly competent along multiple dimensions, they were met with disbelief. As a 1.5-generation woman said,

> A lot of the times most of the people in our communities see us, as you know, housewives. They probably think that my dad and my brother does everything here you know? . . . And then I was talking to, actually, a good friend of mine, and I told him I'm the one that goes and gets the insurance quotes and what I do here. And he says, "Really!?" I said, "Yeah!" I mean, I line up things when there's an annual review of our property insurance because it's quite a lot of money involved.

This owner's heavy involvement in running her motel was an exception to the norm (and she, notably, had been raised in the United States and was not married).

Reasons for a gendered division of labor   Women worked outside of the leading positions for a number of reasons. With regard to the front stage, women had, on average, less education than men and weaker English skills and therefore had difficulty engaging in "professional" interactions with customers. This was particularly true of the older generation. As one proprietor said of his mother, who assisted with the motel and lived on the premises,

> Early morning I need two people to clean up motel. Rest of time only need one. But must speak English. My mom doesn't speak English. I cannot leave my mom here and go outside. So that's my problem. I went to

[a fast-food sandwich restaurant] to pick up my wife [where she worked] and someone came in and asked for a smoking room. [My mother] couldn't take the money.

Another rationale for women's lack of authority stemmed less from treatment by guests than from external vendors and institutions. A female owner near Cleveland shared the following anecdote:

> I was, um, ready to order the pictures that go on top of the bed [in my motel rooms], and I had a company I called. And, I told them give me the best price that you could and I'm ready to order. He still give me the price, and then when [my husband] called they gave him a lower price.

Such experiences contributed to men's dominant role front stage and women's role backstage.[9]

Even women highly involved in their business found reasons to defer to their husbands. For instance, one immigrant female owner ran the front desk of her lower-budget franchise and spoke easily of franchise regulations, rate differences across various websites, and other business affairs beyond housekeeping. When she and her husband built a new motel years ago, she was "heavily involved." She said, "Where the bathrooms were supposed to be, what kind of decorations that you want to do. Of course we did that, you know. So whenever I can, I did it." Still, her husband had final authority on business decisions. She offered various reasons for this:

> Yah, because you know when I got married, I never finished the college. I did not have the college education. . . . He does his work, I do mine. We keep ourselves busy. A lot of things he would not understand in day-to-day operations at the front desk, but any renovation he has to do or buying another property or anything, we do talk about it. Before he used to be heavily involved into the maintenance or buying, and all that. Because he, being a man, he knows, he talks to the other people in same business. They talk about where to get it cheaper and all that. So he has a better idea.

The gendered division of labor, which persisted despite some women's accomplishments, is commonplace within U.S. capitalism, which supports male dominance through segregating the workforce (Padavic and Reskin 2002). But it also carried a cultural dimension. A 1.5-generation woman worked at her parents' motel and said of Indian and Indian American wives' impressions of housekeeping:

> They feel humiliated if husbands do it. It's dirty. And we learn that guys shouldn't do it, so we don't let our father do laundry or bathroom. . . . If my mother is out of town then we, me and my sisters, help do it. . . . All the office-related work dad ends up doing mainly. All the laundry area [and] back areas, girls, ladies end up doing it.[10]

In this case the ethnic norms that gave women a sense of comfort and continuity in the diaspora contributed to their secondary status (Assar 2000). Men did not refuse to do this "dirty work" in response to a loss of gender privilege upon immigration, as is common in other ethnic households (George 2005). Women went out of their way to say that they did not want men doing such work, while acknowledging that husbands often resisted too.

The effect of these pressures was women's diminished confidence in their ability to run their motel as well as their husbands could, despite their immense accomplishments. A female motelier who led women's meetings within AAHOA gave a passionate critique of this situation.

> Women are the backbone of the industry. They will be always the backbone of this industry. Because if it wasn't for the women holding the big operational part of the business and the balance of life—whether it be family, social, kids, you know, everything else that's involved—I don't think the males can dominate in their own business success without them. . . .
>
> When we went across the country [with AAHOA], we asked women, . . . which direction do you want us to go into? All we heard was connectivity: connecting with each other, networking, and building

confidence, you know. We had someone say that we are afraid to step out because we don't have the courage.

Gains are being made, albeit slowly. For example, more women are running for motel leadership positions within AAHOA, but none have been elected to top levels.

Women and men divided the tasks of running a motel along gender lines so as to satisfy guests, grow the motel, and adhere to traditional norms. Because families did so much of the work, how they organized it was critical to their day-to-day performance and satisfaction.

Conforming to and contesting patriarchy   Female informants dealt with the gendered stratification partly by rationalizing it through a transnational lens and partly by resisting it, but they almost always accepted its constraints. As is common for immigrant women, they downplayed domestic inequality by comparing their lives with those of peers in the homeland. The woman quoted earlier who took pride in knowing each department of her motel argued that her role in the business, even if less authoritative than her husband's role, still constituted gender equality as compared to her hypothetical life in India. So she had little reason to contest the division of labor.

> One time one customer came in and we were talking about India and what do you like about this country. I said for me, I would say opportunity, because if I was in India, back in India, at the most what would I have achieved? The kids and the family and that's it. Over here you get the opportunity to get to meet the people and all that, which I would not have achieved if I were in India because in those days the girls don't go out and work where I came from. . . . The motel is added responsibility. But then you get used to. It becomes daily routine that you get used to it.

Her statement "in those days the girls don't go out and work where I came from" refers to a time in Gujarat, starting in the 1930s and still ongoing, when Patidar males were hoping to increase their social status, and minimizing women's labor was a mark of distinction in furtherance of their cause (Gidwani 2000).[11] With this being said, they are not one-sided in their appraisal of their diasporic lives. Besides being an "opportunity," working outside the home is a burden that one must "get used to."

Women also exerted agency from their backstage roles. The literature on women's agency within ethnic businesses has focused on flexible schedules that facilitate a balance of home and work duties (Chin 2005; Zhou 1992). Rather than frame wives as increasingly powerful and comfortable in the family business or continually exploited based on domestic inequalities, it is necessary to recognize women's agency within a sustained hierarchy (Ram and Holliday 1993). My focus is on women's role in decision making.

Women's agency within constraints is seen in families' decision making processes. The vast majority of owners, both men and women, said that although men and women discuss business needs, men have the "final say." For example, one female owner of an independent motel explained her and her husband's decision to change the carpeting in some of the rooms:

> He calls the carpet company and I choose which carpet and which color. He always asks me, which carpet should we use. Which color. He didn't decide by himself. Sometimes the man doesn't think about which color carpet goes with the drapes. He says we'll change the carpet. He calls and gets carpets. I choose the color. Work together. Seems equal. I just say, I like this one and the color and everything. And he ordered everything. He choose the quality and the price. Sometimes I don't know what quality is good.

Here the wife merely decided the color of the carpet, and the husband decided the price, selection, and even whether the carpets should ultimately be changed or not. Given that wives typically spend more time in the rooms than do husbands, it would be logical that she would decide whether to change the carpet or at least have a larger say in that decision. Still, she said that they "work together" and the power "seems equal." Referring to their partnership as "equal" seems like a generous interpretation. Instead, it is a "family myth" that partners often use to reconcile different perspectives on gender relations (Hochschild 1989).

Nevertheless, women's agency should not be dismissed. The selection of carpets could not take place without her input, and the husband deferred to her in some element of that process. Motel rooms are part of a motel's front-stage appearance, creating a lasting impression. Another woman said that women help in subtle ways to make decisions, such as bringing the need for upgrades to their husbands' attention.

Nor were women simply confined to offering advice to husbands who then ran the front stage alone. They also strategized with one another on successful business practices. When I asked the proprietor of an independent motel near Toledo how often she met with other women, she replied,

> Whoever is in the town. We meet at the temple. There was a lot of Indians [who] own the motel. So most of the motels here are owned by Indians. When we get together we talk about all this stuff. Get together once a month with people I know well. We ask about how business is doing, what can we do together to improve business. We say that if we advertise this way, we can get more business. They tell me something to do, and I tell them. We talk about what customers like. We talk about business to close friends. We tell them, we did this and you can make improvements to your motel.

This informant ran the motel while her husband maintained his day job as an engineer. Such women did not necessarily receive greater recognition as workers from their husbands compared with those whose husbands worked in the motel (Assar 2000); nevertheless, she had a more thorough understanding of the business than many other women. And her network of women shows she is not alone.

One owner actually played up her role as a backstage, immigrant woman so as to have an active role in her business. She went out of her way to be mistaken as part of the cleaning staff, which was relatively easy because of the seemingly "natural" association of women of color with low-status service positions. She and her husband co-owned a middle-higher-budget franchise with another friend. When I met her at her motel, she was dressed in a maid's uniform, she wore little jewelry, and her hair was unkempt. Her employees believed that she was good friends with the owner's wife (that is, herself), which she explained enabled her to run the motel better than if she worked front stage.

> That's what we told [the employees]—the owner's wife and I are very good friends. So they know that I talk to his wife and I am going to tell them that [something wrong] is happening, and then they find out and [the culprits] get fired. So they are scared of me. They know that much. See that's the thing that happens when you work by yourself. You want to increase your business, you try to make your place clean, neat, comfortable for the guests. They keep coming back, and I have so many guests who have been coming here because of [me]. Because they don't know that I am the owner.

By reinforcing gender and racial stereotypes, she actually augmented her power in the motel and also "increased [her] business."

Within owners' pervasive concern of saving money and generating a profit, they settled into a gendered family labor routine considered conducive to that. By staying either backstage and/or outside the entrepreneurial side of the business, women lacked the authority of their husbands in running motels. As is common for women of color, they accepted a patriarchy in order to help move their families forward. Yet they found agency within their roles, which assisted their motels. Without their input, motels would lack in sophisticated decision making and owners would have to pay for additional labor. They also strategized how to be active players in the business. Framing women only as lacking power misrepresents the situation, as does framing the family enterprise as a cohesive unit. In the same way that owners handled racial hierarchies by hiring white desk clerks, female owners found opportunities within the towering, embedded hierarchies. This process involved accepting a subjugation while still weakening its effect and assisting their motel.

Paid Backstage Labor

A final dimension of how owners used labor to create a nonethnic front stage and so increase profits involved their choice of paid backstage employees, namely, housekeepers and maintenance persons. Sixty-four percent of owners interviewed had paid employees (not including temporary workers for particular projects, such as renovations). Just as owners had a rationale for privileging whites front stage, they found reasons to employ mostly—although by no means exclusively—minorities backstage. As is common for non-Indian businesses as well, these owners used preexisting hierarchies to save money and create a desired outward appearance.

Owners employed predominantly female labor and often, but not only, women of color as housekeepers. In Ohio, given its racial demographics, there were a number of white women along with African American women and a smaller proportion of Latinas and Indian American women working backstage. The demographics of the area influenced who was available to hire. But owners often had preferences. Like so many other types of business owners, they constructed a racial preference ladder (Waldinger and Lichter 2003; Yoon 1997). Employers do not simply refuse to hire a particular group. Instead, they often hire such a group for low-status jobs rather than for high-status jobs.

African Americans ended up on the bottom of the racial preference ladder, which is the norm in the hospitality industry (Stepick and Grenier 1994). One stereotype held by an owner of a lower-budget franchise was typical: "Nobody wants [these jobs]. Reliability is the big deal. Blacks would not work for six dollars and fifty cents anyway; they can make more than that on welfare." Latinas were a very common labor source outside the Midwest and South (and increasingly inside). They worked predominantly backstage due to language barriers, networks, previous work experience, and racial presumptions by owners. Part of the incentive to hire Latinas was their presumed cultural similarities with Indian Americans. And employers believed immigrants in general worked harder than native-born Americans without complaining of limited upward mobility (Waldinger and Lichter 2003). An owner of a lower-budget franchise said,

> They are hard working, they are long-term employees. They have good family culture, family structure so you see their abilities—if he lost his job, they will tell you, do you have any other opening? I can bring these people in. They are like us, they pull their relatives in, their countrymen.

The employment of Latina/os is so common that a Gujarati-Spanish dictionary is available for owners.[12] Owners support more immigration and a guest worker program. Capitalists in general prefer greater immigration in order to create surplus labor, which keeps wages down and increases the talent pool. Indian American owners were no different.

Employing co-ethnics (or not)   The relationship between owners and co-ethnic employees, within owners' goals of ensuring profits by limiting costs and creating "professional" establishments, merits attention. Scholars debate the benefit of working for co-ethnics in terms of wage compensation, opportunities for mobility, and degree of exploitation (Kwong 1996; Nee, Sanders, and Sernau 1994; Portes and Bach 1985; Sanders and Nee 1996). Rather than engage in that debate, however, I focus on the overall subjective experience of both hiring and working for a co-ethnic. As did many other ethnic entrepreneurs, such as Iranians, Koreans, and Chinese-Vietnamese, Indian Americans relied mostly on laborers not of their own ethnicity (Min and Bozorgmehr 2000). Still, co-ethnics figured prominently in how owners framed desired employees.

Owners revealed a paradoxical dynamic of privileging whites front stage but trusting co-ethnics more. An independent owner in Alabama detailed the pros and cons of whites versus Indians:

> We had a white manager for eight years, behind the desk. We [Indian Americans] are best at controlling the money and managing. But because he's white, he has better results. When it comes to marketing, there's no comparison. If I go around trying to market this motel, and he goes around, there's no comparison. I couldn't get even 50 percent result, like he can. These are the things we face. We would

like to see a white person at our desk, for the sake of the feeling of the customer. As far as taking care of our motel and watching the motel, he cannot do the job like an Indian can. He cannot do the long hours like an Indian can. I can leave an Indian guy here and go out of town, and all will be fine when I get back. Americans, you can't trust to take care of it.

Despite co-ethnics' assumed dependability and disposition to working "long hours," owners recognized the power of white/American privilege and so employed co-ethnics primarily backstage.

Nevertheless, owners believed that they were assisting such workers. They oftentimes allowed workers to live on the premises, which owners believed more than compensated for a backstage role and ensured grateful workers. One franchise owner in a Cleveland suburb listed the cost of living for the average Indian immigrant employee in the Cleveland area and then said,

So basically you have $1,200 monthly expense. That's $15,000 a year, right? Now if they live in a hotel, they save everything but food—like $300 a month. So now this couple who's brand new to America, and they never dreamed about having their own business one day. And they say, if I spend four years here I'm gonna save $100,000 because I have no liability for any utilities, any rent. And, that's the kind of couple I'm looking for. And what they do is they know that they don't have expenses, so they are not looking for a huge salary. . . . To me it's a big saving because I can write about $15,000 in the business expense. And I don't have to pay in too much. I don't have to worry about training for two years until they decide they are ready to move on. . . . I mean, a fifteen-shift package [at eight hours per shift] would be maybe $30,000 [per year].

Q: *Yeah, that's a good idea. Do you ever think that maybe it's taking advantage of people as immigrants? Or—*

It's a win-win situation. An eight-year job in corporate places has one-hour lunch and a one-hour commute on average. You're spending ten hours out of the house, while he's only working eight hours. So he's saving two hours every day. . . . He is averaging about seven dollars an hour. But, in effect, he's making twelve dollars.

The other side of the "win-win" situation was for the owners. Ethnic entrepreneurs typically view co-ethnic laborers as hardworking, trustworthy, and less likely to protest their conditions or pay (Kwong 1996; Yoon 1997). Many motel owners reported difficulty in finding labor to work for six or seven dollars an hour, which was a common wage for the cleaning staff in Ohio in 2007. Paying more would be difficult, according to the owners. As mentioned in Chapter 3, motel staff also rarely receive health insurance, despite frequently carrying heavy loads and doing much manual labor (such as cleaning rooms), which also made it difficult to find committed native-born labor. Immigrant employees have fewer expectations. Also, having employees live in the hotel provided key benefits. One franchise owner explained,

Well, they live on the property, number one. [Second,] all these [American] people that have [submitted] job applications, half won't come for an interview. The other half that do won't show up for work. All of them, there are probably only one or two people I will hire, that will qualify. [Indian Americans] are more dedicated. They need a job because they have expenses, and they do have responsibilities back home to pay and you know.

Q: *They live on the premises. Why is that?*

Incentive. Because they don't pay utilities and secondly, if you need them they are right there.

Indian Americans served, then, as surplus labor to fill in gaps when necessary. This is not to suggest that owners treated co-ethnic labor as servants. When asked if he would call up such a worker at night if a problem arose, the same owner went on to say, "Not in the middle of the night, no. If the shift is finished, it's finished. He's got his life, I've got my life. . . . We'll have dinner together once in a while, whatever."

These workers were seen as dependable partly because of their ethnic background. Arguably, capitalist interests more than long-standing cultural ties shape co-ethnic relations (Bodnar 1985), but the two work together. Immigrant employees often had debts from their travel, responsibilities to family back in the homeland, and daily expenses in the United States. Ethnic commonalties added to their reliability. Hiring is "an investment in uncertainty," and owners felt more secure in their choice if they knew some background characteristics (Waldinger and Lichter 2003, p. 136). Owners believed co-ethnics also approached the job differently. As a second-generation owner said,

> I think that Indian employees take more ownership over a problem. They go the extra mile to please guests. I have to go through a lot more conversations with white staff. They are brought up in this country and ask, "What can you do for me?" I had one white person at the front desk and told him how he could answer a call differently to bring in more business. The response was, "Well, if you paid me more money, I would [do] a better job," which I think a lot of whites would say. Whereas an Indian would say, if I do a better job, they may pay me more money.

Not only were co-ethnic workers read as dependable, industrious, and accepting of base wages, they could end up saving owners money in other ways. As one owner explained, some employees worked off the books and could be paid in ways that other labor could not.

> You can get a better work out of an Indian. If you have an Indian, you don't have to worry about overtime. Sometime they get a flat rate for rooms. You can do a lot of jiggling with the law. You give them more work but not paying overtime [time and a half]. I'll give you three, four dollars per room. That same guy will have his own motel in five years. And you give him a room. They will work seven days a week because they want to earn money. I'll pay the Indian same as Caucasian. If you make X number of rooms, you can stay here and get $1,200 or $1,400 a month. Cheaper for the owner than hiring a Caucasian. . . . Indians never go to court, never file for unemployment, so won't lose money

that way. Don't sue one another. If threaten too, pressured by community not to.

Such laborers work more and don't expect the same strict compensation that native-born employees expect. This framing is similar to that of undocumented Latino laborers by Korean American merchants (Min 2008). Although most Indian American laborers are documented immigrants, their work status may still be precarious. A few owners employed Indian college and graduate students who had emigrated to study. These students are in the United States on student visas and legally are not allowed to work. (This is a group that is completely overlooked in the national conversation on undocumented labor.) In this way the owners found labor with needed skills, such as English fluency, while avoiding paying a wage that legal workers would require. Because of the skill set of students, they could be placed front stage. The savings resulting from having an Indian immigrant rather than a white person work at the front desk was worth the risk of possible loss of business. According to this owner, the reason more Indian Americans did not have co-ethnic employees is because they cannot find them, for so many Indians have moved on to own motels.

On the other hand, some refused to hire co-ethnics, even backstage. A younger man in his early thirties felt culturally handicapped in dealing with co-ethnics, especially those older than he.

> [I employ] fifteen people. No Indians. Don't want them. I cannot say anything to them. If it is American people, I can fire them, hire them right away. With Indians I have certain limits to telling them. Indians also expect a lot more. They expect more money, less work, you pay for their groceries, and give them place to live.

As seen in the second part of the quote, there was a sense that co-ethnics made too many demands on owners. The very qualities that made co-ethnics appealing workers also made them more challenging: they served as a reliable source of labor for years, akin to relatives, and so expected greater acknowledgment and more privileges in return. Other owners assumed that co-ethnics would eventually leave and start their own businesses and so chose not to hire them.

Co-ethnic employees' reactions   Indian American employees appreciated the free accommodations and found their jobs generally tolerable. Language commonalties helped as well. Because the laborers saw themselves as attached to the owner and often heard about the job through a personal contact of the employer, they had little incentive to critique the wages or working conditions (Bonacich and Modell 1980; Zhou 1992). It was not uncommon to see married couples working together. Still, working for a co-ethnic was most appealing because of the possibility of owning a motel one day. Co-ethnic laborers knew they might be taken advantage of. Yet giving in to the hierarchy rather than contesting it was worthwhile if it meant eventually being able to run their own place. As an owner of a higher-middle-budget franchise said,

> A lot of those Indians are friends, relatives of Indians that are over here already. [The sponsored relatives] may not have a formal education and they may have no way to earn money. So usually, the owners get a husband and wife team in there and work twelve hours a day. And they don't pay as much, and they are just like, work and work and work.

By working long days, the family can eventually afford its own motel, and the cycle of labor immigration continues. This contributes to the problem of oversaturation, as explained in Chapter 3. But for the owners, it was worthwhile in the short run, and if one was assisting one's own family members, it was worthwhile in the long run as well.

Although employees hoped to eventually purchase their own motel, their day-to-day work lives were defined more by the content of the job itself and their relations with their employers. The decision to work for co-ethnics did not rest so much on ethnic solidarity as on convenience. In the end, most employees viewed their work as just a job, which otherwise could be hard to find (Yoon 1997). One Indian worker who ran the front desk and did the housekeeping for an Indian-owned motel said,

If it's a small organization, may be better to work for an Indian because of communication. But my wife was working for Kmart, and she never had any problems with a big organization. . . . When you are a worker, people expect lots of stuff from you. . . . It's like working anywhere else.

Indian American workers may not receive high wages, but other employment could be difficult to attain, given their lack of strong English skills and social networks outside the Indian community. For example, one man I met spoke just a little English, and his wife barely spoke any. Both were housekeepers. He communicated with the American workers through simple phrases, key words relevant for the job, and body language. The wife did not communicate with them at all. Other options for such employees included working for big box retail or fast food establishments, and even these may be out of reach depending on English skills and networks. These factors, along with the general preference to work with co-ethnics, made the motel backstage job an appealing option.

Although employees recognized their constraints in finding other jobs, they did not want to work for just any Indian American owner; they did not want to be taken advantage of. More than ethnicity, workers cared about how well they were treated, as mentioned in Chapter 3. In talking with African American, Indian, Latino/a, and white employees of motels, they appreciated owners who were communicative and straightforward and offered fair wages and opportunities for advancement. Indian American owners varied in how they treated employees, as do all small-business owners. Some were known for being miserly, others for being fair or even generous.

As we have seen, the picture of co-ethnic employees is not simply one of marginalization or one of mobility. It is a picture of both trends at work simultaneously. On the one hand, the deployment of co-ethnic labor backstage and their distinct working conditions underscore the racial and cultural hierarchies that privilege white labor. Ultimately, the upper hand belongs to the employer, who can use co-ethnic labor to fill in gaps and run motels at lower costs. Studies emphasizing only the solidarity between owners and workers paint too rosy a picture (Portes and Bach 1985), and those emphasizing the exploitation are too cynical (Kwong 1996), at least for this case. Rather than simply being taken advantage of, co-ethnic workers accrue some benefits in the process. From young students to elder immigrants, recent arrivals can gain housing and employment that may otherwise be difficult to acquire. Some may become motel owners themselves one day. Thus the integration narrative of Indian Americans is furthered by their finding advantages within a lower occupational status.

AAHOA Promoting Professionalism

AAHOA has pushed for owners to professionalize into a more corporate model of management, which owners have responded to. One of its mottoes is "excellence through education," meant to overcome the image of mom-and-pop, slovenly run establishments. Conventions have well-attended sessions on marketing, managing employees, negotiating contracts, and more. AAHOA also promotes training programs, at times in concert with university hospitality schools. For example, it offers a Certified Hotel Owners (CHO) program.[13] At a CHO training session that I attended, participants were given general management suggestions aimed at franchises with paid employees, such as tips for managing employees, running the front office, being cost effective, and marketing the motel.[14] In addition, AAHOA has had videos on its website and articles in its monthly magazine on marketing and using the Internet. Notably, few materials refer to the ethnic or other social differences likely to exist between the Indian owner, the paid staff, and the customers.

AAHOA, which markets a professional, assimilated image of itself, has done a significant amount of charity work. For example, it offered free rooms to active-duty members of the U.S. military and raised money for victims of Hurricane Katrina, comparing that with its transnational charity. As quoted in an article by Ela Dutt:

> "We, the AAHOA members, are part of a diverse American culture, which has enabled us to achieve our 'American Dream,'" and the orga-

nization exhorts its members, "To show our commitment, loyalty and solidarity with our fellow Americans we have launched a campaign to raise funds for the victims of Hurricane Katrina in the Gulf States." . . . "This will be more than the drives we have held for India," Rama [then president of AAHOA] said.[15]

These efforts can help define Indian American establishments as "American-owned" motels, not based on birthplace or skin color, but based on their commitment to the nation and their ability to give.

In addition to pushing owners to embrace Americanized ways, AAHOA pushes dominant organizations, namely, franchises and the government, to better account for the needs of owners. It represents owner-operators, rather than management corporations, franchisors, or other parties. Like a labor union, it argues for the general fairness for owners, again regardless of ethnicity. For example, it promotes a "fair franchising" plan that encourages corporations to respond to owners' concerns (examined in Chapter 3), such as the clustering of comparable brands within a corporation's portfolio, franchisor fees, and more.[16]

The organization has recorded notable achievements on behalf of franchisees. One franchise owner said,

> We get free consultation [from AAHOA]. Suppose if business is going down and you want to change the brand. You have ten-year contract and you have only six years. There are so many rules, you have to pay four years of the name. But AAHOA fought with them and finally came to the agreement that if someone's revenue is going down and is below certain amount of occupancy, person can go to another franchise without paying penalty. That is one advantage. Provided you keep a B average on motel. . . . AAHOA can put pressure on the franchise.

AAHOA also gives owners opportunities to buy goods directly from vendors, such as at their conventions, in order to secure better deals than franchisors offer.

AAHOA works with government institutions in much the same manner, which aids both independents and franchisees. When owners complain of restrictive ordinances or have trouble communicating with representatives because of language barriers, AAHOA representatives step in (see also Min 2008). Representatives convey their substantial footing in the motel industry, contributions to local economies, number of persons employed, and other economic factors that gain political respect. AAHOA also engages in direct action on behalf of moteliers. For example, the AAHOA representative for Michigan in 2007 explained a situation there affecting independent moteliers (not only Indians):

> Basically [the police] give tickets [to owners] when there's a violation. Like [the owner] rents a room without [customer] ID. Or doesn't take the second person's ID. And [the police] park a patrol car in the parking lot. So that's getting the business away. . . . And when the guest would exit the room, if there's two people that come out of the room, [the police] would approach the guest directly and ask them what they were doing. . . . And [AAHOA representatives] went there and had a meeting with the owners and the police chief, city attorney. You got to help us, we'll help you, but you're driving our business away. And they did work with us and that stopped, basically. That stopped. And right now it's been okay.

AAHOA works with the federal government to promote standard capitalist interests, such as not raising the minimum wage, fewer restrictions on immigration, highway transportation improvements, and restrictions to the Americans with Disabilities Act. A key part of AAHOA's national political strategy has been its political action committee. Money talks in government, and AAHOA works within the political system to advance its members' needs. Members have appreciated the organization's efforts. As an owner of a lower-budget franchise with about fifty rooms said of AAHOA,

> [It is the] best thing that happened. Putting lobbying in Washington. Right now they are debating the Disability Act. It is so bad and severe, it hurts the small businesses. For a 500-room hotel, adding another two rooms is no big deal. But for here adding that is expensive. I just spent

$5,000 for special room. Door has to open up more. How many handi-caps come here? They can walk from outside of door to bed, but because of the law you have so many things. . . . This is where lobbying comes into the picture. These [owners] cannot afford. AAHOA represents the practicality of the business.

In pushing its goals, AAHOA at times also joins with mainstream hos-pitality organizations, such as the American Hospitality and Lodging Association.[17]

Incorporating Ethnicity

AAHOA is a professional organization run like comparable bodies. Still, ethnic culture manifests within the organization's internal opera-tion and in dealings with franchisors and the government. The result complicates its goal of presenting Americanized owners.

Among its more symbolic means of displaying ethnicity internally, such as Gujarati food at motel conventions, AAHOA draws from the postcolonial history of its members to encourage collective action. Mo-tel owners' solidarity results in part from a common historical struggle against imperial forces. For example, in pushing for its fair franchising plan at the 1999 AAHOA convention, then AAHOA chairman Mike Patel compared the franchises to the imperial British, as written in *Franchise Times.*

> He needed to make a point to ensure the membership understood what was at stake. So at the convention, he aired a clip from the movie *Gandhi*, about the legendary Indian lawyer who fought British rule with nonviolent means. In the film clip, Gandhi told the English, "I hope you have enough bullets" to stop the entire population from rebelling. By casting franchisors in the role of British imperialists in India, Patel cre-ated a rallying point for members.[18]

Within its domestic agenda, AAHOA invokes a model minority image, consciously or not. According to a consultant for AAHOA, it could make sense for AAHOA representatives to allude to the large body of Indian Americans who are professionals (doctors, engineers, computer programmers, business owners) when dealing with senators and members of Congress, who would appreciate entrée into the financially rich community. Similarly, according to Ohio's only Indian American state representative, Indian Americans' ethnic background could not sway legislation because any proposed bill must be valid on its own merits. But politicians' awareness of Indian Americans' financial background could help draw their attention to proposed legislation in the first place. Put another way, a model minority's endorsement of a piece of legislation will not get it passed, but it does not hurt. For their part, politicians also looked for ways to connect to the ethnic group. For example, at a fund-raiser for the Indian American Ohio representative, other state representatives (all white men) stopped by to meet the motel owner attendees. Each politician was introduced by the organizer as "a friend to the Indian community" in order to build that politician's relationship with the ethnic group.[19] Ethnicity was less relevant when AAHOA dealt with bureaucracies that had no connection to the political process.

The model minority image became even more effective when represented by white Americans on behalf of AAHOA. Two of the organization's main representatives are white: the president and the chief legal counsel. Although hired and retained solely on the basis of their professional qualifications and records, their race adds to their presence in select dealings with (mostly white) industry and government officials. As an AAHOA representative said about the white president:

> Yeah, in him representing us there is the benefit of having the Caucasian. But you know, I will tell you one thing—in the general public, yes, but in the mainstream of the industry—I think everybody that's associated in the industry knows exactly [his] position. He is the president of AAHOA and he reports to the board of directors and the membership, [which] is, you know, 95 plus percent Indian. . . . [But] I'll grant that the initial approach to a person who doesn't have the AAHOA profile, [him being white] does work to our advantage—that's fair.

The message of the model minority becomes even stronger if represented by members of the majority to other members of the majority.

In addition, AAHOA leaders can get government officials to acknowledge the racial implications of their actions. For example, an AAHOA regional representative at the 2006 annual convention in Las Vegas spoke of a local ordinance that was being considered in his area that would require extra security guards at motels. This would financially cripple these businesses. The representative did not believe that the crackdown was simply racially motivated. Still, he said, it was important to remind government representatives of the political implications of the action, of being seen as targeting minority owners. So although AAHOA primarily dealt with officials and franchisors on economic or legal grounds, its ethnic background played a role.

In effect, AAHOA sliced the model minority stereotype into parts, honing in on the most positive aspects while challenging the notion of Indian Americans as passive. Because they challenge their foreignness, they resist being seen as only foreigners and refute a complete differential inclusion. In the process, however, race and ethnicity were not made irrelevant but instead invoked in subtle ways to defend why Indian Americans deserve equal treatment. That is, representatives utilized prevailing and almost inescapable racial notions rather than always confronting them directly. The popularity of the model minority image explains why other ethnic groups have embraced it as well (Hintzen 2001).

AAHOA leaders are using their domestic accomplishments to further transnational goals, further solidifying their image as *ethnic* entrepreneurs. AAHOA has led a few delegations of franchise executives to key tourist regions within India, including Gujarat, to discuss investment opportunities in the hospitality industry. India has a growing tourism market—including domestic tourism—that is underserved by the existing number of hotels.[20] AAHOA's transnational interests go beyond the economic. The organization promotes U.S. foreign policy goals that they view as supportive of India. It uses its economic and political achievements domestically to pursue international agendas. A prime example was the United States–India nuclear power agreement in 2008. A statement released by the organization said, "For the past several years, AAHOA leaders have actively promoted the approval of the Agreement by participating in many high-level meetings and conference calls with the White House and representatives from the Department of State."[21] Such actions cement the transnational links at the political level that have been in play at the personal network level for decades. Also, in 2005 AAHOA tried to bring in Gujarat chief minister Narendra Modi as the keynote speaker of its annual convention. Modi was denied a visa and spoke to the audience via a monitor.[22] AAHOA also endorses candidates for office. This has included practically all Indian Americans running for national office, seemingly regardless of political party or stated stance on motel-related concerns. The belief is that an Indian American will take care of fellow Indian Americans and of India.

As do individual owners and employees, AAHOA and its leaders work within existing hierarchies to advance the goals of the organization. It has promoted a professional approach to motel management and effectively defended its members, but it has also run up against the entrenched racial discourse that framed Indian Americans as inherently "ethnic" rather than fully American. According to this discourse, it is ethnicity that helps make Indian Americans successful capitalists, which defines them as apart from the standard citizen (Chang 2000; Park 2005). The organization's strategies with local leaders and their transnational links inadvertently, perhaps unavoidably, conform to this overdetermined view of Indian Americans as inherently hardworking and successful, even as the organization publicizes its members' commitment to America. As Waldinger and Lichter (2003) argue, the skills and temperaments that make immigrants good workers may also define them as deviant from the nation. This has the indirect effect of contributing to the racialization tied to capitalism. To the extent that capitalism depends on the racial stereotyping and segregation of competing groups, the notion of the model minority will remain active. The more that Indian Americans own motels, the more they become racially stereotyped as natural fits for that position, and they grow in the industry. They become perceived as good moteliers, just as Latinos become good service workers, Third World women become good assembly-line workers, and so on. In addition, for capitalism to be accepted despite the inequalities that it creates, the public needs to be convinced that the system is fair. The model minority stereotype offers this idea, thereby contributing to capitalism's hegemony. In the process, members benefit in relation to franchises or governments that come to value owners not only because of their management skills but also simply because of their background. By using rather than entirely challenging or ignoring racial hierarchies, owners are assisted in their immediate goals but remain marked by their "difference."

Given the entrenched nature of capitalist, racial, cultural, and gender hierarchies, everyday owners, workers, and AAHOA representatives worked within them rather than refuting them entirely. The result resolves the paradox of their simultaneous integration akin to the American dream and entrenched marginalization as immigrant minority men and women, without prioritizing one side over the other. AAHOA representatives and owners, in particular men, achieved greater respect from franchises and the government, fewer criticisms from customers, greater profits, and greater agency in the workplace. Employees similarly adjusted to racial, class, and other hierarchies, for otherwise they faced a secondary labor market without the long-term prospect of owning their own motel. In these primarily micro-level ways, Indian American owners and employees furthered their occupational integration. So despite the explicit challenges revealed in Chapter 3, Indian Americans move toward the American dream.

However, a consequence of these efforts, in particular on the part of individual owners, was the inadvertent continuation of racialization, cultural normativeness, and patriarchy, all of which sustain Indian Americans' marginalization. Owners and employees could not overturn the basis of their various subjugations. Whites, men, Anglo-dominant culture, and business owners have their respective privileges reinforced as informants work within the surrounding hierarchies.

The results of integrating within existing hierarchies included an endurable citizenship, financial gains, and rising social prestige. Yet legitimacy still had to be defended. Therefore, owners and workers simply trying harder in what they were already doing would not lead to the American dream without these accompanying challenges, although it would edge them closer toward that goal.

I now turn to how owners adopted a similar approach of giving in to hierarchies in order to advance their personal lives.

5 The Possibility of Belonging

ONE AFTERNOON IN MARCH 2006, I interviewed an elderly immigrant couple in their independent motel. It was located near an exit ramp intersection off an interstate highway in a rural stretch between Akron and Cleveland. There was a single restaurant in the vicinity and no tourist attractions. This was one of the more isolated areas that I had visited.

The couple lived on-site, and we talked inside their sparsely decorated apartment as they tidied up and looked after their grandchildren. The grandfather was putting away the vacuum cleaner while the grandmother finished cleaning the kitchen. The setting was uninspiring. When the couple first arrived in the United States in 1981, they lived in California with relatives. They soon moved to Illinois to purchase their first motel, despite not knowing anyone there, eventually ending up in Ohio. When I asked them if they had been worried about moving to places where they would find fewer and fewer Indians than in California, the wife replied tersely, "No. No concerns because we need the business. We are poor." This straightforward answer reveals the motivation of many Indian American owners to move across the country, even to rural parts of Ohio. Yet owners wanted to form a sense of attachment to their locality. How is this possible under conditions such as these?

Owners' relations to locals, to co-ethnics, and even to family members take place within a capitalist enterprise that hovers over interpersonal dynamics (Bodnar 1985). How does an immigrant group create a cultural citizenship—that is, form a sense of belonging as full members of their public space—when they are both a cultural/racial minority and scattered geographically? More specifically, how do they form connections with native-born locals? How do they form personal relationships with co-ethnic owners when engaged in business competition? And how does one create a sense of home when living in a motel, apart from residential areas?

Local Community

Indian Americans encountered their share of cultural and racial tensions with locals. Such tensions are common for ethnic entrepreneurs, in particular middleman minorities (Gold 2010). Locals often feel that immigrant owners are "taking over" their area and possibly disrespecting customers (Capeci 1985). Owners of lower-budget motels in particular could be viewed as polluters of the area. Cheaper motels—regardless of owner—can bring down the quality of a neighborhood by "inviting" nefarious activities through their low prices and owners' presumed lack of oversight. Numerous examples of tensions exist.[1] For example, an Indian American–owned independent motel in East Cleveland (a city on the eastern border of Cleveland) became associated with prostitution and drug dealing and had been the scene of violent crimes. A couple of days after a white, approximately 30-year-old prostitute was found tied up and dead in her room at the motel, local residents and the mayor promised to shut the motel down. As written in the Cleveland *Plain Dealer* in 2007,

> "Nothing else goes on over there but drugs and prostitution," said Andrew Maloney, who runs Andrew's Auto Service across the street from the motel. Mayor Eric Brewer was similarly uncomplimentary, saying the place was poorly run. Brewer promised that city inspectors will be aggressive in citing building-code violations, and he plans to "hammer

them until they are found to be a nuisance," which would allow the city to take the business to court.[2]

The mayor's explicit goal was to close the motel regardless of changes the owner would make, with the assumption that doing so would eliminate a blight in the community. Yet this tactic does not address the causes of crime. Still, longtime residents of economically struggling towns across the country have been known to blame Indian motel owners for their city's conditions. And although locals' impressions of these motels as moral polluters are not limited to Indian American–owned places—lower-budget motels encounter such critiques regardless of owners' ethnicity—Indian Americans' immigrant minority status makes them easier targets for such concerns.[3] Purchasing cheaper motels catalyzed Indian Americans' prolific growth, but such motels were also a source of these stereotypes and challenges.

This stereotyping of Indian American motels resembles the racialization of Chinatowns of old (and still today, to a degree), for the space itself becomes viewed as corrupting. Furthermore, the form of pollution seen to be associated with these spaces is similar, that of a hypersexualized environment that threatens neighbors' purity, safety, and health (Shah 2001). Like urban enclaves, people live in or spend the night in these businesses, including the owners themselves. So both motels and Chinatowns house social ills. Lower-budget owners often exist in a sharply different hierarchy than their co-ethnic model minority in higher-budget establishments, who are not polluters but welcome to areas according to public rhetoric.[4]

This awkward relationship of Indian American motel owners and locals was not defined simply by their being motel owners, nor was it limited to lower-budget owners. The overwhelming majority of Gujarati owners, including among informants, are Hindu, which places them apart from standard culture. In Ohio, for example, public references to Christianity extend beyond church signs and talk radio. Although this practice is arguably less prevalent than in Bible Belt states, it is a marked departure from the cosmopolitan sites of other research on Indian

America. Some vivid examples are in the town of Lima, Ohio. As one nears the exit for Lima driving south on Interstate 75, one sees on the right a corporate building with a large, highly visible sign on its left side that reads, "Christ Is the Answer." Another on its right side reads, "United States Plastic Corp." For a while a strip mall had a sign near the street that, as one might expect, advertised deals in the stores—it also proselytized that one should believe in Christianity. This is in addition to the number of churches in the town. Christianity is dominant throughout the United States, but one difference in the heartland is the lack of obvious religious heterogeneity. There are Hindu temples, mosques, synagogues, and the like in Ohio. Still, a Christian normativeness pervades public discourse on religion and the landscape; non-Christian religions are noteworthy for their differences.

Creating Ties

Indian American owners and their families could have sequestered themselves within their community, connecting with locals only when necessary.[5] When immigrant minorities, whether affluent or working class, face hostility from another race, they are less likely to forge a relationship with them. Instead, they identify with their ethnic group apart from the mainstream or they reject their ethnic background in an attempt to join with their host country (Portes and Zhou 1993; Waters 1999). Even affluent immigrants and their descendants experience tensions with locals, which leads them to affirm ties to their ethnic group (Kibria 2002; Purkayastha 2005; Tuan 1998). Because so much scholarship explains why ethnic solidarity persists despite immigration, groups' relations with locals have been overlooked. As a result, it is hard to understand how ethnic groups create ties to others despite tensions with them.

Indian American owners of all economic levels sought meaningful relations with locals but did not signal an assimilation trajectory. Their manner and results varied depending on their resources and acculturation. As is common with immigrant professionals, owners with greater resources took on a model minority image, that of a minority group whose economic accomplishments make them worthwhile additions to a local environment, especially compared with native minorities (Hintzen 2001). Owners with stronger English skills and a more secure economic footing claimed a model minority status in establishing relationships with political and economic leaders. An owner of two motels in the Akron/Canton area said, "Indian people have made friends. Developers are friends. City mayors are friends. Government people. So they have made a name, which we didn't have that many years ago." An owner of a higher-middle-budget motel near Columbus explained how his immigrant status raised his profile among locals:

> When you are self-made and you have your own [business]—and interestingly that is higher [from] non-Indians, that perception of [you]— they put you on a higher pedestal. Because I come from another culture and I made it here in this culture. So that factors in to the general people, the nonimmigrant population, the non-Indian population. They look at that and say, "Whoa, you made it."

This owner felt respected *as* an ethnic minority.

Rather than try to appear comparable with the majority only as successful entrepreneurs, informants also publicly expressed their culture. They wanted to create a shared respect for their heritage and thereby diminish barriers from the mainstream. Those with the most resources, in this case English skills and opportunities to interact with locals (that is, well-established immigrants and the second generation), more often attempted multiculturalism. On occasion individuals displayed their culture publicly with peers. One second-generation teenage girl in Lima spoke enthusiastically of her cultural performances at her school:

> I love being Indian. It's different. I was in a talent show and did an Indian dance. It's my talent. I love the culture. It's different. . . . In school they sometimes refer to India. . . . I enjoy hearing about it. I'm an Indian. I'm from there. . . . I don't try to hide it.

For the most part, though, Indian Americans shared their background in one-on-one interactions. First-generation owners would sometimes discuss their homeland with inquisitive customers. The 1.5 and second generation had more opportunities for dialogue with classmates and friends. A young woman in Lima who had spent half of her life in India and half in the United States said,

> I only have a couple of friends who are really interested in India. They could care less, but they are good friends of mine. They know I am Indian and I have my own things to do, and they have their own things to do. But there are a few that really like to get involved, and they like to try food and come to functions and things like that.

Youth bonded with locals as ethnic Americans. Even in a town like Lima—predominantly white and not particularly cosmopolitan—they encountered not ridicule of their background but reactions ranging from indifference to interest.

Lower-budget motels and immigrants with limited acculturation also bonded with their locality apart from co-ethnics. Generally, such entrepreneurs and middleman minorities are expected to have weak, if any, ties to locals because of the criticisms and prejudice of customers along with their often limited proficiency in American culture (Duany 1989; Levine 1977; Zenner 1980). They presumably live as "potential wanderers" and "strangers" within their area (Min 1996; Wolff 1950, cited in Bonacich 1973). They may never move out of their area but always hold on to the possibility. They are not motivated to learn about local customs or exchange a meaningful dialogue about lifestyles. Literature on the children of entrepreneurs highlights their distance from other groups partly because of their upbringing in a small business (Park 2005; Song 1999).

Despite these predictions, lower-budget owners found the basis for a professional and lifestyle link to the mainstream. They asserted that as business owners, they deserved full citizenship. As one owner of a low-budget franchise in a Cleveland suburb said,

> Motel owners [of all levels] are respected. Whether you are a PhD or a motel owner, you did the same thing. The PhD—you have to work six, seven years. The motel owner also worked hard. You own your own

business and worked hard. You are a businessman. That is respected. . . . Customers learn from all around that Indians are good, hardworking professionals, business owners. Prejudice goes down gradually.

Even though lower-budget owners in effect invoked the same model minority stereotype as higher-budget owners, they had a different definition of what belonging meant. They did not count on warm collegiality with local leaders to signal acceptance. Instead, without a higher social status or English fluency, they felt well received when simply not mistreated as foreigners. As the proprietor of an independent motel in Lima said,

> [I] feel like equal member of Lima. This is our hometown. As long as nobody bothers or gives a hard time, you feel good. . . . If [white motel owners] don't listen and cause problems, [we] can say look, you're U.S. citizens, we're U.S. citizens. . . . If customers come, we chat with them. Say, if you need anything, we can help you.

By promoting a positive image as law-abiding minorities, especially compared with other immigrants, Indian Americans raised their status in the eyes of customers and government agencies. A recent immigrant in Toledo, who lacked fluency in English, said,

> [Indian Americans have a] good image. [Other Indian Americans tell me] that's a good image, so I think it's a good image. . . . I do not have any American friends. . . . [Americans are] nice. Every time I go anywhere, they help me out. When I come [to the United States], I don't speak English very well. When I go to the bank, everywhere, they help me out. They don't think that if he don't speak English—they don't laugh at you.

The lack of negative treatment signaled a welcoming space. Although relatively cursory, such incidents helped informants feel part of their area and less wary of outsiders.[6]

Regarding cultural differences, owners with less acculturation or fewer resources did not feel as comfortable advocating multiculturalism.

Instead, they engaged in the reverse: they conceived of mainstream norms as already inclusive of their own. This required some creative cognitive work at times. They found support for their culinary and religious preferences within mainstream culture. Food is a fundamental component of culture. Many Indian Americans are vegetarian. Few restaurants in non-metropolitan areas, however, are such or even offer significant vegetarian options. Rather than dwell on this, informants highlighted the selections available with a glass-half-full attitude. For example, one owner grew up mostly in India before moving to Chicago as a young man. Now in Lima, Ohio, he missed the urban life with its variety of dining options. Still, he embraced the area. "I go to Mexican restaurant and eat vegetarian. I go to Taco Bell and get things with beans. Burger King has a veggie patty. I don't think that for 10 percent of the population you have to change everything." Here *Burger King* became a vegetarian-friendly place. This is a far cry from the Indian ethnic enclaves of Jackson Heights in New York City and Devon Street in Chicago. The owners demonstrate an everyday agency in their ability to construct an alternative meaning to their geography, namely, meat-based restaurants (de Certeau 1984).

Similarly, an immigrant owner in Lima was a practicing Hindu but did not mind seeing the public signs of Christianity mentioned earlier. In fact, he actually appreciated them:

> I like the signs. They inform you, here is a god. You follow the god rules. . . . I'm living here; all people are Christians. [Still,] no one forces me. Whatever I like, I do it. They are saying go this way to god. If you don't like this way, don't worry.

Religion distinguished Hindus from the Christian majority, but religious differences need not result only in separation. Indian Americans can create ties to the mainstream as Hindus by accentuating their traditional values and heritage within a multicultural format, especially post-9/11, in which Islam has become the religion of the enemy. Hinduism facilitates these connections because it does not rely on a single text or doctrine. Being a religious minority without local institutional support (for example, a temple or cultural association) was easier to handle if immigrants felt tied to the majority religion. Their efforts made them feel part of their town, even if locals were unaware of it.

Limitations to Local Ties

Informants' attempts to connect with locals, rather than only with their ethnic community, created an attachment to their surroundings. Yet their efforts can have the unintended consequence of curbing acceptance of other minorities and themselves as equal residents. Regarding those with more resources, the model minority stereotype is one of the few means Indian Americans have to bolster their social image. This is especially true in places like Ohio that lack a deep history or nuanced understanding of the race. But the stereotype reinforces a racial hierarchy of African Americans and Latinos on the bottom and also undermines Indian Americans' efforts to achieve full belonging. It suggests that their presumed foreign character makes them successful, as discussed in Chapter 4 (also see Park 2005). It is this same foreign character that perpetuated informants' negative encounters with government agencies, franchisors, and others. The respect owners have earned has depended on their estrangement, at least in theory, from being full Americans. They could have a difficult time undermining stereotypes as foreigners, especially when it is not in others' interests to befriend them. The same outcome pertains to owners with fewer resources who are successful in framing themselves as the model minority.

The cultural displays of informants with greater resources also, and unavoidably, affirmed a benign multiculturalism, that is, an acceptance of immigrants' cultural aspects that ultimately supports the dominant group's norms and institutions rather than creating deep cultural respect (Wolfe 2000). In regions that lack significant diversity and a history of immigration, advocating for true multiculturalism proves difficult. So informants came to expect a limited degree of cultural acceptance. For example, the 1.5-generation Indian American woman quoted earlier accepted religious barriers with her Christian friends in one-on-one interactions. Unlike other research findings, she reported no outright hostility toward Hinduism (Kurien 2007). Still, even those few who took an interest in her background did not want to discuss religion. She reported, "They know what I think about [religion], so they won't say much to me, because they know that what I think, I'll stick with it." The devaluing of non-Christian faiths at the public level in her town continued in the private level. A silencing of religious diversity occurs frequently for religious minorities, despite their own attempts to create a dialogue across faiths. A full sense of belonging becomes less likely under such conditions.

The dance performance by the teenage girl at her school also advocated for a restricted cultural acceptance, even as it pushed cultural boundaries. She referred to her background as "my talent," which made being of Indian descent comparable with other talents, such as playing guitar. In other words, it can be enjoyed by others at an aesthetic level devoid of a history. The movements of this Bollywood-inspired dance stem more from MTV than from Indian classical form (Chatterjea 2004). The audience applauded a cultural display that appears benign yet is still exotic, even as it was meaningful and artistic for the performer. This impression of ethnicity makes it harder for ethnic minorities to gain acceptance when asserting substantive or controversial differences, like religion. Even this girl recognized a possible limit to interracial acceptance despite her justified pride in her intercultural performances. She said, "It's going to be awkward. . . . I don't think we're ever *really* going to belong because this is America. But we can try."

The efforts by owners with fewer resources also facilitated a local citizenship to a degree but recognized their secondary social status. Not being ridiculed or forced to incorporate meat into one's diet or told to adopt a different religion is one thing. But being able to fully express one's cuisine or faith at the public and interpersonal levels is something else entirely and was something that informants could rarely do. Many believed that as recent immigrants, they were akin to guests who should make themselves comfortable in someone else's home. Overall, informants created a deeper level of integration than normally expected for immigrants, but it depended on a lack of full inclusion rather than signaling a trajectory of full equality.

Ethnic Community

More central to informants' sense of belonging were their connections to co-ethnics. The assumption in most discussions of immigrant community life is that there is a supportive network of co-ethnics who are brought together through ethnic spaces, celebrations, and friendships and who provide each other with economic and emotional support (Ling 2004; Logan, Zhang, and Alba 2002; Zhou 1992). A less popular—and counter—framing of ethnic communities emphasizes their fissures, such as labor exploitation between co-ethnic workers and bosses, and job competition between workers (Kwong 1996; Mahler 1995). Ethnic entrepreneurs are portrayed similarly, either as primarily sharing social and economic resources and organizing for common interests or as divided because of rivalries over the same customers and a desire for higher class status (Abelmann and Lie 1995; Bonacich and Modell 1980; Light 1972; Min 2008; Yoon 1997; Zhou 2004).

Recognizing the deficiency of this collegiality-versus-conflict framing, some researchers have considered both dynamics as applicable to ethnic communities. Most relevant to this research on motel owners, Parreñas (2001) argues that Filipina domestic servants in the diaspora experience both ethnic solidarity and anomie. The co-ethnic bonds come from a shared background, reliance on each other for jobs, and shared investment in business. Yet this harmony is challenged, if not undermined, by the competition between one another for jobs and by their commercial treatment of one another within their micro businesses. In other words, much of what unites them also divides them.

Co-ethnic Competition and Schisms

Despite a culture of mutual assistance, business competition and other schisms created hurdles in owners forming close relations with other owners unless they were already connected as kin or longtime friends (Jain 1989). Neither independent owners nor franchise owners were immune from business rivalries. Independent owners could not count on brand loyalty to limit the need to compete with other owners. Franchisees depended on brand loyalty and service and often claimed that they did not worry about other motels in their market. Theoretically each brand serves a different segment of the market. Yet such distinctions can be lost on customers, as explained in Chapter 4.

The degree of competition between owners varied by geography. Owners agreed that the tension among owners in the South was much more intense because of its high density of Indian American owners. Still, tensions could be anywhere. An owner of a middle-budget franchise in South Bend, Indiana, would go online to check the room rates of another franchise that was located right next to his. He claimed the rivalry prevented him and the other owner from being friends. Owners also tried to convince customers that their motel was a better deal than a neighboring competitor. For example, I heard a franchisee in Ohio tell a customer whose friend was staying at a nearby establishment that he could give the friend a better rate and overall experience, which the customer should relay.[7] Lowering rates to beat one's competition was not uncommon, especially as the number of fellow Indian owners in one's vicinity increased. An elder motelier who typically highlighted the camaraderie among Indian American owners nevertheless had this to say:

> Indian can lower rates when preferable. . . . Will say, don't let the customer walk out. An Indian knows how to do that. If got a lot of room vacant, will lower rate. . . . It's a rule—you got six Indians on a block, you're going to have a rate war.

Owners with few motels in their vicinity rarely changed their rates. In other words, greater competition trumped the possibility of greater camaraderie.

Owners of clearly different budget levels could form ties with one another more easily because of their lack of direct competition. For example, an owner of a lower-budget franchise outside Cleveland socialized on occasion with an owner of a middle-budget franchise about a half-mile away. As he said, "I am at a different level than [the other motel]. So no competition." Yet the differences between owning a lower-budget motel and owning a middle-budget motel led to such distinct experiences as to preclude deep commonalties. As one owner of a middle-lower-budget franchise in Toledo said about an independent owner he was related to,

> There's a big difference [between] running a hotel like this and then going over to [my relative's independent motel] or something like that. I mean, whatever you're going to have [in common] is a coincidence. . . . He doesn't even know what franchise fees are, not even a taste. It's too different.

In effect, the more that owners had in common, the more competition they experienced, as capitalism constrained relations (Bodnar 1985). Nor did owners find camaraderie with non-Indian motel owners (typically whites) (Dhingra 2009b).

The differences between middle-budget/higher-budget and lower-budget owners were reflected in how they ran their businesses. According to lower-budget owners, they needed to cut costs to make a profit given their fewer rooms and lower prices, but hopefully without damaging the quality of the establishment. A frequent habit was monitoring the usage of utilities. For example, one proprietor said, "Cut down water bill, electric. Turn heat on five rooms, rent those. Then turn another five rooms. Some people rent a room in small motel and turn heat on quick right after rented. Tell wife to turn on." No expense was too small.

In contrast, owners of middle- and upper-budget motels prioritized different kinds of work. Instead of spending time mowing the lawn, checking in guests, and turning off lights, middle- and higher-budget owners engaged in training employees, marketing, negotiating better contracts with banks, researching other investment opportunities, and so on. In this sense they were akin to white owners. A white manager of a middle-budget franchise said in response to how he tried to increase profit,

Be involved in the community, keep up on sales calls. Visit with businesses if interested in staying here. Clean rooms. Community involvement in projects: projects with the school, teacher of the year. Gives word out to the community [about the motel]. . . . [Because] someone has to tell [outsiders] the best place to stay.

Notably, he did not mention cutting costs. When I pointed out to a second-generation owner that many immigrants seemed to view motels as a livelihood to protect, whereas the children considered it as a business to buy and sell, he replied,

Bingo. When you think of something as an investment, you think of it from a revenue perspective. The first generation thinks of it from a cost perspective: if I live on the premises, I save money. If I fire my front desk person, I save 7 dollars an hour.

The division between owners also reflected ontological differences about the nature of one's work. Higher-budget owners did not define themselves as motel owners but as professional businesspeople, whose line of business happened to be motels. They were in the real estate and hospitality industries. One second-generation female motelier emulated Donald Trump and other large-scale real estate capitalists.[8] These owners did not just "work" but engaged in "intellectual labor," and they referred to rooms as "products" and "commodities."

The different approaches to running their business could lead to schisms among owners, most often across generations. As a second-generation proprietor of a middle-higher-budget motel said,

The problem is that [lower-budget immigrant owners] have never taken the time to further their education from a business standpoint, from a real estate type of standpoint. All they know is that we build hotel rooms and we sell them. So the way they speak about their industry is very amateur. Their focus is on—oh, that guy dropped his rate ten bucks, I'm dropping mine lower. . . . Because they don't understand that you have got to drive rates. OK? You've got to have rate integrity. . . . The only person you are going to hurt is yourself and the whole market. And that's why there was a lot of backlash with Americans. There are these Indians coming in and destroying the market.

According to this logic, immigrants created their own problems by focusing on cutting costs.

It was not just the second generation offering up these criticisms. Immigrants with middle- and higher-budget franchises also criticized lower-budget owners as unprofessional even while they respected their hard work. An owner of a middle-higher-budget motel near Columbus talked about independent motel owners who had been targeted by a city government in Ohio for closure. He felt these owners could have prevented the government's action.

> Some of [these targeted motels] do need to be shut down because [the owners] have sucked every drop of blood from the hotel. And they don't put money into it. . . . It is happening all over where they are shutting down these hotels because they know that the person on the other side of the hotel is defenseless. . . . So if you are invested in the system and you are a good neighbor, then you meet with the clergy and the neighborhood association and they will see [your] face also [and work with you].

Run-down places were not the norm, but their very existence fit a stereotype that resonated. Such critiques pertained to owners who had not kept up their properties as much as possible. Yet many run-down motels required more maintenance than owners with limited revenue or capital to secure loans could afford, which some higher-budget motel owners did not always recognize.

Disagreements over management styles could lead to friction within families because parents typically owned or had heavily invested in their children's motel. For example, at an AAHOA convention, a second-generation woman who ran an economy motel in New York City, confided that she constantly argued with her father over her style of management. The father felt that when she was out of the motel, she was not working, whereas she said that she could be productive from home and that she felt it necessary to attend meetings and events outside the motel. One second-generation owner actually regretted his upbringing within an Indian-owned motel. When asked what impact his upbringing in a motel had, he replied,

> I think it's actually a detriment. . . . I think that what it makes us end up doing is we keep wanting to do things—we keep reverting back to doing things the way they did them. Well, you know, to give you an example. My dad painted the entire motel himself in 1974. Right? I'm never going to do that. But if it's painting room 107 and it's going to cost me a couple hundred bucks, I'll be like yeah, I'm not doing anything this weekend, why don't I just go paint it. And that really—you don't think it's taking away from you because it's just a weekend day or it's just two hours to fix the lock or I just got to sit at the desk for four hours, you don't think it's taking a lot out of you. But it is because it's time that you could be spending doing something else.

Another owner similarly referred to his mimicking of his parents' do-it-yourself style as a "trap that I fell into. . . . And those days are really over, but it's hard to let go, I guess."

Just as the second generation judged the first, the first judged the second. An owner of a lower-budget franchise near Cleveland shared her impression of the second generation:

> But the kids these days, they don't want to do this business. The few who are still in the business—the new generation—they don't have to work as hard as we did. Because most of them—we started out independent. These days it's all franchise. . . . Plus they are born into [some wealth], so they don't have to work as hard. While my son is handling the business, he's not going to go and do the laundry or—at the most he will do the front desk when you need somebody.

Whereas many immigrants entered the industry because they could live in the motel and attend to their families without needing child care, few in the second generation treated it as a family space. It was a workplace just like any other professional, corporate site.

Gendered practices also limited social engagements for women. Some wives explained their less amount of leisure time relative to their husbands as their own preference. One female owner south of Toledo offered this:

> Everyone is busy. Running from motel to home to kids' school to mother's appointment. We don't have time. Men and women have different kinds of habits. . . . Women get together less than men. Men go outside in evening time, get a drink together. Most of the women don't drink. . . . Adult parties I don't like to go. I go once in a while, but I keep worrying about my kids.

Other wives referenced gender hierarchy. An owner near Cleveland noted:

> [Even if women plan to get together,] they have to look after the kids, look after the in-laws, they have to cook for the guests. They have other responsibilities. Men can get up and go. [Women] will do three or four weeks and they will fall out. "Oh, I cannot go, my in-laws are coming. I cannot go, my kids are . . ."

Immigrant women often experience greater—not complete—domestic freedoms once they are living and working in the United States than when in their homeland. Small business owners, however, may experience a divergent trend as the patriarchy common in families carries over to their work lives (Baines and Wheelock 1998; Lee 2005). The result is possibly less of a community engagement than preferred.

Transnational, Virtual, and Regional Ties

Tensions between Indian American owners, along with their busy schedules, often precluded their becoming friends. Furthermore, friendships between owners and Indian Americans of other professions were limited due to occupational and status differences (Dhingra 2009b). As a result, Indian Americans often turned outward for a sense of community, to family and friends abroad, mostly in India. In Ohio, their transnationalism took place at the individual rather than the group level, that is, they connected to India but not through local or regional organizations. Besides communicating by phone and email, owners visited India every few years (if that often—it was extremely difficult to leave the motel for any length of time), typically in the winter and usually for a wedding or some other family ceremony. They also sent remittances to family in Gujarat. And Gujarat is encouraging nonresident Indians to travel to and invest in their homeland, such as through financial assistance, guarantees of electricity stability, and more.[9]

Television created a more consistent transnational linkage (Dudrah 2002).[10] In nearly every living room of the motel homes that I visited, there was little furniture except for a sofa, a chair, a coffee table, and a large-screen television. These televisions were frequently on. And almost everyone subscribed to Dish network, which provided up to sixteen television and radio stations, primarily in Hindi.[11] These stations offer Indian soap operas, comedies, movies, news, sports, and religious programming as well as local and U.S.-based programming. One network, TV Asia, specializes in diasporic programming, including AAHOA events. I spoke with a TV Asia representative. She estimated that half of the stories she covered involved AAHOA, including coverage of its regional conventions throughout the country.

> [The channel is popular because] it's the only channel that serves the local Indian community. Nobody else does it. . . . [Viewers] want to see . . . their faces, let's put it that way. They want to see their town, their events, their children on TV Asia.

In a medium that portrays Americans as white and Indians as living in India, attention to the diaspora filled a niche for viewers. And because these owners lived in their workplace and spent all of their time in a single setting, a large-screen television seemed to be a worthwhile investment.

These relatively standard sources of transnationalism connected individuals to India but not to social networks within the United States, which they also sought. The academic emphasis on the transnational and the local has overlooked the regional as a meaningful geographic space. Informants referred to relatives living a few hours away as part of their close network (Dhingra 2009b). Organized means of associating with those of their ancestral villages and marriage circles were also popular. Some Patels (more specifically, various subsets of Patels) held occasional village reunions in the United States and took part in network associations and related conventions.[12] Owners also had directories of U.S. Patels of their particular ancestry. The directory lists families' names, parents' occupations, and age and gender of children. One owner took pride in demonstrating how she could learn about people and eventually arrange marriages. These associations and publications provided the structure for network building within the United States, helping to expand networks as well as providing social support within an otherwise possibly isolated immigrant experience arising not only from being away from the homeland but also, for many, from being located in a rural area.

Occupational and Social Bonds Among Local Owners

Despite these alternative forms of community, the most significant source of ethnic ties involved one's local peers.[13] Even with the tensions between owners discussed previously, informants wanted camaraderie locally and depended on one another as ethnic resources in order to survive in the industry. They accomplished this through professional interactions and through social interactions revolving around rituals.

Business oppositions shaped but did not define relations among owners. Informants recognized one another not merely as competition but also as ethnic resources. Gujarati owners were more likely to help one another than they were to help non-Gujarati owners (Kalnins and Chung 2006). As is common for ethnic entrepreneurs, motel owners came together when responding to external pressures, such as from franchisors and the government. Such social capital proved essential for running a profitable motel. This support manifested itself in a variety of ways, including suggestions for whom to hire or call for repairs, where to purchase supplies, and even when to expect bureaucratic hurdles. For example, during my interview of an independent owner in Lima, he received a phone call from an owner of a peer establishment, who told him that a government representative was making the rounds to inspect motels. Another owner with few connections to others in the city received a similar phone call. Comparable calls were not made to non-Indian owners. Assisting a co-ethnic owner helped ensure reciprocated support down the line. These owners also turned to AAHOA as a resource, to find vendors, to talk with mortgage brokers and other financial representatives, and more.

Also, despite a schism with some immigrants, the second generation appreciated aspects of their work strategy. Even the informant who expressed regret at growing up in a small motel noted,

> The fundamentals of the business of strong customer service, of making sure you understand your numbers, what rates you can charge—those fundamentals are still the same [as for immigrant owners]. . . . I went back to that base knowledge when I came back from business school. We had a property that was severely underperforming. It's twenty-five rooms, dumpy, one-star property in a very, very good market. And all I did was work through those numbers the way that my dad did, you know. . . . I cut [all the amenities] out. . . . So that was pretty much purely from that fundamental knowledge. It has nothing to do with my M.B.A.; it has nothing to do with my education.

As far as the differences between lower-budget and middle-/higher-budget motels discussed earlier, they do exist. But there is also a certain amount of overlap in their management techniques. Higher-budget motels and hotels (regardless of owner) engage in their own cost-saving strategies (Stepick and Grenier 1994). Owners employ primarily part-time workers. Employees could be paid less than the minimum wage and have illegal deductions taken out of their checks, such as for scheduled breaks. Health and safety standards could be compromised as well. In other words, lower-budget owners' practices of keeping the lights off or not renovating frequently fits a broader pattern found in more "respectable" businesses and should be seen as such.

Also, many if not most owners used a combination of "physical" and "intellectual" business tactics. For instance, an immigrant owner of a lower-budget franchise in Toledo strategized on how to drive up occupancy through marketing:

> Coupons, newspapers, AAA books, signs, fliers. Special newspaper comes out. . . . [Still,] our goal is less towards marketing and more towards cutting costs. If have to run with American staff, you won't meet costs.

The ubiquitous signs for lodging on interstate highways also constituted basic-level marketing. One independent motelier near Toledo said that his sign on the highway and the second one on the exit ramp cost him around a thousand dollars per year. Lower-budget owners may not have prioritized marketing or the like as much, but they may not benefit as much from such strategies. Also, independent motels indirectly help franchises, and so they work together in the hospitality industry. They serve a poorer clientele, which alleviates franchises from criticism of pricing out a customer segment. So, professional ties could be found even across budget levels.

Further connecting owners were social engagements outside the workplace. In order to create solidarity despite competition and schisms, they often depended on ritualistic interactions, which does not always mean religious or ceremonial affairs set aside from daily life. A ritual is any symbolic and structured practice indicative of social relations that commands attention and communicates a shared moral order, in this case shaped by ethnoreligious ties (Wuthnow 1989). As people become engaged in the ritual at hand, they pay less attention to their other interests (Collins 1994). As such, ritualistic settings can allow for both social capital and social distance between participants, which suited owners who wanted to socialize despite their rivalries in business.

A key social ritual for Gujarati men was volleyball.[14] Only men participated, about twenty at each of the five games I attended.[15] They rented out public and private volleyball courts in their local towns for weekly or biweekly games. The men ranged in age from early twenties to upper fifties. Players typically divided into three teams. One team would watch and then take the place of the team that lost. A game was constantly going on, so people could not sit removed from the activity for too long. Two men from the team not currently playing served as line judges.

The volleyball games enabled social bonding because they functioned as more than just a leisure sport. They served as a ritualistic encounter. And the more effort required for a ritual, the more belonging it produces for participants (Marshall 2002). The games took place during early evening, usually for a period of about two hours. The same people typically attended. Meaningful divisions between owners—such as whether one was the first or second generation or owned a franchise or an independent (most players had lower-budget motels, whether independent or franchise)—did not impact the match. Instead, having put their cell phones and keys aside and wearing short-sleeved T-shirts and shorts or sweatpants, players competed side-by-side. They were engaged in the action, taking points won and lost seriously. They pushed teammates to play harder and smarter. They apologized for mistakes and applauded teammates for good shots. I was struck by how intently they focused on what could have been a very casual leisure activity. In addition, the activity was reminiscent of the masculine, ethnic culture of Gujarat. The game is popular in Gujarat, and owners played it here as in Gujarat, in a style one player called "direct" as opposed to the American "indirect" manner: players did not set up teammates to get a penetrating shot, as is typical in American-style volleyball. Instead, every time the ball came over the net, a player hit it back to the other side, like tennis. That most profane of subjects, business, was seldom discussed during the ritual. In fact, those who were playing rarely spoke at all except to correct a teammate or make an occasional light-hearted comment in reference to the game. Those sitting and watching talked more. They talked about the game that was in play, they joked around with each other, and occasionally there would be some generic motel-related conversation, like vague complaints about staff.

An interest in community solidarity, rather than in a sports or leisure activity per se, motivated people to attend the games. For example, when I asked a 1.5-generation owner of a higher-low-budget franchise in

Toledo if he was comfortable in his city, given the fewer Indian Americans there, he replied tersely,

> Why do you think we [Indian owners] hang out with each other? Play volleyball couple times a week; we cook out. I don't see any [white] Americans there. No blacks there. That creates comfort. Why do I go to India every year?

The game is comparable to trips to India. It was not the game that mattered but the social support it created.

Most of motel owners' social interactions took place in gender-segregated spaces, partly because of cultural norms and partly because of staffing needs at the motel. I did not have access to women-only spaces. Women claimed that they socialized less frequently than did their husbands, which men mostly confirmed. There was no comparable scheduled outing like volleyball games for most women. Their socializing primarily took place as mothers, that is, with children. Women came together in late afternoons in one another's motels or homes when possible, more as a personal gathering than as a formal group. They also congregated at temples if one was nearby and/or in people's homes or motels for prayer meetings.

A main site for public social gatherings that involved both women and men was the Hindu temple. Husbands and wives came to the temple together and/or with their children, and mothers came with their children. If there was one in their area, many Gujarati Hindus attended a Swaminarayan temple. Swaminarayan is a particular sect of Hinduism. There are about sixty-five Swaminarayan temples in the United States and three in Ohio as of 2009, near the major cities of Cincinnati/Dayton, Cleveland, and Columbus.[16] This form of Hinduism practices even more elaborate ritual ceremonies than do other Hindu sects popular in the United States (Kurien 2007). The standard services across all Hindu temples take place Sunday mornings and/or evenings and are followed by a meal. The ritual aspect of temple services encouraged a social cohesion among attendees that required an investment of only part of themselves, their ethnoreligious background. Even for those not engaged in its rituals, the temple reminded them of their other commonalties.

Limits to the Co-ethnic Motel Owner Community

Informants' efforts to create strong ties did not overcome the structural impediments facing them. Actual bonds could remain limited, especially if people were not related or lacked ancestral ties. Occupational solidarity was not a guarantee of strong social ties. For example, owners who belonged to AAHOA did not cite closer relations to members than to nonmembers. Similarly, owners who called one another to pass on business-related information did not necessarily come together socially. The shared identity of ethnic owner was situational. As it dissipated from one context to the next, so did the unity. Relations across budget levels were easier to maintain because there was little competition. But as indicated earlier, such relations often lacked depth because of the very element that made them comfortable.

Similarly, ritualistic practices created social capital but did not necessarily result in strong relations. Rituals, because they are removed from the rest of daily life, provide a social cohesion but do not alter the group dynamic outside the spaces where they occur. Owners remained in a struggle for customers. As one owner said,

> We don't have [a] bunch of friends where you can hang out. You have a business and family, and you have to take care of that first. There is always time for socializing in weddings and picnics and volleyball. You don't want to call someone and say hello. We don't want gossip going on. . . . If I need help or they need, then you call.

Talking too much created the risk of revealing too much about one's own life ("gossip"), whether personal or professional.

Even when engaged in a ritualistic community, my observations and informants' comments confirm the absence of closeness between owners who lacked other types of connections (for example, the connection of kin). For example, in the parking lot after a volleyball game in Toledo, a franchisee pointed to an independent owner driving a newly purchased SUV, probably only a couple of years old, and asked rhetorically how he could afford that as an independent owner.[17] The question served as both a judgment of the owner's possibly questionable business practices and an indication of knowing little about this peer despite their playing together every week. Also, people generally dispersed after games. One player in Toledo was young, sociable, and in the same age range as some of the others, but he was not related to anyone. He commented that living in this area "sucks. No one likes to go to party. They all stay home. After game, they don't want to go to dinner or anything. Just want to go home." He did not even know that some people actually went out to dinner together after the match, including people his own age (who were related to one another). The smaller ethnic community in the area led to this predicament. Even when informants claimed to be friends with another, further conversation sometimes suggested otherwise. I would be asked by an owner what another charged per room, or even asked how many motels a person, considered a "friend," owned. In this sense rituals differ from personal conversations, gatherings with friends, and other commonplace activities that build deeper relationships. This is not to suggest that owners lacked these deeper relationships entirely. Many had them. But they typically involved members of one's extended family or friends from one's Gujarati village.

The lack of ethnic infrastructure in Ohio further limited people's opportunities to create even ritualistic bonds. Access to a temple proved difficult for many people because they were few and far between. Nor is convenience guaranteed as more temples are built. As mentioned in the Introduction, a new Hindu temple is to be constructed in Richfield, a rural/suburban village in northeastern Ohio that sits about halfway between Cleveland and Akron. Whether residents of Cleveland, Akron, or their suburbs will have the time and energy to drive the more than twenty miles each way to Richfield just for a temple service is unclear.

Business constraints also prevented some owners from forming ritualistic connections to co-ethnics. Those in independent motels needed at least one person in the motel at all times. Often the wife was relegated to staying in the motel. In addition to a lack of time, she might not know how to drive or feel confident communicating in English.

One owner had an upbeat attitude toward this. When I asked her if she got bored staying in the motel all day, she responded, "I have TV!" She watched Indian rather than American television shows. In effect, she is referring to virtual people rather than to real guests at her motel as breaking up her isolation.

The result for owners is the possibility of community. They found creative ways to create an ethnic community—in the diaspora, regionally, and locally—while sensing some distance from it. The "either/or" framing that currently dominates the literature on ethnic communities should be changed to a "both/and" framing. Communities entail both camaraderie and competition. Here we see *how* they coexist, not just that they can. Owners reached beyond their local vicinity, found business support, and engaged in ritual encounters. This perspective on how immigrants handle both their competition and their camaraderie can apply to ethnic entrepreneurs in larger cities as well. Such persons can more easily form ethnic ties given the much greater number of ethnic people and organizations in their area. Still, they, too, face barriers to a complete solidarity (Abelmann and Lie 1995; Yoon 1997). They may handle this duality with a reliance on rituals and other techniques.

Although such practices create solidarity, they do not create robust relations. The economic needs of owners limited close camaraderie, especially when revenue was down. Informants accepted that competition and schisms hovered above community dynamics, and they built meaningful relations within those limits. In other words, people form ethnic relations that can remain partially hypothetical.

Home

The other part of informants' personal lives is their home. Independent and lower-budget franchise owners often live in their motels as a means to save money. Among my informants, just over half lived in their motels, and all of those were immigrants. On the one hand, within an integration perspective, this is viewed as necessary but temporary for middleman minorities—the second generation rarely follows suit. On the other hand, if the American dream includes a house in the suburbs, then living in one's motel signifies a dream deferred. Viewed from this perspective, this strategy to save money led to a diminished sense of "home" for both parents and children because they had to constantly consider work and customers. In effect, they lived under surveillance. Yet owners create a meaningful sense of home within these constraints, one they thought others should envy. As for other aspects of owners' personal lives, their home experiences defy easy categorization.

Echoing the literature on stay-at-home employees and entrepreneurs, motel owners—in particular women—voiced the challenges in separating and balancing home and work, especially given the nature of running a twenty-four-hour/seven-day establishment (Duxbury, Higgins, and Thomas 1996; Loscocco 1997). Complaints by owners fell into three broad categories: (1) incessant work demands, (2) the geography surrounding the motels, and (3) the possibility of illegal and/or sexual activity on the premises, all of which broke down a desired notion of home.

Parents decried that the daily demands of owning a business took time away from their children and from relaxation. One owner of an independent motel lived in a separate home. She used to own a franchise that she lived in. She explained the differences in living situations:

> If I live in motel, it's easy. I can do housework during day. . . . [But,] it wasn't like home, home. . . . When at home you think of your family, not about work. When I was living in motel, I was thinking of customers might come. If helping kids with homework, a phone call could come at any moment. You can't focus on two things at once. . . . Now that living at home, it's different. At least for a little while the motel is out of my mind. When I lived there, the office is next door. After I sold the motel, I was still answering the phone [saying the franchise name]. You are always part of it.

Many of the strategies that lower-budget owners, in particular independents, initiated to save money on labor had the latent effect of making work further dominate the home sphere. As an independent proprietor in Lima claimed with a sense of pride over his ingenuity,

> I'm going to save the labor. When people come in and want to rent a room, they press a button. I hear a buzzer in my room [at home in the motel]. I set up a phone system. I don't have to answer every call. If they call and want to talk to a room, they can do that themselves. . . . I also carry a phone with me and can answer the phone anywhere.

Owners faced a trade-off between saving money and having real private time, and they almost always chose the former. Such owners spent a considerable amount of time in their homes. They had no choice. An independent owner with no paid staff felt resigned to this fact: "Thing is, when you don't have employees, you do a lot of things on your own. Like here, me and my wife, we are here twenty-four hours. Someone has to stay here, not matter if someone's checking in or not."

While in the motel, owners could sit and watch television, cook lunch, even take a nap, all while still technically working. Yet ironically, being at home so much meant getting used to lacking a private life. Guests were a constant disruption to private time. On occasion I showed up unannounced to motels. Once a husband was taking a nap, according to his wife. Owners in their apartments could often see or hear customers driving in and so had to stop what they were doing to attend. At first such instances struck me as unpredictable interruptions in one's day, but I soon gathered that the episodes were so common, albeit unscheduled, as to be how owners understood what daily life meant. Owners complained of the interruptions and appreciated their absence when they moved into separate homes, but they did not dwell on them as problems within motel life. When I was inside people's apartments for tea or interviews, the phone would ring as guests called for supplies, and it was taken in stride. When having tea in one family's motel apartment, the mother asked her teenage daughter to get her sari for her as they prepared to get ready for an outing that evening.[18] Soon after, the phone rang, which the daughter answered. She hung up and casually told her mother that some guests needed towels, which the mother, without looking up, then directed her to tell another employee to get. A private life was built around work intrusions that were heightened by required cost-cutting strategies.

Although guest intrusions are unpredictable, there is a standard time when guests check in, during late afternoon. Owners would try to finish some chores before that. One such chore was cooking dinner (Kang 2010). Owners cooked at whatever time they could. They ran large fans in the lobby to dispel cooking odors. Some preferred to finish earlier in the day so that the aroma of Indian food would not be noticeable during check-in time. Customers looked down on "curry motels." As one owner said of her cooking at her home behind the check-in desk,

> Customers don't like Indian cooking, makes big smell. Behind the office was living room and kitchen. Turn on fan, open the door. You are losing the business. If I have a choice, I don't live at motel. It makes a big difference to customer. Once they step outside the office, they criticize it.

Franchise owners with paid staff also had troubles relaxing when living in their motels. An owner in northeast Ohio grew up in a motel and lived in one for a while as an owner until moving to a separate house. He said of living in a motel as a franchise owner,

> It sucks basically. [Laughs] Well, you know, if you're at the property, you can't really sit at the hotel and do something else. If you're sittin' there for a few minutes and not doing things, you gotta say, "Well, let me see what's going on downstairs." The other thing is, which is an unfortunate thing, with employees. If they know that you're on-site, instead of taking the steps forward in doing their own problem solving and stuff, they'll just call you up. So like, we'll get a lot of customers they don't realize that you know, umm, even though we run a hotel, we have a life too, just like they do.

Customers, employees, and even owners themselves blur the boundaries between home and work, to the detriment of the private sphere. Even if a staff member was on duty, owners in lower-budget and even middle-budget motels still needed to be available for daily chores. If a guest requests a rollaway bed, the owner might have to interrupt his/her dinner to deliver it because the front-desk clerk cannot leave the post.

Children typically lamented growing up in a motel but did not resent their parents, for they understood the economic necessity behind the lifestyle (Park 2005; Song 1999). Like children growing up in any small family-owned business, many complained of having to chip in. As one informant said, "[I] grew up in motel. Helped out a lot. Like any small business, you help out." Girls and boys had similar degrees of work responsibilities, although their tasks were often gendered like their parents'. Parents emphasized that education was their top priority for their children but that children lent a hand in the motel when necessary.

The geographic location of motels also prevented a "normal home" for families. Those who grew up in motels were not idealistic about residential life; they knew that there were those who had less inviting homes. But it was still easy for them to believe the grass was greener on the other side of the lawn, a lawn they did not even have. As the daughter of owners said of growing up in an independent motel:

> It's different. You don't have a backyard or front yard. It's not a house. But it could be better than a house, when you see some houses. I wish I had an upstairs. But oh well, I don't have some things. If I had a backyard, I could have a swing set or something. In a motel you're obviously not going to have that.

It was not just growing up in a workplace that bothered them, it was *not* growing up in a residential district, where children were expected to grow up. An owner in Delaware believed that living in a motel deprived him of a "normal childhood":

> The opportunity to play with other kids and to have friends that live next door or across the street, rather than seeing different places every day and not having a friend close by that you can go to easily. . . . You know . . . with the neighborhood, or trick-or-treating for that matter.

Indicative of a lack of a "normal childhood," in visiting the motel apartments of families with children, I only occasionally saw children's toys

These are the "neighbors" of a franchise owner and his family, who live on-site in their motel in Ohio.

outside the apartment, that is, within public view. Instead, children's paraphernalia sat inside the home, including computers, televisions, books, games, tricycles, and so on. In effect, being a child and doing the things that children do was not allowed in most of the space in which the families spent their day. Parents wanted to give their children a more standard home environment. The notion of home is so powerful within the literature on immigration and Asian American studies partly because it is an elusive concept. "Home" is typically framed as nostalgia for the *homeland*. Here, the problem was not being too American but not being American enough, that is, not having the stereotypical suburban experience that "Americans" had.

More than the imposition of work and the workplace generally, some aspects of simply owning a motel broke down the ideal notion of home. In particular, illegal and/or sexual activities by customers in the rooms threatened the atmosphere parents hoped to build for their children. Owners criticized the use of motel rooms for sex, including the "quickie" business of prostitution, partly for its impact on children. As one said,

> I don't like the quickie business, so my kids are not there anymore. Some people tell their kids to check the rooms and see the crazy movie on. And kids watch that. Doesn't make sense to come to this country but lose your child to this. If that happens you don't make anything in life.

Immigrant parents in general worry about their children becoming too assimilated. Here, that threat came from within one's own home rather than only from the outside. An independent owner recounted a few instances at her motel that made her wish her children could have grown up in a residential area.

> Atmosphere is—business has bad image. One [motel] across the street has police problems. Drug problems at place across street. We had one time [a guest] checked in. And then some cars come. We called police and said there is something going on in this room. You can take care of it but not involve us. Police took him; they were looking for him. . . . Older son was living in motel; it was a run-down business. If I live in an apartment or house, he can enjoy with other kids. My older kid watches TV and playing games, [because] no one was around [in the motel]. I don't like my kids seeing police coming. After a while the kid was running around after us into the motel to clean up. He would see dirty movies and dirty magazines. I would cover it up but he would see it. At this motel, problem is still there. People are same everywhere. You can't control it.

A "proper" home meant a space that would not have such risks. Although other family-run businesses have their share of undesirable behavior, few also double as the owners' homes.

This framing of those living in their motels is not meant to romanticize those living in separate homes. Such owners could not totally avoid the "twenty-four-hour headache," as they put it, even when they had staff that would attend to most issues. They would still be called in at night on occasion. They often did paperwork at night rather than rest. And some had even more involvement. A proprietor of a lower-budget franchise kept his day job. He received calls on average once a week, such as when customers wanted a better deal for a room. When he came home at six o'clock, his job as a motel owner started in full gear. He said,

> We work nights, we work weekends. We do accounting from home. I spend two hours a night making sure the bank balance is not charging more, we have enough inventory, nobody's making the clock, how many rooms sold is the match rates—that's our housekeeping dollars. . . . My free time is going down.

He had installed video cameras at his motel and showed me how he was able to monitor employees through a software program on his home computer, which he frequently did in the evenings. His home computer sat in their living room, making his domestic life akin to owners who lived in their establishments. He would call employees to give advice or correct possible mistakes.

Creating Home

How did owners and their families vie for a private space if they lived at work? How did they continue to make a claim on the "white picket fence" scenario within the American dream? First, they rationalized that their choice was necessary and even beneficial in the long run. Owners could not control what some guests did. As a proprietor in a small town in northern Ohio said,

> This is business, this is how we make a living, we aren't doing anything wrong. . . . The parents don't have any choices really. They have to make money somehow, and that's the only thing that they have found to make money. . . . They would like to move on to a cleaner business, you know what I'm saying?

In terms of the effects on children, parents framed their decisions within an immigrant equation, weighing the pros and cons of raising their children within such an environment versus other alternatives. They often argued that despite the hassles, they raised better, more responsible children if in the motel. A lower-budget franchise owner's children helped in the motel, including with the rooms. When I asked him if they saw inappropriate material, he replied,

> After they become fourteen, fifteen, by then they know things. I know what you mean. We didn't like it but sometimes [from] the financial point of view, we have to save money—we have to do it. We want to pay for their education, we have to do it. I have two daughters who are educated.

This informant connected the sacrifice of his daughters seeing such materials with the opportunity to be educated; the latter was only possible because of the former. A mother pointed out that her husband grew up in a motel and witnessed mature situations and turned out fine as an adult, so having their children witness such materials in their current motel should be okay. Parents also stated that children learned the value of hard work and money by assisting in motels.

In addition, the motel could keep a family together throughout the workday, as is common for small family-owned businesses, in particular immigrant businesses (Bonacich and Modell 1980; Jung 2008). Female owners often cited family togetherness as a key reason for why motels suited them. Having to always be working was better than not having one's kids nearby, despite parents' complaints of work interfering with parenting. One owner in Wisconsin wanted to go into the motel business as a means of attending to her children while earning money. She said of her husband,

> Well, he is an engineer, he has his own good job, you know. And I have two boys, and I don't want to put my kids to the babysitter. So, I go in the motel business. I can take care of the kids at home and learn the motel too. . . . That's how I bought the motel when I have two little kids.

In contrast to motel owners, most other female entrepreneurs start a business when their children are older and they have more free time (Dhaliwal 1998).

Rather than envying others' residential situation, owners believed that others should envy them for their ability to attend to their children. An owner near Cleveland contrasted her enviable situation to the challenges facing working mothers today.

> Here is the thing: these days because I see the younger generation, they have both work and then family, baby. Maybe within a month either they are in day-care center or the grandparents have to help them out. . . . I can take care of the home and I can take care of the family and you know, it worked out for me. It was the best situation. The reason was—is whenever I wanted to get out of here, I could go. Say to somebody look out for my son. When he was growing up, we had a maintenance man. He used to follow him so I don't have a babysitter. [Laughs] And the, you know, schoolwise, I used to take them to school in the morning, drop them off, work whatever in the middle of it pick them up, taking them to the library or to the game. It was perfect.

Women often choose careers based on their schedule flexibility, so as to attend to child care. Because these mothers lived in their motels, they could take care of domestic needs while at work. They had no commute, no need for day care or babysitters, less reliance on prepackaged foods, and so on (Hill, Ferris, and Märtinson 2003; Kang 2010). Working at the motels allowed another enviable element, the ability to teach one's culture to one's children. Owners often commented that they could teach their children the Gujarati language and Gujarati values because they were home even when working.

Instead of just focusing on women's power in either the workplace or the home, we need to see how women's ability to bridge work and home signals their agency and helps make motel life amenable. Many found ways to combine elements of domestic and work obligations. A common example was doing the home laundry and work laundry simultaneously. They also could have their children join them in cleaning rooms and making beds. An elderly immigrant woman in a small independent motel in Lima said,

> I don't separate home and work. I do laundry for motel while cooking lunch or dinner. I like it. Business and residence in the same place—so you do work for both at the same time. It's better for wife to live and work in same place. We work faster.

A woman in Toledo, when talking about her evening plans, had just made her children a snack and then planned to set up some rooms before her sister-in-law arrived for tea. She too moved between domestic and work obligations rather than feeling the need to segregate them, which enabled her to manage her responsibilities more easily. As women work in the family business or even outside it, they do not necessarily accrue more power in the domestic sphere (George 2005; Kibria 1993). These informants could contest the second shift and the burden to work long hours at multiple tasks; instead, they took pride in being able to accomplish this workload "faster" through their enterprising efforts. Importantly, women's negotiation of this stratification allowed families to save money on hiring more staff.

Owners also justified their residential setting by deconstructing the presumed idyllic life of others in the suburbs as not that different from their own. When I asked an owner, who lived in a downtown motel in a city near Cleveland, if he regretted not having neighbors and a "normal" residential experience, he rebutted by asking me how often I socialized with my neighbors. When I replied that it was rare, he looked at me contentedly and said, "See?" Another owner of a lower-budget franchise that bordered a Wendy's fast food restaurant in a different commercial district outside of Cleveland said,

> Do you have to talk to others to feel part of the area? You live in a house. Do you have a talk to neighbors? Do you have to get together? You live your own life. They live their own life. Whatever they do, you have nothing to do with it. Same thing. If I live in this area, should people from another area come here and say "hello, hello"? No. Should I go there and say "hello, hello"? No.

From such a perspective, motel life seemed similar to the standard household.

Families who lived in their motels also responded to the intrusion of work into home through two distinct sets of practices: reversing the dynamic so that home life intruded into work, albeit to a measured extent, and segregating home from work. Owners integrated those aspects of home that did not challenge the standard image of a motel, and they segregated elements that otherwise would diminish the notion of a separate home.

Because owners, especially of independent motels, had broken down the boundary of work and home by making work part of their home lives, it made sense to bring their homes into their work lives. Independent owners did not have to wear a uniform and could more easily move back and forth between work and home spaces. They typically wore casual attire and no name tag. This is in contrast to franchise owners, who did not necessarily wear a uniform but dressed in a more business-casual mode, with shirts tucked into trousers, dress shoes, and so on.

Franchise owners also used their motel as an extension of home, although in ways that did not intrude on the guests' sense of "ownership" over the motel. As a proprietor outside Toledo said,

> We have a pool in the motel. We play with [our children] here. Those times are gone that customers are going to leave because you're seen. Even if today someone leaves because I'm sitting here [in the lobby], that's his problem.

Children in a pool could be anyone's children, not necessarily the owners. An owner of a middle-lower-budget franchise spent part of his morning sitting in the lobby, reading the morning paper and watching CNN on the lobby television while wearing his franchise name tag and attire of khaki pants and red, collared polo shirt.[19] It is a time of the day when new guests rarely check in and those staying can easily be attended to. He and his wife also maintained a small vegetable garden in the back of the motel. A garden beautified the area and so did not create a deviant picture. An independent owner watered plants outside the rooms. Families integrated personal aspects into the work sphere that, for the most part, did not disrupt and possibly enhanced a standard motel lobby or exterior.

Owners also created a sense of home by segregating those components that more clearly designated private interests, often related to ethnicity. This segregation was not simply to protect the business but also
to prevent their sense of home from being overrun by work. It involved
aesthetics and family norms, including a gendered hierarchy of domestic responsibilities. Owners compartmentalized home and work by having different physical aesthetics within each. As an independent owner
said of her home décor within the motel, "Oh yeah, you put your extra
touches in there. You put your wallpaper. Not the motel stuff. Plants,
whatever." Informants could save money on these items by using the
motel variety. But they wanted a break from work to the extent possible.
I saw a NASCAR blanket on a boy's bed, separate glassware and silver-
ware in kitchens, distinct wall hangings in living rooms, and the like. I
saw no motel supplies in people's homes, at least not in the main areas of
living rooms, bedrooms, and kitchens. Instead, these items were in their
offices or storage areas. In other words, it was not apparent within the
motel home that one was in a workplace.

Couples spoke in Gujarati to each other and occasionally to their children. Families used their Gujarati names. They played Indian music,
both religious and popular. They ate predominantly Gujarati and other
Indian foods for breakfast, lunch, and dinner. They also kept the ritual
of having a teatime. They decorated their homes with ethnic, often
Hindu symbols. These included pictures of the goddess Lakshmi, the
Hindu swastika sign, a Hindu calendar, and miniature temples in bedrooms. One home even had an ornate, indoor bench swing popular in
India. The motel homes felt like two-, three- or four-bedroom apartments. One owner said with pride,

> Yeah, we take a shower after we do laundry [and other motel chores],
> and then we sit. And you, like, change. You are the Desi part now.…
> Indian music, Indian TV. I like TV. Everybody has that now. America,
> you know, America is isolated. It's not like India.

As this quote suggests, there is little difference between being sequestered within one's motel apartment and being in a residential neigh-

borhood, for in the United States people are generally isolated. The real contrast in his mind was not between motels and neighborhoods but between the United States and India. Also, as he noted and as noted earlier, the most common way that motel owners and their families affirmed a backstage, ethnic boundary involved watching television.

Another way to create a sense of home involved standardized gender norms within the domestic sphere. The burden to create a "home" typically falls on women. Wives took care of the cooking and cleaning for the most part, despite the fact that husbands occasionally (some, regularly) cleaned motel rooms. An informant's husband had cleaned bathrooms in their motel, but she would not ask him to do the same in the house:

> I don't think I can make him clean the bathroom [inside the home]. This is my personal opinion. My man shouldn't have to do this. He has done it and he'll do it. If I have to do housekeep and he has to help me, I'll put him in vacuuming or making beds. But the dirtier work, I'll do it, I don't mind. When we were running an independent motel, he has done that too. . . . He's cleaning toilets in the business, he doesn't have to do that at home. He can help me, but I wouldn't demand.

The notion of some household chores being too dirty for men to engage in, despite the fact that they have done it for their business, helped separate home and work. As she went on to say,

> Doesn't matter if you're in the motel business or you working for somebody in the office, if you want to help your wife in the home, it has nothing to do with the business. It's something separate.

Other women echoed this attitude, that regardless of where one's work was located or what it entailed, practices there did not impact how a "proper" home should operate.

Limits to Creating a "Home, Home"

Despite informants' efforts to equate motel homes with standard homes and the more general need to deconstruct the middle-America, suburban image, meaningful residential differences exist. Residing in a business district removes one from the possibility of neighborly interactions that could create trust and inter-dependency among diverse groups.[20] Furthermore, it involves hazards, including physical danger, noise pollution, and sexual imagery, that take away from the intended functions of the home as a place of refuge from the "outside world," especially for children. One owner expressed a commonly noted relief about residing outside the motel.

> [Living outside the motel,] I go home [after work], I read my paper, I relax, I play with my kids a little bit sometimes. I'm off work. Once I get home, I go do something else. I'll go for a walk in my neighborhood, things like that. I go over to the gardens.

He could connect to his space in ways that those living in motels could not. They often kept working on the premises, and when they did walk outside their homes, many encountered parking lots, gas stations, and interstate highways.

Motel life represented the only viable option for many owners since they migrated with the intention of opening a motel and living in it. Informants got used to living in the motel and did not mind it much while there. As a second-generation Indian American said, "At that time, you know, I think it was home because that's where I belonged for nearly ten years, so it felt like home." Yet regardless of their efforts, living in the motel did not constitute a "home, home" for the reasons discussed earlier. This same informant went on to say that residing in a motel "sucked," and now he, his spouse, and his children live in a separate home. Still, motel life constituted a meaningful sense of the domestic for Indian Americans, even if not fully satisfactory. As immigrant parents accepted such limitations, they enabled the next generation to avoid them.

A full cultural citizenship for owners and their children may have been elusive but not entirely so. They embraced multiculturalism, the possibility of co-ethnic community, and a relatively comfortable domestic life inside motels. Individuals with greater resources accomplished this to a greater degree. Such efforts moved owners and their families past the isolation and intracommunity friction considered definitive of immigrants' social lives, in particular of ethnic entrepreneurs. They advanced their integration and a somewhat satisfactory private life.

Still, as both "forever foreigners" and owners of lower-budget establishments, many owners and their families experienced somewhat limited community and domestic contentment. Informants' only viable means of asserting their belonging weakened but did not overcome the obstacles facing them. For example, a side effect of downplaying religious differences and cooking in discreet ways was to accept a level of surveillance. Also, the multicultural displays and ritual practices allow for only limited connections to locals and co-ethnics, respectively. As a result, trying even harder to create a fuller sense of comfort would not necessarily accomplish it. That owners, in particular immigrants in lower-budget establishments, might have economic security does not mean they have not had to make sacrifices in the process. Nevertheless, they and their families find ways to significantly lessen their isolation, creating a meaningful private life.

Geography plays a role here as well. Even well into the twenty-first century, the cultural image of the heartland remains quintessentially American with a presumed white homogeneity in its vast rural areas. The demographics of the area compared with the coasts further suggest a limited cosmopolitanism. Informants' determination to create community resulted in greater heterogeneity in the region than would otherwise exist. But it did not overturn this cultural image. Challenging this impression proved difficult, given the ethnic activities available in most of the Midwest. Indian Americans rarely had ethnic engagements in interracial settings, such as public South Asian or Indian parades, museums, and outdoor festivals (Chicago is an exception). This is indicative of their smaller population and lack of ownership over public spaces, in contrast to those in much larger cities or areas with longer Indian histories (for example, Yuba City, California). Instead, they relied on ethnic spaces closed off to others, such as rented-out volleyball courts and temples. These activities assist ethnic communities but leave the broader environment relatively untouched. Groups learn to build ethnic and possibly mainstream lives, but there is little room for a recognized hybridity.

Conclusion

THE ACHIEVEMENTS OF INDIAN AMERICAN MOTELIERS have received well-deserved applause from mainstream media, national politicians, and one another. Owners appear to have attained the American dream and the freedom they sought in emigrating from colonial and postcolonial conditions. Standard theories of ethnic entrepreneurship elucidate how Indian Americans, in particular Gujaratis, attained a prolific representation in the industry. It is a story of significant achievements, enough to enable the next generation to integrate further. Yet underneath these achievements, owners and their families struggled to attain not only financial security but also full citizenship, both publicly and privately. The inequalities do not stem primarily from racist or anti-immigrant or sexist persons. As seen in Chapters 3 and 5, many (not all) of the challenges owners faced had indirect relationships to their immigrant minority background. The bulk of owners and their families lacked racial, gendered, and/or class privileges relative to the institutions and cultures surrounding them.

Rather than assert one characterization over another, *Life Behind the Lobby* presents the full picture of these immigrants' lives. To maintain profitable motels and a desired domestic life, owners and their families carefully created professional appearances, reached out locally, and vied for a sense of the private within their personal lives. A latent effect was the reification of the stratified systems that surrounded them in the first place. They weakened the effect of these embedded inequalities while having little choice but to affirm their existence.

Reassessing Narratives of Success

Recognizing the extent of hierarchies within owners' successes challenges the neoliberal assumptions entrenched in entrepreneurial discourse. Success in small business is possible but not as typically portrayed. It is not simply by being entrepreneurial and hardworking that owners have attained their industry dominance. Instead, community networks, a weary motel market, corporate incentives, global economic imbalances, and more join with this community's industriousness to explain their presence in the industry. Owners' continued achievements speak more to their micro-level agency and organizational efficacy to advance within racial, cultural, gender, and other hierarchies than to the openness of a U.S. meritocracy and civil society. Most scholars deconstruct the neoliberal agenda by documenting the experiences and protests of highly marginalized groups. *Life Behind the Lobby* provides a new focus on this shared agenda. Although nonimpoverished immigrant communities, including lower-budget motel owners, are rarely as politicized as those under more pronounced subjugation, it is still necessary to analyze their economic and social conditions as a way to dismantle institutionalized privileges.

The effort required to operate a motel, the industry's unstable economic returns, and the challenging personal lives similarly elucidate the American dream. The American dream rhetoric of abundant opportunity and equality is rarely realized. Yet cases such as those described in *Life Behind the Lobby* suggest that the dream occurs frequently. It is insincere to dismiss the American dream by downplaying Indian Americans' successes, for evidence of their accomplishments is ample. Instead, it is more appropriate to reevaluate what the American dream truly is. Because it is inherently tied to the inequalities owners must navigate, it is not a stable outcome. Instead, personal struggles, embedded hierarchies, and economic insecurity (witness the current economic downturn) that never go away but can seem tamed for stretches of time represent the reality of most American dreams more accurately than does a rags-to-riches scenario. Appreciating the context surrounding motel owners' and their families' hard work more fully recognizes their accomplishments.

As immigrant entrepreneurs get closer to the American dream of a house, a stable business, and a content family life, their community moves closer to a full citizenship, that is, equal opportunity to pursue their economic, cultural, social, and other interests. Indian Americans fought for full citizenship every day when they navigated institutionalized realms, like dealing with local governments, and interpersonal interactions, like checking guests into their motel. As Indian Americans successfully negotiate these hierarchies, they achieve an endurable citizenship. That is, they get by in their day-to-day lives with franchisors, politicians, banks, customers, locals, peers, and family members. For owners, this sufficed—they did not dwell on exclusions.

Of course a number of motel owners have gone on to attain significant financial returns and social prestige in their industry, their local community, and beyond. These persons affirm the model minority image practically synonymous with Asian Americans in general and Indian Americans in particular. But the owners who are working day and night to maintain their working-class or middle-class status should not be seen as the exception to the rule for Indian Americans. Historically, Indian America has been a working-class population. And even the American dream scenario of the most accomplished individuals is subject to market downturns. Thus, the owner of an economy franchise off an interstate highway may represent the community as well as her/his co-ethnic physician with a practice in the nearest metropolitan area.

Reassessing Adaptation

Even as prevailing theories of adaptation avoid simplistic portrayals, they end up privileging either a group's integration or its subjugation and resistance, depending on its circumstances. Because competing theories of adaptation find relevance in this case, it is impossible to choose a single trajectory of gradual integration or sustained subjugation, as is often the case for immigrant minorities. Informants weaken the effect of the inequalities facing them even as they affirm their basis. The result, then, is a back-and-forth process of adaptation. Rather than leading to tidy conclusions and grand theoretical assertions, the real process of adaptation is much messier and much more unpredictable. Analyzing how macro-, meso-, and micro-level factors intersect to create this messiness should be our focus.

At issue is how to analyze and measure adaptation. In assessing adaptation, the most common question has been how much of a certain variable (education, income, interracial friendships, respect) a group has attained. As a group achieves more—more education, more income, and so on—the implication is integration and equality. If a group does not achieve more, the implication is that an external impediment or a lack of resources is hindering integration and equality. Much of the debate on immigrants' adaptation and the effects of race and imperialism has been around how much or how little a group has attained. Similarly, within diaspora studies, the strength of the diaspora is assessed by how strongly a group maintains its ties to the homeland—the preservation of its culture, frequent visits back, remittances to family still living there, and the like.

As I have argued elsewhere (Dhingra 2007), it is necessary to move past the question of how much and instead ask *how* groups achieve their goals, if they do. Motel owners can claim considerable success as a group and offer clear support for social mobility. Yet how they accomplished these goals—that is, not simply utilizing ethnic resources and opportunities but also working within existing hierarchies—explicates the relevance of critical and anti-imperialist perspectives. We need to analyze how groups can move forward economically and/or socially, and the analysis needs to include the power of race, gender, and other hierarchies as being constitutive of that forward movement. This is instead of only acknowledging the power of stratification systems by arguing that a group either failed to achieve its goal or sacrificed tremendously for that goal. By asking how groups maneuver, we can move away from assessing outcomes based on whether an increased stratification or an increased integration is more pronounced.

This revised approach to assessing the experiences of diasporic communities brings together discourses on immigrant adaptation and racial inequality, which typically take place separately. When we discuss the differences between "minorities" and whites, we focus on the power of race. When we discuss the differences between "immigrants" and natives, we focus on the power of culture. Although not ignorant of the fact that immigrants experience racial hierarchies and minorities have cultural differences, scholars stress one kind of conversation with each group. *Life Behind the Lobby* is part of a larger effort in the literature to move past this exclusive framing. We must theorize race and racial inequality within analyses of immigrant adaptation. It is not sufficient to merely refer to immigrants' minority status. Nor is it enough to frame a minority within its political economy as a function of historic and contemporary discrimination without attending to the power of culture, group resources, and possible transnational ties. Models of immigrant adaptation should recognize the social inequalities (race, gender, sexuality, class) and ethnic resources within global capitalism.

Reassessing Regionalism

Although *Life Behind the Lobby* does not take on the Midwest as its central orienting concern, the region plays an important role in shaping the lives of its inhabitants.[1] Critical regionalism as a field examines regions as cultural constructs rather than as essentialized spaces. Attention is paid to cultural artifacts as telling signs of broader forces inside and outside the region (Powell 2007). This is distinct from a place having a singular culture. With this in mind, it is necessary to attend to the role of geography in shaping interethnic relations. It is too simplistic to evaluate the effect of geography by looking for either a tolerance or an intolerance of difference. Such a question assumes that the cultural makeup of a region's inhabitants make them inherently more or less welcoming to newcomers, which downplays how the economy, organizations and associations, political interests, and cultural norms together shape these exchanges.

Instead, we must ask how these forces within a geography influence how tolerance operates and the ways in which immigrant groups respond.

For Ohio and the Midwest, the notion of being the heartland defines its cultural significance to the nation. The location of Ohio played a background yet active role in shaping owners' public and private citizenship. The heartland has served to define a traditional "American" character of a supposed commitment to family values (rarely defined), individual rights, independent determination, and military pride. The image is entrenched in how the United States wants to define itself to the world, so as to advance its war on terror in defense of its "wholesome" way of life. The freedom that Indian American pioneers sought seems best encapsulated in this region, despite their settling in California. At a time when "American values" are extolled in the specter of global terrorism post-9/11, the heartland takes on an even stronger romanticization than normal. Part of this image stems from the presumed white racial homogeneity of the area. The large rural sections in particular suggest a simple, wholesome way of life. With immigrants of color from Asia, the Caribbean, and Latin America dominating the population changes of the coasts, the Midwest becomes even more of a "true American" marker (Frey 2002). The loss of jobs in the Rust Belt cities can be viewed as supportive of this nationalistic image: the main U.S. manufacturing industries are in decline because of the threat of global business practices that undermine U.S. values of fair pay and acceptable working conditions. The murder in Detroit of Chinese American Vincent Chin by two white former autoworkers in the 1980s is a vivid reminder of the kinds of outcomes to which this narrative can lead.[2]

Indian Americans and other immigrant communities (notably Arab Americans in Illinois, Michigan, and Ohio) disrupt this singular image of the heartland. They forge ties to their localities despite their occupational status as middleman minorities. Informants learned to navigate the cultural normativeness of their area in how they ate at restaurants, made sense of religious symbolism, performed cultural programs, and dealt with racial categories. They complicate the heartland image by introducing greater heterogeneity, but they do not overturn it. Indian Americans had few opportunities to openly confront such a simplistic notion of public culture. They rarely had ethnic engagements in interracial settings. This is indicative of their smaller population and lack of ownership over public spaces, in contrast to those in larger cities (for example, the public South Asian and Indian parades, museums, and outdoor festivals in New York City). Instead, they relied on ethnic spaces closed off to others, such as rented-out volleyball courts, temples, and homes. Because Indian Americans' communal gatherings took place primarily in private settings, their community formations did not alter the dominant representation of the region.[3] While some customers in Ohio (as elsewhere) disliked staying at an Indian-owned motel, they rarely expressed an intrinsic and open hostility toward Indians' cultural differences. Owners' efforts helped them gain acceptance while still upholding the heartland's definition of proper citizenship. Overall, we need to consider the various ways that immigrants construct meanings about and navigate their environment so as to understand how hierarchies reproduce themselves while being traversed.

Notes

Introduction

1. Ela Dutt, "Al Gore urges Indian Americans to engage in politics," *News India–Times*, May 3, 2002, p. 8.

2. "New survey showcases unprecedented impact of AAHOA members," May 27, 2010. Available at www.aahoa.com/AM/Template.cfm?Section=Press _Releases1&TEMPLATE=/CM/ContentDisplay.cfm&CONTENTID=4717.

3. "Gingrich to AAHOA: Politics is like running a hotel," *Indus Business Journal*, May 1, 2004.

4. Joseph Berger, "Rooms to succeed: For the children of Indian-American hoteliers, all is possible," *New York Times*, February 3, 2004.

5. Roger Yu, "Indian-Americans book years of success in hotel business," *USA Today*, April 18, 2007.

6. Comparable news stories have appeared elsewhere, at times with the same title, for example, Laura Sydell, "Indian immigrants find niche in hotels," National Public Radio, August 16, 2004; Jon Herskovitz, "Indian immigrants find niche in hotels," Reuters News Service, May 2, 2004.

7. Berger, "Rooms to succeed."

8. This statistic comes from surveys conducted by PKF Hospitality Research. According to PKF, AAHOA members (most of whom are Indian) owned 20,156 properties in the United States as of April 2009. This, of course, does not include the many Indian Americans who are not members of AAHOA. According to the American Hotel and Lodging Association, there were 49,505 lodging

establishments in the United States at the end of 2008, which means that 40.7 percent of all establishments were owned by AAHOA members. More information is available at www.aahoa.com/AM/Template.cfm?Section=Press_Releases1 &TEMPLATE=/CM/ContentDisplay.cfm&CONTENTID=4717.

9. "New survey showcases unprecedented impact of AAHOA members."

10. Yu, "Indian-Americans book years of success"; Govind Bhakta, *Patels: A Gujarati Community History in the United States* (Los Angeles: University of California, Asian American Studies Center Press, 2002).

11. Tunku Varadarajan, "A Patel motel cartel?" *New York Times Sunday Magazine*, July 4, 1999.

12. The definition of a small business is debatable (Blackford 1991). According to the government definition, a business with five hundred employees or fewer is a small business. Most motels have a fraction of that. And owners of small businesses are typically familiar with the operations and employees of the business, which also applies to motel owners.

13. Field notes, AAHOA annual convention, Chicago, June 18, 2010.

14. Gary Gates, "Income of gay men lags behind that of men partnered with women," Urban Institute Research of Record, June 13, 2003. Gays and lesbians are desired residents partly for their disposable income. But gays aged twenty-five to fifty-four with partners earn on average $3,000 less than men with female partners.

15. Current standard assimilation theory (Alba and Nee 2003) differs from a paradigm emphasizing diverse "modes of incorporation" among immigrants (Portes and Rumbaut 2006) in that the former emphasizes the benefits of adopting mainstream culture and downplays hurdles to equality compared with the latter, even as both perspectives agree that hurdles to full acceptance and to successful integration can be overcome if a group has the right resources.

16. The authors refer to Portes and Rumbaut and their emphasis on segmented assimilation as representative of racialization rather than of assimilation because the authors allow for race to matter more, especially for Mexican Americans, than do straight-line assimilation authors (e.g., Alba and Nee 2003). As explained earlier, I recognize the differences between straight-line and segmented assimilation theories, including that segmented assimilation theories take racism more into account. Portes and Rumbaut still emphasize the general assimilation process and mostly agree with Alba and Nee's formu-

lation (Portes, "Author meets critic session on Richard Alba and Victor Nee, *Remaking the American mainstream: Assimilation and contemporary immigration*," presented at the American Sociological Association Meeting, Philadelphia, August 2005). They do not assume that race has inherent effects and are not as critical about U.S. racial dynamics as scholars in the critical race camp (Espiritu 2009). For these reasons, I place Portes and Rumbaut in the integrationist camp.

17. Another attempt to move past this theoretical dichotomy argues that ethnic minorities can become like the white, middle-class mainstream by adopting racist practices toward native minorities (Loewen 1971). In this case, integration and active racism go hand in hand. Groups attain greater equality with whites by denigrating other minorities, thereby minimizing how much they are framed as minorities themselves. Although informative, this formulation does not address the issue of individuals experiencing both marginalization and assimilation.

18. Lavina Melwani, "The Gujaratis," *Little India*, February 2002.

19. "New survey showcases unprecedented impact of AAHOA members."

20. For instance, the Taj Hotel line, a brand of high-budget hotels, is owned by the Indian company Tata.

21. Yu, "Indian-Americans book years of success."

22. Field notes, AAHOA regional convention, Chicago, March 30, 2005.

23. "New survey showcases unprecedented impact of AAHOA members."

24. Adam Piore, "Latest immigrant wave: Indian hotel developers," *The Real Deal*, February 1, 2007.

25. U.S. Census Bureau, "State & Country QuickFacts: Ohio," June 3, 2011. Available at http://quickfacts.census.gov/qfd/states/39000.html.

26. Ibid.

27. U.S. Census Bureau, Data Set: Census 2000 Summary File 2 (SF2) 100 Percent Data, Table PCT1. Available at http://factfinder.census.gov.

28. Ibid.

29. However, unlike in Chicago, New York, and other major cities, South Asian Americans in Ohio's metropolitan areas do not dominate the taxi-driving sector or the very small retail sector (e.g., newspaper stands).

30. U.S. Census Bureau, Data Set: Census 2000 Summary File 1 (SF1) 100 Percent Data, Table PCT6. Available at http://factfinder.census.gov.

31. U.S. Census Bureau, Data Set: Census 2000 Summary File 2 (SF2) 100 Percent Data, Table PCT1. Available at http://factfinder.census.gov.

32. Robert L. Smith, "Indian immigrants find niche in hotels: Cultural, practical reasons lead many to hospitality business here, across U.S.," *Plain Dealer*, December 10, 2004.

33. U.S. Census Bureau, Data Set: Census 2000 Summary File 4 (SF4)—Sample Data Table PCT1. Available at http://factfinder.census.gov.

34. Ibid.

35. U.S. Census Bureau, Data Set: Census 2000 Demographic Profile Highlights: Selected Population Group: Asian Indian alone or in any combination. Available at http://factfinder.census.gov.

36. Fact Sheet, Ohio, U.S. Census Bureau, Data Set: Census 2000 Demographic Profile Highlights: Selected Population Group: Asian Indian alone or in any combination. Available at http://factfinder.census.gov.

37. In 2000, only .25 percent of Indian American households were listed as living below the poverty level. Ibid.

38. U.S. Census Bureau, Data Set: Census 2000 Summary File 4 (SF4)—Sample Data Table PCT87. Available at http://factfinder.census.gov. These percentages refer to the number of people self-employed within the total population of self-employed for each race and sex group, excluding those involved in agriculture, forestry, fishing and hunting, and mining.

39. "Indian-Americans make their presence felt at Democratic convention," August 26, 2008. Available at www.rediff.com/news/2008/aug/26slde2.htm.

40. Most Hindu temples are ecumenical. For example, a Cincinnati ecumenical Hindu temple has deities from various regions with exactly the same dimensions and no hierarchies.

41. The attorney for those representing residents against the building of the temple, Leland Cole, is quoted as saying, "The concern that I think a lot of us feel is that the technical requirements are being very closely adhered to." He continues, "However, the fundamental basis of the zoning use—is it harmonious in the area—seems to be ignored. It's not an engineering project. It's a determination of whether this particular building, this temple, located in this area, in a residential area, is really harmonious." (Mike D'Agruma, "Richfield PZC gives Hindu temple final blessing," May 29, 2008. Available at www.akron.com/akron-ohio-community-news.asp?aID=2517.)

Chapter 1

1. Kadva Patel Samaj, August 6, 2009. Available at http://kadvapatelsamaj
.blogspot.com/2009/08/kadva-patel-history.html.

2. Ibid.

3. Patels from distinct districts still seek one another out and congregate when possible, even in the United States, where caste and regional distinctions among Indian immigrants has become less important. For instance, the Leva Patel community in the United States has its own monthly magazine and conventions.

4. In fact, Patidars had entered trade within Gujarat, even as farming predominated (Tambs Lyche 1982). Trade was a respected activity for them by this time.

5. Kanjibhai Desai was referred to as Kanjibhai Patel in Stanley Turkel, *Great American Hoteliers: Pioneers of the Hotel Industry* (Bloomington, IN: AuthorHouse, 2009).

6. These migrants must leave the country if their work ends, and their spouses (arriving under an H-4 visa) cannot work. The spouse is seen not as a person but as an appendage of the worker.

Chapter 2

1. Tunku Varadarajan, "A Patel motel cartel?" *New York Times Sunday Magazine*, July 4, 1999.

2. In 1998, Rama and his family started a scholarship program, the Rama Scholarship for the American Dream, which awards scholarships to Indians and other minorities who are studying hospitality management at the undergraduate or graduate level. Information on the program is available at www
.ahlef.org/content.aspx?id=19820&terms=rama.

3. As another example, a 1996 article in *India Worldwide* reported:

Ramesh Gokal was recently appointed president of Knights Lodging a brand of Hospitality Franchise System; Harish Pattni is chairman elect for the small property Advertisement Committee of the American Hotel & Motel Association. (Shanker Patel, "Hotels, motels and Patels: Guys from Gujarat make it big in the New World," November 30, p. 4)

Similarly, in 2009 Bakulesh "Buggsi" Patel was elected to the owners' association of the InterContinental Hotels Group, and both Alpesh Patel and Jaydeep

Patel were elected to the Choice Hotels Owners' Council. These are just a few examples of the national motel/hotel franchise industry's recognition of Indian Americans.

4. Bonacich (1973) states that middleman minorities are typically sojourners. Waldinger, Aldrich, and Ward (1990) critique this notion by arguing that sojourners would be less likely than settlers to want to invest money in a business as a means of accruing income with the goal of leaving. Part of Bonacich's point with the sojourner type is that owning a business as a middleman minority often invites host hostility, and only those who planned on leaving quickly would tolerate that as well as have the incentive to reinvest their earnings back into the business in order to make sufficient profit. Indian American interviewees did not claim to start a business because of their intention to eventually leave the United States, unlike the classic sojourner. Still, they prioritized business growth and revolved their lives around the business rather than on becoming full members of their area. This "outsider" perspective proves useful for their means of business management. As seen later in the text, owners move beyond this outsider perspective as well, for it does not define them totally even as it continues to be relevant.

5. This business transfer from European immigrants to Asian immigrants is not unique. For example, Korean Americans took over businesses from second- and third-generation Jewish Americans whose children did not want to run them (Park 1997; Steinberg 1986).

6. Korean Americans cite the same advantage to working with poorer African American customers as opposed to working with middle-class white customers (Lee 2002).

7. Field notes, August 6, 2009.

8. Varadarajan, "A Patel motel cartel?"

9. Part of the reason that brands come and go has been increased market segmentation by franchisors. Hotel operators constantly start new brands targeted to very specific niches, such as extended stays on a lower versus a higher-budget, full-service hotels at middle-budget prices, and establishments located in rural areas versus off interstate highways versus in urban centers. Not all new brands can survive, which means that some franchisees find themselves in financial straits. See Mike Sheridan, "Hotel franchising: Let's play the name game!" *National Real Estate Investor*, September 1, 1996.

10. Edwin McDowell, "Hospitality is their business: One ethnic group's rooms-to-riches success story," *New York Times*, March 21, 1996.

11. About Boston: see Jenifer B. McKim, "A room to call home," *Boston Globe*, June 24, 2009, p. A1. About Anaheim, California: see Erik Eckholm, "As jobs vanish, motel rooms become home," *New York Times*, March 11, 2009, p. A1. About New York City: see Jess Wisloski, "Motel housing homeless draws wrath of neighbors," *Daily News*, October 10, 2007.

12. In fact, Indian American hotel owners in San Francisco in the early 1980s faced criticism for how they treated homeless guests subsidized by city government at a rate well below market value (Jain 1989). Tensions became so severe that then mayor Diane Feinstein had to publicly denounce the racist attacks on Patels and defend their contribution to the city for taking in low-income residents.

13. Monua Janah, "Indian immigrants find room to grow beyond motels," *Wall Street Journal*, August 25, 1989, p. B2.

14. Independent motels continue to be more likely than franchised places to open in low-income and rural areas (Kalnins and Chung 2006).

15. Stanley Turkel, "From ragas to riches, part I: A wonderful American immigrant success story," May 2003. Available at www.ishc.com/Article-Search .aspx?search=turkel.

16. Sunita Sohrabji, "Motel owner sues AAA citing discrimination," *India West* 15, no. 16 (1990): 29.

17. T. Green, "Foreigners buying up U.S. motels," *Los Angeles Times*, May 29, 1977, p. C5.

18. Fred Schwartz, "Getting to know the Asian American Hotel Owners Association," *Franchising World*, March 1, 2005.

19. Informants stressed that they started motels because others they knew had already done so successfully. Classical economic and sociological theories on entrepreneurship, influenced greatly by Joseph Schumpeter, emphasize the individual character of the entrepreneur as a risk taker and innovator (Blaug 2000). Immigrants are supposedly more open to taking risks because they are not completely socialized into the norms of their host society. The impression of Gujaratis about themselves is in contrast to this, with an emphasis instead on their "herd mentality" and avoidance of risk, as seen in this chapter. Although some pioneers clearly took on a great number of unknowns to enter the hotel and motel industry, the characterization of risk taker cannot be applied to the community as a whole.

20. Motel owners' networks were not diverse but were highly dependable, and so facilitated a solid return on their investment (Burt 2000).

21. Rangaswamy (2007) finds a comparable trend for Gujaratis migrating to the Midwest to work in Gujarati American–owned Dunkin' Donut shops.

22. This narrow conception of the job market is typical of immigrants with less human and cultural capital (Massey 2003).

23. As of 2010, the criteria included employing at least ten nonrelative, U.S. workers and investing $1,000,000 or $500,000 in targeted areas. Complete information is available at www.uscis.gov.

24. This is akin to the rotating credit systems found among other ethnic entrepreneurs (Bonacich and Modell 1980; Light 1972).

25. According to a few informants, compared with other immigrants, Indian Americans have made only moderate use of government programs, such as assistance from the Minority Business Development Agency of the U.S. Department of Commerce (Min and Bozorgmehr 2000). The paperwork is intense for such programs. So despite many native groups' belief that ethnic entrepreneurs receive special incentives to start businesses, this happens infrequently (Lee 2002).

26. An independent, Indian-owned bank in Anaheim, California, was started by a Patel in part to focus on lending money to motels. As quoted in M. Potts, "First Indian-owned bank opened in Anaheim," *India West* 27, no. 18 (2002): B6, the banking entrepreneur stated:

> I understand their business, so in terms of lending requirements, we would be a little more flexible in customizing the financing of motels. . . . Motel financing is very complicated and not many banks do that. . . . We will consider a motel loan, where most other banks would not, because I seem to understand the industry. [I speak] both Hindi and Gujarati, which makes them feel a little more comfortable discussing their business and their finances, as opposed to someone they cannot relate to.

In contrast to this entrepreneur's statements, however, most owners said it is little problem today acquiring loans from mainstream banks if one's plan is sound. According to informants, other Indian Americans have followed suit and plan to open their own banks.

27. This was not as high as he would like because their gross income was eaten up partly by their high mortgage rate.

28. Joseph George, "The future is young, says Secretary Mehul Patel," *India Abroad*, July 2, 2010, p. A16.

29. A conception of small business as an alternative to the job market, as opposed to a last resort that should be avoided, helps explain why later-generation

Indian Americans did not look down on business ownership as their career plans faltered. Like many Latino entrepreneurs (Raijman and Tienda 2000), Indian immigrants did not enter small business because of a complete lack of other options. In contrast, Korean immigrants mostly saw a small business as a means to overcome a blocked labor market, and they expected their children to enter "safe" professions (Kim 2006).

30. The children of Indian immigrants viewed self-employment as both an economic and a personal opportunity, as common for middle-class entrepreneurs generally (Valdez 2010).

31. Leaders of the National Association of Black Hotel Owners, Operators and Developers attend AAHOA conventions and have invited AAHOA leaders to speak at their conventions.

Chapter 3

1. Aziz Haniffa, "AAHOA celebrates its 10th anniversary," *India Abroad,* March 26, 1999, p. 32.

2. AAHOA representatives have also criticized this trend. See "From the Chairman: Challenges for 2006 and beyond," *AAHOA Lodging Business,* March 2006. Owners sometimes found ways around the problem of buying supplies only from franchise-sanctioned vendors, but it still created negative feelings.

3. Barbara DeLollis, "Budget hotels going more upscale: Flat-screen TVs, granite counters, sleek looks, same prices," *USA Today,* March 24, 2008.

4. Barbara DeLollis, "Motel 6 pushes ahead with edgy revamp after recession slows progress," *USA Today,* June 20, 2010.

5. This feeling of being squeezed was echoed by many informants. In fact, this point took up quite a bit of time at the 2005 AAHOA convention during a moderated conversation between four franchise corporation representatives and two successful Indian American franchisees. A chairman of one major motel conglomerate said that *maybe* it was a good idea to take away some requirements as they add others (e.g., a coffeemaker in each room). The room filled with applause from owners.

6. For instance, a lower-budget franchise owner at the 2006 AAHOA convention in Charlotte, North Carolina, explained that he attended the convention primarily to see the latest options from vendors. When I asked him why, given that the franchise notified him of needed upgrades, he responded that his goal is to satisfy the customer, not the franchise. And to do that, he had to pursue different and possibly more amenities than required.

7. Other common complaints included liquidation damage fees for leaving a franchise, monthly fees to the franchise without a guarantee of revenue engendered from belonging to the franchise, seemingly unfair inspections by franchisors, the lack of disclosure of the fees' results, costs to transfer a motel to a third party, and fees levied from customer complaints.

8. Field notes, AAHOA annual convention, Chicago, April 23, 2010. For instance, one owner said that the franchisors were correct in that they do not raise fees during financially good times but still thought the executives' responses came across as insensitive.

9. Field notes, AAHOA annual convention, Chicago, April 23, 2010.

10. Field notes, AAHOA annual convention, Las Vegas, March 23, 2006.

11. Field notes, AAHOA annual convention, Charlotte, NC, March 9, 2007.

12. Field notes, AAHOA regional convention, Lima, OH, September 21, 2006.

13. Blue MauMau staff, "Franchisee clubs clash, CHOC chair resigns," April 4, 2010. Available at www.bluemaumau.org/8728/hotel_franchisee_organizations _clash_choc_chair_resigns. (Blue MauMau is a blog and news website for the franchisee community.)

14. Ibid.

15. See also Dean Narciso, "Motel's tenants pack their bags," *Columbus Dispatch*, December 3, 1995, p. C2.

16. Anjetta Mcqueen, "Motel owner flees meeting on crime," *Plain Dealer*, February 8, 1996.

17. Similar efforts in New Jersey have taken place, according to an AAHOA representative at the 2005 annual convention. City ordinances in select areas there required cars to face outward rather than inward in motel parking lots so police can check for expired license plates. The background, according to the representative, is that the city wants to tear down the motels for a development project. Police have come to the motels because of owners' calls reporting illegal activities in the rooms. The city frames the motels as crime sites rather than thanking the owners for reporting the crimes taking place there. In effect, owners are punished for reporting crimes. The latent effect is for owners to not report illegal activities.

In addition, an AAHOA representative told of a local ordinance in a town in Michigan, indicative of how extreme the challenges to owners can become in choosing to run an economical rather than an expensive lodging establishment.

There was actually, there's an ordinance there saying that whoever checks into a room and takes a lady inside must be married. . . . There could be times where if you refuse somebody to give them a room, [the customer] could sue you. And don't get me wrong, there are hotels that try to run a clean business. But they can't refuse service to anybody. They can't just assume they're a prostitute or drug dealer or whatever, unless they have a track record or something. . . . The police don't really understand. Really the police are supposed to follow the innkeeper law. And they don't do it.

The owner is caught in the middle of the expectations of customers and the almost idiosyncratic preferences of local government. Nor is this ordinance rare in its putative effects on owners.

18. Extended stays have been the source of other problems for owners. In Ohio, for example, extended stays in motels not designed for that purpose led to tensions with the state fire marshal, who worried about the hazards from cooking and living in such establishments. Only with the intervention of the state legislature did the problem get resolved, notably with the assistance of the state's only Indian American state representative. AAHOA worked with Ohio state representatives and the fire marshal to alter the twenty-eight-day restriction on extended stays in most motels. Field notes: Toledo, October 11, 2007; Cleveland, June 18, 2008.

19. Personal communication with freelance journalist Chris Maag about his interviews with white residents of Breezewood, Pennsylvania, regarding their city's loss of population and declining quality of life. Maag's interviews revealed a significant prejudice against Indian American motel owners. Residents blamed these motel owners in particular, not owners generally, for driving down the quality of the motels and the city itself. Residents ignored the structural conditions that have hurt towns in the Midwest and Northeast for the past few decades, such as the decline of manufacturing jobs and the lack of infrastructure investment and ensuing job opportunities. I later went to Breezewood and chatted informally with some Indian American owners, who expressed surprise and distress at hearing these comments.

20. Viji Sundaram, "Arizona Republic story angers Indian community," *India West* 15, no. 16 (1990): 25.

21. Richard Springer, "Indo-American motel association sues Oakland for discrimination," *India West* 24, no. 44 (1999): A1.

22. Kate Zernike, "A.C.L.U. says ethnic bias steered Georgia drug sting," *New York Times*, April 6, 2006; Racial Justice Campaign Against Operation Meth Merchant blogsite staff, "Introducing Operation Meth Merchant," December 22, 2005. Available at www.stopoperationmethmerchant.org/blog/2005 /12/introducing-operation-meth-merchant.html.

23. South Asian Americans Leading Together, webinar on racial profiling, November 19, 2009. Webinar held at www.saalt.org.

24. Although such nativist signs are indeed less common today than in the 1980s, they still exist and can garner national attention. See Hilary Hylton, "No-tell motels," *Time*, August 9, 2007. Ironically (or not), the title of this article on Patel motels refers to seedy establishments where people may be engaging in illegal acts, such as prostitution. The article itself illuminates one challenge to Indian immigrant owners, that of prejudiced non-Indian owners and customers.

25. Charlie LeDuff, "When origin becomes a competitive issue," *New York Times*, May 11, 2002, p. A10.

26. Jim Conkle, "Non-native motel owners deserve your support," *Route 66 Pulse*, January 23, 2008.

27. One Indian owner of a motel on Route 66 in California has decorated the motel in a traditional Americana motif, with countless pieces of memorabilia from the time when the iconic highway was in its glory (Wood and Wood 2004).

28. Bureau of Labor Statistics, Regional and State Unemployment (Annual), 1992–2010. Available at www.bls.gov/schedule/archives/all_nr.htm#SRGUNE.

29. Ohio Labor Market Information, http://ohiolmi.com/research/2009 OhioEconomicAnalysis.pdf.

30. John Gruner, "Ohio tourism holds its own in slow economy," *Plain Dealer*, November 21, 2008. Available at www.cleveland.com/travel/index.ssf/2008/11 /economys_silver_lining_ohio_to.html.

31. Ohio Hotel & Lodging Association, STR Report, "State of the Industry," OH&LA Annual Conference, November 2009.

32. For example, about 50 percent of Great Wraps franchises, whose corporate headquarters is in Atlanta, are owned by Indian Americans, many of whom either also own motels or sold their motels. See Michel Potts, "From hotels to franchises; great wraps, batteries plus attract Indian Americans," *India West* 28, no. 53 (2003): B1.

Chapter 4

1. For instance, the National Association of Black Hotel Owners, Operators, and Developers has sought guidance from AAHOA.

2. This could be a generational preference—younger moteliers were less likely to have changed their names.

3. Starting in 2008, in San Jose, California, and Boston, a small number of Indian American owners have started putting copies of the Bhagavad-Gita in their motel rooms, next to copies of the Gideon Bible. These are mostly in independent lower-budget franchise motels. This movement is sponsored by the Panchajanya Project. Their documents suggest that guests, including non-Indians, have appreciated finding the Bhagavad-Gitas. Questions remain on this project, such as how owners reconcile this activity with concerns of appearing too foreign, whether the generally lower-budget scale of these motels allows these owners to have such ethnic symbols given that customers with low incomes have fewer lodging options, if owners approached by the project ever turn down the Bhagavad-Gitas, and whether these locations are more prone than other geographies to allow this. In any case, that this program has received any success signifies that the dominating presence of Indian American proprietors at the lower-budget level is now allowing some owners a bit more leeway in representations of ethnicity.

4. This owner's ethnic reference, however, misrepresents how other groups ran their motels. In talking with white managers (not owners) of lower-budget motels, the differences across ethnic lines were less obvious. They claimed to have to always be available. One white informant who managed a lower-budget franchise lived at the motel and went home on weekends to stay with her family. Similar to Indian American owners, she tried to manage costs by employing few staff. However, her family did not play much of a role in running the motel. She said, "[Employing family is] not a good policy. [The franchise] don't like you to do it. OK if have one or two. Family not allowed on the premises without written notice." Indians talked about the differences but did not necessarily know many whites for real-life comparisons. But at franchise conventions, Indian American and other owners would exchange tips, signifying that the line between types of owners was not as defined as some might think.

5. I do not have information on the gendered dynamics between second-generation husbands and wives. Based on other research, respondents of that

generation neither expected nor wanted the same degree of gendered relations as common among their parents, but gender imbalances often remain (Dhingra 2007).

6. This section discusses the roles of the adults. Children's roles receive attention in the next chapter.

7. Those families that had sponsored migrants, and so had greater economic strain, may have had a stricter gendered division of labor (Assar 2000).

8. Dhaliwal (1998) goes on to argue that even South Asian British women running their own business, separate from their families, deferred to their husbands regarding financial matters.

9. Notably, no owners claimed explicit racial discrimination from vendors, as occurs for other entrepreneurs (Min 2008).

10. Notably, one male owner of an independent motel was in charge of cleaning the bathrooms and rooms. He took great pride in how clean he got them and once contested a customer's complaint of a dirty bathtub.

11. Women in the small business sector in India are working to have their contributions better recognized. The Self-Employed Women's Association supports the efforts of women laborers both inside and outside the domestic sphere (Desai 2002).

12. "Motel operators turn to Gujarati-Spanish phrasebook," August 10, 2006. Available at http://news.oneindia.in/2006/08/10/motel-operators-gujarati -spanish-phrasebook.html.

13. Full information on this program is available on the AAHOA website, at www.aahoa.com/AM/Template.cfm?Section=CHO_Program.

14. Field notes, November 2005.

15. Ela Dutt, "Hotel owners give rooms, board free to victims," September 16, 2005. Available at http://epaper.desitalk.com/dit/2005/09/16/focus12-094051.html.

16. AAHOA chairmen also have suggested various initiatives to continue pressure on the franchisors. These include surveys to owners to grade their franchise, as a corollary to franchisors' inspection and grading of owners.

17. See, for example, Ralph Nurnberger, "Hospitality industry leadership experiences workings on the Hill firsthand," February 11, 2005 (updated April 25, 2005). Available at www.collegecostshowmuch.com/2005/p_news/nit/iacpa -archieve/2005/02/11/summit1-11022005.html.

18. Nancy Weingartner, "Making the '12 points': Mike and R.C. Patel go from 'zee to 'zor to prove fairness is a two-way street," *Franchise Times*, June– July 2007.

As another example, at the 1994 AAHOA convention, the keynote speaker was the Bollywood film icon and fellow Gujarati Amitabh Bachchan. According to an account in *India West,*

> "He emphasized that our growth, our hard work, and our family values have helped us to grow in a foreign country to a level where we have almost 50 percent of the lodging economy and he said that requires guts," [AAHOA chairman] Shah recounted.
>
> After reciting poems by his father, a famed poet in his own right, the Hindi film star gave a motivational speech on "Agnipath," whose message of walking through fire to achieve success was derived from the famous film of the same name. Urging Indian hoteliers not to give up the fight they have been waging for more than ten years to take their rightful place within the hotel industry, Bachchan, with both fists raised and slowly bringing them to his chest, chanted, "Agnipath, agnipath, agnipath."
>
> "The crowd just went crazy," Shah recalled. (Michel Potts, "Indian, Asian hotel owners groups join forces at meet," *India West* 20, no. 5 [December 16, 1994]: C53)

The AAHOA audience drew from a collective memory of resistance, which motivated solidarity.

19. Field notes, June 18, 2008.

20. Aziz Haniffa, "Indian hospitality industry is clearly poised for tremendous growth," *India Abroad* 40, no. 24 (2010): A20.

21. Ashfaque Swapan, "Elated community hails n-deal," *India West* 33, no. 46 (2008): A1.

22. The United States denied Modi's visa for entry. It based the decision on "a finding by the Indian National Human Rights Commission" that linked Modi to the massacre and rape of Muslims in Gujarat in 2002 (www.frontlineonnet.com/fl2208/stories/20050422000704700.htm). In fact, according to *Samar* magazine, "In 2002, the U.S. Commission on International Religious Freedom recommended that India be listed as a Country of Particular Concern by the U.S. State Department, and in 2004, it was added to the list" (www.samarmagazine.org/archive/article.php?id=195). AAHOA members and leaders remained bitter about the denial of the visa. Furthermore, as a result of pressure from religious freedom and South Asian organizations, numerous speakers canceled their appearances, and major businesses pulled their sponsorship.

Chapter 5

1. Richard Springer, "Indo-American motel association sues Oakland for discrimination," *India West* 24, no. 44 (1999): A1; Viji Sundaram, "Arizona Republic story angers Indian community," *India West* 15, no. 16 (1990): 25; Michelle Hunter, "Metairie motels seized, owners arrested on prostitution, tax charges," *Times-Picayune*, March 26, 2010; Drew Brooks, "Police seek court action against Fayetteville motel," *Fayetteville Observer*, May 5, 2011; Ed Treleven, "Madison seeks to close troubled Beltline motel," *Wisconsin State Journal*, April 25, 2011.

2. John Caniglia, "Neighborhood woes laid at motel's door: Business faulted for drugs, prostitution," *Plain Dealer*, October 9, 2007.

3. See Chapter 3, footnote 19, as well as Jain (1989) regarding incidents in California.

4. For instance, the building of new, higher-budget motels receives positive attention in local newspapers, including how many employees will be hired. For example, see www.timesrecordnews.com/news/2008/oct/28/marriott-be-next -one-several-jack-box-sites/ and www.tulsaworld.com/business/article.aspx ?subjectid=32&articleid=20100209_32_E1_Fairfi846957.

5. Portions of this section have previously been published: Pawan Dhingra, "Hospitable to others: Indian American motel owners create boundaries and belonging in the heartland," *Ethnic and Racial Studies* 33, no. 6 (2010): 1088–107. Reprinted here with permission.

6. As another example of such daily interactions, in Toledo, five owners—of mostly lower-budget motels—and I went out for dinner (field notes, September 24, 2005) after playing volleyball. We could have opted for an Indian restaurant where we would have been among co-ethnics, but instead we went to a local sports-themed restaurant, which was near the Indian establishment. We were the only nonwhites in the crowded restaurant, but the owners indicated no concern whatsoever. They spoke in Gujarati with one another at times, joked with the waitress (in a nonsexual manner), and behaved like any other table of men would behave. Although such a dinner can be read as mundane and therefore not worth mentioning, it is precisely because of its pedestrian nature that I draw attention to it. Everyday interactions create the meanings people assign to their environment.

7. Field notes, March 2, 2006.

8. For example, at a motel convention in Las Vegas (March 22–24, 2006), one participant of the second generation complained about the choice of key-note speaker, ABC news correspondent Sam Donaldson, as being unrelated to business. She would have preferred Donald Trump or some other celebrity entrepreneur who could model successful real estate business techniques.

9. See www.ibef.org/download/Gujarat_190111.pdf.

10. The Internet was more popular among the younger generation. Given that they lived in relatively isolated areas, in time it may provide another type of transnational connection but to date had not.

11. There is also a twenty-four-hour Gujarati-language news channel, broadcasting news from Gujarat.

12. Some owners came together through the Charotar Patidar Samaj, a network association of Patidars in the United States. One of the express purposes of its annual conventions is to help arrange marriages within the 1.5 generation and the second generation. The Leuva Patidar Samaj of the USA attracts thousands to its annual conventions, where sessions to discuss children's marriages are popular as well. Most members of both organizations are tied to the motel industry.

13. Portions of this section have already been published, under Dhingra 2009b. Reprinted here with permission.

14. Volleyball games are so popular among male owners that AAHOA conventions sponsor them.

15. I attended four in Toledo and one in Anniston, Alabama.

16. Each of these is of the subsect Bochasanwasi Akshar Purushottam Sanstha.

17. Field notes, November 21, 2005.

18. Field notes, November 5, 2005.

19. Field notes, September 24, 2005,

20. This is not to suggest that residing near whites necessarily leads to intergroup camaraderie and cannot create its own tensions, but at least the possibility of interethnic dialogue exists (Putnam 2007).

Conclusion

1. Portions of this section have already been published under Dhingra 2009a. Reprinted here with permission.

2. Vincent Chin was mistaken for a Japanese American. Because Japan was the target of Detroit's ire at the time, Chin became the target of misplaced aggressions fueled by the global economy.

3. The growth of Hindu temples and other non-Christian religious spaces marks the cultural and racial heterogeneity of the region. But because they serve only followers of those faiths, despite these spaces' open-door policies, most persons bypass them without reflecting on their religious assumptions.

Bibliography

Abelmann, Nancy, and John Lie. 1995. *Blue Dreams: Korean Americans and the Los Angeles Riots*. Cambridge, MA: Harvard University Press.

Alba, Richard, and Victor Nee. 2003. *Remaking the American Mainstream: Assimilation and Contemporary Immigration*. Cambridge, MA: Harvard University Press.

Aldrich, Howard, Trevor Jones, and David McEvoy. 1984. "Ethnic Advantage and Minority Business Development." In *Ethnic Communities in Business: Strategies for Economic Survival*, ed. Robin Ward and Richard Jenkins, 189–210. Cambridge: Cambridge University Press.

Aldrich, Howard, and Roger Waldinger. 1990. "Ethnicity and Entrepreneurship." *Annual Review of Sociology* 16: 111–35.

Ancheta, Angelo. 1998. *Race, Rights, and the Asian American Experience*. New Brunswick, NJ: Rutgers University Press.

Assar, Nandini. 2000. "Gender Hierarchy Among Gujarati Immigrants: Linking Immigration Rules and Ethnic Norms," PhD diss., Virginia Polytechnic Institute and State University.

Bailey, Thomas, and Roger Waldinger. 1991. "Primary, Secondary, and Enclave Labor Markets: A Training Systems Approach." *American Sociological Review* 56, 4: 432–45.

Baines, Susan, and Jane Wheelock. 1998. "Reinventing Traditional Solutions: Job Creations, Gender, and the Micro-Business Household." *Work, Employment and Society* 12, 4: 579–601.

Bal, Gurpreet. 2006. "Entrepreneurship Among Diasporic Communities: A Comparative Examination of Patidars of Gujarat and Jats of Punjab." *Journal of Entrepreneurship* 15, 2: 181–203.

Bald, Vivek. 2007. "'Lost' in the City: Spaces and Stories of South Asian New York, 1917–1965." *South Asian Popular Culture* 5, 1: 59–76.

Barringer, Herbert, and Gene Kassebaum. 1989. "Asian Indians as a Minority in the United States: The Effect of Education, Occupations, and Gender on Income." *Sociological Perspectives* 32, 4: 501–20.

Bastos, Susana, and Jose Bastos. 2005. "'Our Colonisers Were Better Than Yours': Identity Debates in Greater London." *Journal of Ethnic and Migration Studies* 31, 1: 79–98.

Basu, Anuradha. 1998. "An Exploration of Entrepreneurial Activity Among Asian Small Businesses in Britain." *Small Business Economics* 10: 313–26.

Bates, Crispin. 1981. "The Nature of Social Change in Rural Gujarat: The Kheda District, 1818–1918." *Modern Asian Studies* 15, 4: 771–821.

Baum, Joel, and Heather Haveman. 1997. "Love Thy Neighbor? Differentiation and Spatial Agglomeration in the Manhattan Hotel Industry." *Administrative Science Quarterly* 42: 304–38.

Bhachu, Parminder. 1985. *Twice Migrants: East African Sikh Settlers in Britain*. London: Tavistock Publications.

Bhakta, Govind. 2002. *Patels: A Gujarati Community History in the United States*. Los Angeles: University of California Asian American Studies Center.

Blackford, Mansel. 1991. *History of Small Business in America*. New York: Twayne Publishers.

Blaug, Mark. 2000. "Entrepreneurship Before and After Schumpeter." In *Entrepreneurship: The Social Science View*, ed. Richard Swedberg, 51–75. New York: Oxford University Press.

Bodnar, John. 1985. *The Transplanted: A History of Immigrants in Urban America*. Bloomington: Indiana University Press.

Bonacich, Edna. 1973. "A Theory of Middleman Minorities." *American Sociological Review* 38, 5: 583–94.

———. 1987. "'Making It' in America: A Social Evaluation of the Ethics of Immigrant Entrepreneurship." *Sociological Perspectives* 30, 4: 446–66.

Bonacich, Edna, and John Modell. 1980. *The Economic Basis of Ethnic Solidarity: Small Business in the Japanese American Community*. Berkeley: University of California Press.

Bonilla Silva, Eduardo. 2003. *Racism Without Racists: Color-Blind Racism and the Persistence of Racial Inequality in the United States*. Lanham, MD: Rowman & Littlefield.

Brah, Avtar. 2008. "The 'Asian' in Britain." In *A Post-Colonial People: South Asians in Britain*, ed. N. Ali, V. S. Karla, and S. Sayyid, 35–61. London: Hurst and Company.

Breman, Jan. 1996. *Footloose Labour: Working in India's Informal Economy*. Cambridge: Cambridge University Press.

———. 2007. *The Poverty Regime in Village India: Half a Century of Work and Life at the Bottom of the Rural Economy in South Gujarat*. New York: Oxford University Press.

Brennan, Lance. 1998. "Across the *Kali Pani*: An Introduction." *South Asia* 21: 1–18.

Brown, Wendy. 2006. "American Nightmare: Neoliberalism, Neoconservatism, and De-Democratization." *Political Theory* 34, 6: 690–714.

Burt, Ronald. 2000. "The Network Entrepreneur." In *Entrepreneurship: The Social Science View*, ed. Richard Swedberg, 281–307. New York: Oxford University Press.

Capeci, Dominic. 1985. "Black-Jewish Relations in Wartime Detroit: The Marsh, Loving, Wolf Surveys and the Race Riot of 1943." *Jewish Social Studies* 47, 3/4: 221–42.

Chandras, Kananur. 1978. "East Indian Americans." In *Racial Discrimination Against Neither-White-Nor-Black American Minorities*, ed. Kananur Chandras, 80–96. San Francisco: R and E Research Associates.

Chandrasekhar, S. 1982. *From India to America: A Brief History of Immigration, Problems of Discrimination, Admission, and Assimilation*. La Jolla, CA: Population Review Publications.

Chang, Robert. 2000. *Disoriented: Asian Americans, Law, and the Nation-State*. New York: New York University Press.

Chatterjea, Ananya. 2004. *Butting Out: Reading Resistive Choreographies Through Works by Jawole Willa Jo Zollar and Chandralekha*. Middletown, CT: Wesleyan University Press.

Chaturvedi, Vinayak. 2007. *Peasant Pasts: History and Memory in Western India*. Berkeley: University of California Press.

Chin, Margaret. 2005. *Sewing Women: Immigrants and the New York City Garment Industry*. New York: Columbia University.

Chou, Rosalind, and Joe Feagin. 2008. *The Myth of the Model Minority: Asian Americans Facing Racism.* Herndon, VA: Paradigm Publishers.

Cobas, Jose. 1989. "Six Problems in the Sociology of the Ethnic Economy." *Sociological Perspectives* 32, 2: 201–14.

Cohen, Yinon, and Andrea Tyree. 1994. "Palestinian and Jewish Israeli-Born Immigrants in the U.S." *International Migration Review* 28: 243–55.

Collins, Randal. 1994. *Four Sociological Traditions.* New York: Oxford University Press.

Crewe, Emma, and Uma Kothari. 1998. "Gujarati Migrants' Search for Modernity in Britain." In *Gender and Migration,* ed. Caroline Sweetman, 13–20. Oxford: Oxfam.

Culbertson, Hugh, Dennis Jeffers, Donna Stone, and Martin Terrell. 1993. *Social, Political, and Economic Contexts in Public Relations: Theory and Cases.* Hillsdale, NJ: Lawrence Erlbaum Associates.

Daniels, Roger. 1989. *History of Indian Immigration to the United States: An Interpretive Essay.* New York: The Asia Society.

Das Gupta, Monisha. 2006. *Unruly Immigrants: Rights, Activism, and Transnational South Asian Politics in the United States.* Durham, NC: Duke University Press.

de Certeau, Michel. 1984. *The Practice of Everyday Life.* Berkeley: University of California Press.

Desai, Manisha. 2002. "Transnational Solidarity: Women's Agency, Structural Adjustment, and Globalization." In *Women's Activism and Globalization: Linking Local Struggles and Transnational Politics,* ed. Naples Nancy and Manisha Desai, 15–33. New York: Routledge.

Dhaliwal, Spinder. 1998. "Silent Contributors: Asian Female Entrepreneurs and Women in Business." *Women's Studies International Forum* 21, 5: 463–74.

Dhingra, Pawan. 2007. *Managing Multicultural Lives: Asian American Professionals and the Challenge of Multiple Identities.* Stanford, CA: Stanford University Press.

———. 2008. "Committed to Ethnicity, Committed to America: How Second-Generation Indian Americans' Ethnic Boundaries Further Their Americanisation." *Journal of Intercultural Studies* 29, 1: 41–63.

———. 2009a. "Introduction to Special Issue on the Midwest." *Journal of Asian American Studies* 12, 3: 239–46.

———. 2009b. "The Possibility of Community: How Indian American Motel Owners Negotiate Competition and Solidarity." *Journal of Asian American Studies* 12, 3: 321–46.

Dholakia, Ravindra. 2008. "Macroeconomic Framework for Development in Gujarat." In *Gujarat: Perspectives of the Future,* ed. R. Swaminathan, 105–50. New Delhi: Academic Foundation.

Duany, Jorge. 1989. "The Cuban Community in Puerto Rico: A Comparative Caribbean Perspective." *Ethnic and Racial Studies* 12, 1: 36–46.

Dudrah, R. K. 2002. "Zee TV-Europe and the Construction of a Pan-European South Asian Identity." *Contemporary South Asia* 11, 2: 163–81.

Duxbury, Linda, C. A. Higgins, and Roland Thomas. 1996. "Work and Family Environments and the Adoption of Computer-Supported Supplemental Work-at-Home." *Journal of Vocational Behavior* 49, 1: 1–23.

Ehrenreich, Barbara. 2001. *Nickel and Dimed: On (Not) Getting By in America.* New York: Metropolitan Books.

Espiritu, Yen Le. 2003. *Home Bound.* Berkeley: University of California Press.

———. 2009. "'They're Coming to America': Immigration, Settlement, and Citizenship." *Qualitative Sociology* 32, 2: 221–27.

Fernandez, Marilyn, and Kwang Chung Kim. 1998. "Self-Employment Rates of Asian Immigrant Groups: An Analysis of Intragroup and Intergroup Differences." *International Migration Review* 32, 3: 654–81.

Foner, Nancy. 1998. "Benefits and Burdens: Immigrant Women and Work in New York City." *Gender Issues* 16, 4: 5–24.

Fortney, Judith. 1970. "International Migration of Professionals." *Population Studies* 24, 2: 217–32.

Foucault, Michel. 1977. *Discipline and Punish: The Birth of the Modern Prison.* New York: Vintage.

Frey, William. 2002. "Three Americas: The Rising Significance of Regions." *Journal of the American Planning Association* 68, 4: 349–56.

George, Sheba. 2005. *When Women Come First: Gender and Class in Transnational Migration.* Berkeley: University of California Press.

Gibson, Margaret. 1988. *Accommodation Without Assimilation: Sikh Immigrants in an American High School.* Ithaca, NY: Cornell University Press.

Gidwani, Vinay. 2000. "Quest for Distinction: A Reappraisal of the Rural Labor Process in Kheda District." *Economic Geography* 76, 2: 145–68.

Glenn, Evelyn Nakano. 2002. *Unequal Freedom: How Race and Gender Shaped American Citizenship and Labor.* Cambridge, MA: Harvard University Press.

Glick Schiller, Nina. 2005. "Racialized Nations, Evangelizing Christianity, Police States, and Imperial Power." *American Ethnologist* 32, 4: 526–32.

Goffman, Erving. [1967] 2005. *Interaction Ritual: Essays in Face-to-Face Behavior.* New Brunswick, NJ: Transaction Publishers.

Golash-Boza, Tanya. 2006. "Dropping the Hyphen? Becoming Latino(a)-American Through Racialized Assimilation." *Social Forces* 85, 1: 27–55.

Gold, Steven. 1995. *From the Workers' State to the Golden State: Jews from the Former Soviet Union in California.* Boston: Allyn and Bacon.

———. 2010. *The Store in the Hood: A Century of Ethnic Business and Conflict.* Lanham, MD: Rowman & Littlefield Publishers.

Gold, Steven, Ivan Light, and M. Francis Johnston. "The Second Generation and Self-Employment." *Migration Information Source*, March 2006. www.migrationinformation.org/Feature/display.cfm?id=447.

Grewal, Inerpal. 2005. *Transnational America: Feminisms, Diasporas, Neoliberalisms.* Durham, NC: Duke University Press.

Groth, Paul. 1999. *Living Downtown: The History of Residential Hotels in the United States.* Berkeley: University of California Press.

Hardiman, David. 1981. *Peasant Nationalists of Gujarat: Kheda District, 1917–1934.* New Delhi: Oxford University Press.

Harvey, David. 2005. *A Brief History of Neoliberalism.* New York: Oxford University Press.

Helweg, Arthur, and Usha Helweg. 1990. *An Immigrant Success Story: East Indians in America.* Philadelphia: University of Pennsylvania Press.

Hess, Gary. 1974. "The Forgotten Asian Americans: The East Indian Community in the United States." *Pacific Historical Review* 43, 4: 576–96.

Hill, E. Jeffrey, Maria Ferris, and Vjollca Märtinson. 2003. "Does It Matter Where You Work?" *Journal of Vocational Behavior* 63, 2: 220–41.

Hintzen, Percy. 2001. *West Indians in the West: Self Representations in a Migrant Community.* New York: New York University Press.

Hochschild, Arlie. 1983. *The Managed Heart: Commercialization of Human Feeling.* Berkeley: University of California Press.

———. 1989. *The Second Shift.* New York: Viking.

Hout, Michael. 1984. "Status, Autonomy, and Training in Occupational Mobility." *American Journal of Sociology* 89, 6: 1379–409.

Hout, Michael, and Harvey Rosen. 2000. "Self-Employment, Family Background, and Race." *Journal of Human Resources* 35, 4: 670–92.

Jain, Usha. 1989. *The Gujaratis of San Francisco*. New York: AMS Press.

Jakle, John, Keith Sculle, and Jefferson Rogers. 2002. *The Motel in America*. Baltimore, MD: Johns Hopkins University Press.

Jensen, Joan. 1988. *Passage from India: Asian Indian Immigrants in North America*. New Haven, CT: Yale University Press.

Jones, Carol, George Taylor, and Dennis Nickson. 1997. "Whatever It Takes? Managing 'Empowered' Employees and the Service Encounter in an International Hotel Chain." *Work, Employment & Society* 11, 3: 541–54.

Jung, John. 2008. *Southern Fried Rice: Life in a Chinese Laundry in the Deep South*. Raleigh, NC: Lulu Press.

Kalita, S. Mitra. 2003. *Suburban Sahibs: Three Immigrant Families and Their Passage from India to America*. New Brunswick, NJ: Rutgers University Press.

Kalnins, Arturs, and Wilbur Chung. 2006. "Social Capital, Geography, and Survival: Gujarati Immigrant Entrepreneurs in the U.S. Lodging Industry." *Management Science* 52, 2: 233–47.

Kang, Miliann. 2010. *The Managed Hand: Race, Gender, and the Body in Beauty Service Work*. Berkeley: University of California Press.

Kasinitz, Philip, John Mollenkopf, Mary Waters, and Jennifer Holdaway. 2008. *Inheriting the City: The Children of Immigrants Come of Age*. Cambridge, MA: Harvard University Press.

Khandelwal, Madhulika. 2002. *Becoming American, Being Indian: An Immigrant Community in New York City*. Ithaca, NY: Cornell University Press.

Kibria, Nazli. 1993. *Family Tightrope: The Changing Lives of Vietnamese Americans*. Princeton, NJ: Princeton University Press.

———. 2002. *Becoming Asian American: Second Generation Chinese and Korean American Identities*. Baltimore, MD: Johns Hopkins University Press.

Kim, Claire. 1999. "The Racial Triangulation of Asian Americans." *Politics and Society* 27: 105.

———. 2000. *Bitter Fruit: The Politics of Black-Korean Conflict in New York City*. New Haven, CT: Yale University Press.

Kim, Dae Young. 2006. "Stepping-Stone to Intergenerational Mobility? The Springboard, Safety Net, or Mobility Trap Functions of Korean Immigrant Entrepreneurship for the Second Generation." *International Migration Review* 40, 4: 927–62.

Kim, Illsoo. 1981. *New Urban Immigrants: The Korean Community in New York.* Princeton, NJ: Princeton University Press.

Kim, Kwang, Won Hurh, and Marilyn Fernandez. 1989. "Intra-Group Differences in Business Participation: Three Asian Immigrant Groups." *International Migration Review* 23, 1: 73–95.

Kim, Nadia. 2008. *Imperial Citizens: Koreans and Race from Seoul to LA.* Stanford, CA: Stanford University Press.

Kitano, Henry, and Roger Daniels. 1995. *Asian Americans: Emerging Minorities.* Englewood Cliffs, NJ: Prentice Hall.

Kurien, Prema. 2007. *A Place at the Multicultural Table: The Development of an American Hinduism.* New Brunswick, NJ: Rutgers University Press.

Kwong, Peter. 1996. *The New Chinatown.* New York: Macmillan.

Lakdawala, D. T. 1982. *Gujarat Economy: Problems and Prospects.* Ahmedabad, Gujarat: Sardar Patel Institute of Economic and Social Research.

Lal, Vinay. 2008. *The Other Indians: A Political and Cultural History of South Asians in America.* Los Angeles: UCLA Asian American Studies Center.

Landolt, Patricia, Lilian Autler, and Sonia Baires. 1999. "From Hermano Lejano to Hermano Mayor: The Dialectics of Salvadoran Transnationalism." *Ethnic and Racial Studies* 22, 2: 290–315.

Leckie, Jacqueline. 1998. "The Southernmost Indian Diaspora: From Gujarat to Aotearoa." *South Asia* 21: 161–80.

Lee, Eunju. 2005. *Gendered Processes: Korean Immigrant Small Business Ownership.* New York: LFB Scholarly Publishing.

Lee, Jennifer. 2002. *Civility in the City: Blacks, Jews, and Koreans in Urban America.* Cambridge, MA: Harvard University Press.

Levine, Donald. 1977. "Simmel at a Distance: On the History and Systematics of the Sociology of the Stranger." *Sociological Focus* 10, 1: 15–29.

Levitt, Peggy. 2001. *Transnational Villagers.* Berkeley: University of California Press.

———. 2007. *God Needs No Passport: Immigrants and the Changing American Religious Landscape.* New York: New Press.

Light, Ivan. 1972. *Ethnic Enterprise in America.* Berkeley: University of California Press.

Light, Ivan, and Edna Bonacich. 1991. *Immigrant Entrepreneurs: Koreans in Los Angeles, 1965–1982.* Berkeley: University of California Press.

Light, Ivan, and Steven Gold. 2000. *Ethnic Economies.* San Diego, CA: Academic Press.

Ling, Huping. 2004. *Chinese St. Louis: From Enclave to Cultural Community.* Philadelphia: Temple University Press.

Lipsitz, George. 1998. *The Possessive Investment in Whiteness: How White People Profit from Identity Politics.* Philadelphia: Temple University Press.

Loewen, James. 1971. *The Mississippi Chinese: Between Black and White.* Cambridge, MA: Harvard University Press.

Logan, John, Wenquan Zhang, and Richard Alba. 2002. "Immigrant Enclaves and Ethnic Communities in New York and Los Angeles." *American Sociological Review* 67, 2: 299–322.

Logan, John R., and Richard D. Alba. 1999. "Minority Niches and Immigrant Enclaves." In *Immigration and Opportunity: Race, Ethnicity, and Employment in the United States*, ed. Frank D. Bean and Stephanie Bell-Rose, 172–93. New York: Russell Sage Foundation Publications.

Loscocco, Karyn. 1997. "Work-Family Linkages Among Self-Employed Women and Men." *Journal of Vocational Behavior* 50, 2: 204–26.

Madhavan, M. C. 1985. "Indian Emigrants: Numbers, Characteristics, and Economic Impact." *Population and Development Review* 11, 3: 457–81.

Mahler, Sarah. 1995. *American Dreaming: Immigrant Life on the Margins.* Princeton, NJ: Princeton University Press.

Maira, Sunaina. 2009. *Missing: Youth, Citizenship, and Empire After 9/11.* Durham, NC: Duke University Press.

Marshall, Douglas. 2002. "Behavior, Belonging, and Belief: A Theory of Ritual Practice." *Sociological Theory* 20, 3: 360–80.

Massey, Douglass. 2003. *Beyond Smoke and Mirrors: Mexican Immigration in an Era of Economic Integration.* New York City: Russell Sage Foundation.

Mathew, Biju. 2005. *Taxi! Cabs and Capitalism in New York City.* Ithaca, NY: Cornell University Press.

Mayer, Peter. 1984. Review of *Peasant Nationalists of Gujarat: Kheda District, 1917–1934*, by David Hardiman. *Pacific Affairs* 57, 2: 344–46.

Mehta, S. S. 1983. "Planning Problems and Prospects." In *Gujarat Economy: Problems and Prospects*, ed. D. T. Lakdawala, 313–18. Ahmedabad, Gujarat: Sardar Patel Institute of Economic and Social Research.

Melamed, Jodi. 2006. "The Spirit of Neoliberalism: From Racial Liberalism to Neoliberal Multiculturalism." *Social Text* 24, 4: 1–24.

Menjívar, Cecilia. 2000. *Fragmented Ties: Salvadoran Immigrant Networks in America.* Berkeley: University of California Press.

Min, Pyong Gap. 1996. *Caught in the Middle: Korean Communities in New York and Los Angeles*. Berkeley: University of California Press.

———. 2008. *Ethnic Solidarity for Economic Survival: Korean Greengrocers in New York City*. New York City: Russell Sage Foundation.

Min, Pyong Gap, and Mehdi Bozorgmehr. 2000. "Immigrant Entrepreneurship and Business Patterns: A Comparison of Koreans and Iranians in Los Angeles." *International Migration Review* 34, 3: 707–38.

Morgan, Howard. 1964. *The Motel Industry in the United States: Small Business in Transition*. Tucson: University of Arizona, Bureau of Business and Public Research.

Nair, Savita. 2001. "Moving Life Histories: Gujarat, East Africa, and the Indian Diaspora, 1880–2000." PhD diss., University of Pennsylvania.

Nee, Victor, Jimy Sanders, and Scott Sernau. 1994. "Job Transitions in an Immigrant Metropolis: Ethnic Boundaries and the Mixed Economy." *American Sociological Review* 59, 6: 849–52.

Okihiro, Gary. 1994. *Margins and Mainstreams: Asians in American History and Culture*. Seattle: University of Washington Press.

Ong, Aihwa. 2003. *Buddha Is Hiding: Refugees, Citizenship, the New America*. Berkeley: University of California Press.

———. 2006. *Neoliberalism as Exception: Mutations in Citizenship and Sovereignty*. Durham, NC: Duke University Press.

Pabrai, Mohnish. 2007. *The Dhandho Investor: The Low-Risk Value Method to High Returns*. Hoboken, NJ: John Wiley.

Padavic, Irene, and Barbara Reskin. 2002. *Women and Men at Work*. Thousand Oaks, CA: Pine Forge Press.

Parekh, Sunil. 2008. "Gujarat's Industrial Development: A Perspective." In *Gujarat: Perspectives of the Future*, ed. R. Swaminathan, 59–104. New Delhi: Academic Foundation.

Park, Kyeyoung. 1997. *The Korean American Dream: Immigrants and Small Business in New York City*. Ithaca, NY: Cornell University Press.

Park, Lisa. 2005. *Consuming Citizenship: Children of Asian Immigrant Entrepreneurs*. Stanford, CA: Stanford University Press.

Parlin, Bradley. 1976. *Immigrant Professionals in the United States: Discrimination in the Scientific Labor Market*. New York: Praeger Publishers.

Parreñas, Rhacel. 2001. *Servants of Globalization: Women, Migration, and Domestic Work*. Stanford, CA: Stanford University Press.

Patel, Anjana, and Natvarbhai Patel. 2001. *The Leva Patidar Patels of Charotar: A Community History.* London: Charotar Patidar Kutumb.

Patel, Pravin, and Mario Rutten. 1999. "Patels of Central Gujarat in Greater London." *Economic and Political Weekly* 34, 16/17: 952–54.

Pease, Donald. 2000. "US Imperialism: Global Dominance Without Colonies." In *A Companion to Post-Colonial Studies*, ed. Henry Schwartz and Sangeeta Ray, 203–20. Malden, MA: Blackwell Publishers.

Pocock, David. 1972. *Kanbi and Patidar: A Study of the Patidar Community of Gujarat.* Oxford: Clarendon Press.

Poros, Maritsa. 2010. *Modern Migrations: Gujarati Indian Networks in New York and London.* Stanford, CA: Stanford University Press.

Portes, Alejandro, and Robert Bach. 1985. *Latin Journey: Cuban and Mexican Immigrants in the United States.* Berkeley: University of California Press.

Portes, Alejandro, Luis E. Guarnizo, and William Haller. 2003. "Assimilation and Transnationalism: Determinants of Transnational Political Action Among Contemporary Migrants." *American Journal of Sociology* 108: 1211–248.

Portes, Alejandro, and Rubin Rumbaut. 2001. *Legacies: The Story of the Immigrant Second Generation.* Berkeley: University of California Press.

———. 2006. *Immigrant America: A Portrait.* 3rd ed. Berkeley: University of California Press.

Portes, Alejandro, and Min Zhou. 1993. "The New Second Generation: Segmented Assimilation and Its Variants." *Annals of the American Academy of Political and Social Science* 530: 74–96.

Posadas, Barbara. 1999. *The Filipino Americans.* Westport, CT: Greenwood Press.

Powell, Douglas. 2007. *Critical Regionalism: Connecting Politics and Culture in the American Landscape.* Chapel Hill: University of North Carolina Press.

Prashad, Vijay. 2000. *The Karma of Brown Folk.* Minneapolis: University of Minnesota Press.

Prus, Robert, and Styllianoss Irini. 1980. *Hookers, Rounders, and Desk Clerks: The Social Organization of the Hotel Community.* Toronto: Gage Publishing.

Purkayastha, Bandana. 2005. *Negotiating Ethnicity: Second-Generation South Asian Americans Traverse a Transnational World.* New Brunswick, NJ: Rutgers University Press.

Putnam, Robert. 2007. "*E Pluribus Unum:* Diversity and Community in the Twenty-first Century—The 2006 Johan Skytte Prize." *Scandinavian Political Studies* 30, 2: 137–74.

Raijman, Rebeca, and Marta Tienda. 2000. "Immigrants' Pathways to Business Ownership: A Comparative Ethnic Perspective." *International Migration Review* 34, 3: 682–706.

Ram, Monder, and Ruth Holliday. 1993. "Relative Merits: Family Culture and Kinship in Small Firms." *Sociology* 27, 4: 629–48.

Ramji, Hasmita. 2006. "Journeys of Difference: The Use of Migratory Narratives Among British Hindu Gujaratis." *Ethnic and Racial Studies* 29, 4: 702–24.

Rangaswamy, Padma. 2007. "South Asians in Dunkin' Donuts: Niche Development in the Franchise Industry." *Journal of Ethnic and Migration Studies* 33, 4: 671–86.

Reddy, Chandan. 2005. "Asian Diasporas, Neoliberalism, and Family: Reviewing the Case for Homosexual Asylum in the Context of Family Rights." *Social Text* 23: 3–4, 84–85, 101–19.

Rosaldo, Renato. 1997. "Cultural Citizenship, Inequality, and Multiculturalism." In *Latino Cultural Citizenship: Claiming Identity, Space, and Rights*, ed. William Flores and Rina Benmayor, 27–38. Boston: Beacon Press.

Ruiz, Vicki. 2008. "Citizen Restaurant: American Imaginaries, American Communities." *American Quarterly* 60, 1: 1–21.

Rutten, Mario. 1995. *Farms and Factories: Social Profile of Large Farmers and Rural Industrialists in West India*. Delhi: Oxford University Press.

Rutten, Mario, and Pravin Patel. 2003. "Indian Migrants in Britain: Mirror Image of Social Linkages Between Gujarat and London." *Asia Europe Journal* 1, 3: 403–17.

Sahay, Anjali. 2007. "Indian Diaspora in the United States and Brain Gain: Remittances, Return and Network Approaches." In *Sociology of Diaspora: A Reader*, ed. Ajaya Kumar Sahoo and Brij Maharaj, vol. 2, 940–74. New Delhi: Rawat Publications.

Sakamoto, Arthur, Kimberly Goyette, and Chang Hwan Kim. 2009. "Socioeconomic Attainments of Asian Americans." *Annual Review of Sociology* 35: 255–76.

Sanders, Jimy, and Victor Nee. 1996. "Immigrant Self-Employment: The Family as Social Capital and the Value of Human Capital." *American Sociological Review* 61, 2: 231–49.

Sengstock, Mary. 1982. *Chaldean-Americans: Changing Conceptions of Ethnic Identity*. Staten Island, NY: Center for Migration Studies.

Shah, Nayan. 2001. *Contagious Divides: Epidemics and Race in San Francisco's Chinatown*. Berkeley: University of California Press.

Shane, Scott. 2003. *A General Theory of Entrepreneurship: The Individual-Opportunity Nexus.* Northampton, MA: Edward Elgar Publishing.

Sherman, Rachel. 2007. *Class Acts: Service and Inequality in Luxury Hotels.* Berkeley: University of California Press.

Sheth, Pravin. 2001. *Indians in America: One Stream, Two Waves, Three Generations.* Jaipur, India: Rawat Publications.

Siu, Lok. 2001. "Diasporic Cultural Citizenship: Chineseness and Belonging in Central America and Panama." *Social Text* 19, 4: 7–28.

Song, Miri. 1999. *Helping Out: Children's Labor in Ethnic Businesses.* Philadelphia: Temple University Press.

Spencer, Ian. 1997. *British Immigration Policy Since 1939: The Making of Multiracial Britain.* New York: Routledge.

Spickard, Paul. 2007. *Almost All Aliens: Immigration, Race, and Colonialism in American History and Identity.* New York: Routledge.

Srivastava, Ravi, and S. K. Sasikumar. June 22–24, 2003. "An Overview of Migration in India, Its Impacts and Key Issues." Paper presented at the Migration, Development, and Pro-Poor Policy Choices in Asia Conference, Dhaka, Bangladesh.

Steinberg, Stephen. 1986. "The Rise of the Jewish Professional: Case Studies in Inter-Generational Mobility." *Ethnic and Racial Studies* 9, 4: 502–13.

Stepick, Alex, and Guillermo Grenier. 1994. "The View from the Back of the House: Restaurants and Hotels in Miami." In *Newcomers in the Workplace: Immigrants and the Restructuring of the U.S. Economy,* ed. Louise Lamphere, Alex Stepick, and Guillermo J. Grenier, 181–98. Philadelphia: Temple University Press.

Streefkerk, Hein. 1997. "Gujarati Entrepreneurship: Historical Continuity Against Changing Perspectives." *Economic and Political Weekly* 32, 8: M2–M10.

Swedberg, Richard. 2000. *Entrepreneurship: The Social Science View.* New York: Oxford University Press.

Takaki, Ronald. 1989. *Strangers from a Different Shore: A History of Asian Americans.* New York: Penguin Books.

Tambs Lyche, Harald. 1982. *The London Patidar.* London: Macmillan.

Telles, Edward, and Vilma Ortiz. 2008. *Generations of Exclusion: Mexican Americans, Assimilation, and Race.* New York: Russell Sage Foundation.

Thandi, Shinder. 2007. "Migrating to the Mother Country: South Asian Settlement and the Post-War Boom 1947–80." In *A South-Asian History of Britain,* ed. Michael Fisher, Shompa Lahiri, and Shinder Thandi, 159–182. Westport, CT: Greenwood World Pub.

Theroux, Paul. 1967. "Hating the Asians." *Transition* 33: 46–51.

Tuan, Mia. 1998. *Forever Foreigners or Honorary Whites? The Asian Ethnic Experience Today.* New Brunswick, NJ: Rutgers University Press.

Valdez, Zulema. 2010. *The New Entrepreneurs: How Race, Class, and Gender Shape American Enterprise.* Stanford, CA: Stanford University Press.

Vishwanath, L. S. 1990. "Peasant Movements in Colonial India: An Examination of Some Conceptual Frameworks." *Economic and Political Weekly* 25, 2: 118–22.

Waldinger, Roger. 1986. *Through the Eye of the Needle: Immigrants and Enterprise in New York's Garment Trades.* New York: New York University Press.

———. 1994. "The Making of an Immigrant Niche." *International Migration Review* 28, 1: 3–30.

Waldinger, Roger, Howard Aldrich, and Robin Ward. 1990. *Ethnic Entrepreneurs: Immigrant Business in Industrial Societies.* Newbury Park, CA: Sage Publications.

Waldinger, Roger, and Michael Lichter. 2003. *How the Other Half Works: Immigration and the Social Organization of Labor.* Berkeley: University of California Press.

Waters, Mary. 1999. *Black Identities: West Indian Immigrant Dreams and American Realities.* Cambridge, MA: Harvard University Press.

Westwood, Sallie, and Parminder Bhachu. 1988. "Introduction." In *Enterprising Women: Ethnicity, Economy, and Gender Relations,* ed. Sallie Westwood and Parminder Bhachu, 1–15. New York: Taylor and Frances.

Whyte, William F. 1946. "When Workers and Customers Meet." In *Industry and Society,* ed. William F. Whyte. New York: McGraw Hill.

Wolfe, Alan. 2000. "Benign Multiculturalism." In *Multiculturalism in the United States,* ed. Peter Kavisito and Georganne Rundblad, 445–54. Thousand Oaks, CA: Pine Forge Press.

Wood, Andrew, and Jenny Wood. 2004. *Motel America: A State-by-State Tour Guide to Nostalgic Stopovers.* Portland, OR: Collectors Press.

Wuthnow, Robert. 1989. *Meaning and Moral Order: Explorations in Cultural Analysis.* Berkeley: University of California Press.

Yoon, In-Joon. 1997. *On My Own: Korean Businesses and Race Relations in America.* Chicago: University of Chicago Press.

Zenner, Walter. 1980. "American Jewry in the Light of Middleman Minority Theories." *Contemporary Jewry* 5, 1: 11–30.

Zhou, Min. 1992. *Chinatown: The Socioeconomic Potential of an Urban Enclave.* Philadelphia: Temple University Press.

———. 2004. "Revisiting Ethnic Entrepreneurship: Convergencies, Controversies, and Conceptual Advancements." *International Migration Review* 38, 3: 1040–74.

Zhou, Min, and C. Bankston. 1998. *Growing Up American: How Vietnamese Children Adapt to Life in the United States.* New York: Russell Sage Foundation.

Zuberi, Dan. 2006. *Differences That Matter: Social Policy and the Working Poor in the United States and Canada.* Ithaca, NY: Cornell University Press.

Zúñiga, Victor, and Rubén Hernández-León. 2005. *New Destinations: Mexican Immigration in the United States.* New York: Russell Sage Foundation.

Index

acculturation, 59, 164, 165–66, 167–71
adaptation, 205–6, 207
advertising, 100, 114
African Americans: discrimination against, 108; Indian Americans and, 108; as labor, 127, 144; in Ohio, 20
"Agnipath," 225n18
Alba, Richard, 212n16
Aldrich, Howard, 216n4
Americana, 223n24
American Automobile Association (AAA), 68
American fever, 41
American Hotel and Lodging Association, 52, 211n8
American Hotel & Motel Association, 215n3
Amin, Idi, 35
Anaheim, California, 218n26
Arab Americans, 108
Asian American Hotel Owners Association (AAHOA), 15, 180; 1994 convention, 225n18; 1999 convention, 88; 2004 convention, 2; 2005 convention, 219n5; 2006 convention, 99–100, 219n6; 2010 convention, 7; charity work by, 152–53; fair franchising plan, 153, 155; franchises and, 97, 102, 153, 155, 219n5, 220n8, 224n16; governments and, 153–56, 157–58, 221n18; lobbying by, 154–55; model minorities and, 155–57; National Association of Black Hotel Owners, Operators and Developers and, 108–9, 219n31, 223n1; on professionalization, 152; property ownership, 211n8; racialization at, 97, 102; significance of, 124; start of, 68; on television, 178; transnational interests, 157–58; volleyball sponsorship by, 227n14; women in, 139–40; young moteliers group in, 80–81

Asian Americans: discrimination against, 13, 25, 46, 47–48, 127; in Ohio, 20, 213n29; racial profiling of, 108; in U.S., 10–11. *See also specific nationalities*
Asiatic Barred Zone Act, 25, 39
assimilation, 164, 212n15, 212n16, 213n17
authenticity, 132
average daily rate (ADR), 118

Bachchan, Amitabh, 225n18
Bal, Gurpreet, 34
bankruptcy: of franchises, 64–65, 93, 119, 120; motels in, 64, 65, 93, 119, 120

245